T0374951

Robert Johnson, Mythmaking, and Contemporary American Culture

Music in American Life

A list of books in the series appears at the end of this book.

Robert Johnson Studio Portrait (Hooks Bros., Memphis, 1935)

Robert Johnson,

Mythmaking, and Contemporary American Culture

Patricia R. Schroeder

University of Illinois Press
Urbana and Chicago

Manufactured in the United States of America
C 5 4 3 2 1

This book is printed on acid-free paper.

Library of Congress Cataloging-in-Publication Data
Schroeder, Patricia R., 1951–
Robert Johnson, mythmaking, and contemporary American culture /
Patricia R. Schroeder.
p. cm. — (Music in American life)
Includes bibliographical references (p.) and index.
ISBN 0-252-02915-1 (cl. : alk. paper)
1. Johnson, Robert, d. 1938—Criticism and interpretation. 2. Blues
(Music)—Social aspects. 3. Blues (Music)—History and criticism.
I.Title. II. Series.
ML420.J735S37 2004
782.421643'092—dc22 2003020027

Contents

Acknowledgments

Many people have contributed to the making of this book. I am, of course, solely responsible for any errors of fact or interpretation within it. But I want to acknowledge the influence of the many people who have helped me, directly and indirectly, and to express my gratitude toward them.

I have long been a passionate fan of the blues, but I did not find an intellectual community in which to discuss blues artists, history, and literature until I attended the 1997 and 1998 meetings of the Delta Studies Symposium, held annually in Jonesboro, Arkansas. Many of the people I met there encouraged my academic interest in the blues and pointed me toward scholarly sources that have informed my thinking in profound ways. Foremost among them is Adam Gussow, with whom I have maintained an ongoing conversation about the blues that seems forever to be taking me in new and rewarding directions. I have also been inspired by the creativity and friendship of Arthur Flowers, Hawkeye Herman, Fruteland Jackson, Roger Wood, William Wiggins, and the symposium organizers, William Clements and Rick Burns. And while they may be surprised to hear it, these pages contain traces of ideas that Vernon Chadwick, Steve Cheseborough, Craig Morrison, and Jerry Wasserman all helped germinate and for which I thank them.

I lament the loss and honor the memory of two friends that I first made at the Delta Studies Symposium, Peter Aschoff and Hank Ballenger, both of whom shared ideas, sources, and their passion for the blues with me. I hope something of their presence lingers in these pages, as in my heart.

In addition to these influences on my thinking about the blues, colleagues from a variety of disciplines helped me develop my ideas about cultural mythology in contemporary American culture. Primary among them is Timothy Raphael, friend and performance studies scholar extraordinaire. Others who graciously helped me find sources, track down facts, or refine ideas include Juli Burk, Peter X. Feng, James V. Hatch, Hawkeye Herman, Margot A. Kelley, and Scott Baretta. Gregory Johnson, curator of the Blues Archive at the J. D. Williams Library, University of Mississippi, helped me track down sources that no one else could find. I am grateful to the staff of the Myrin Library at Ursinus College and especially for the intrepid assistance of Joan Rhodes in filling my often obscure interlibrary loan requests.

Others helped me through the arduous writing process. For reading sections of the manuscript in various stages and offering helpful suggestions, I am indebted to Adam Gussow, Stephen C. LaVere, Christine Levecq, Dick Richards, Melanie Richards, Richard Schroeder, and especially Cidbob, who stuck with me through the entire book and provided a valuable sounding board. I am deeply grateful to Bruce Jackson and Stephen Wade, both of whom read the completed manuscript and helped me shape and focus my sometimes unruly text.

For responding so graciously to my queries about their works, my thanks go out to T. C. Boyle, Alan Rodgers, and especially Alan Greenberg, who was continually generous with his time and support. (And everyone should go and see the film version of *Love in Vain,* being produced by HBO and scheduled for release in the same year as this book.)

For writing letters in support of this project to various granting agencies, I am grateful to Jill Dolan, Adam Gussow, Sally Harrison-Pepper, James V. Hatch, Bruce Jackson, Brenda Murphy, and William Wiggins. I never got the money, but the willingness of colleagues from a variety of disciplines to support my project almost made up for that.

Alan Greenberg, Adam Gussow, Hawkeye Herman, and Alan Rodgers all graciously granted me permission to quote from their personal correspondence. I appreciate Stephen C. LaVere for making the Robert Johnson photographs available and acknowledge the United States Post Office for permission to use the stamp image. Suzanne Noguere's poem "Robert Johnson" is reprinted with the permission of the author and Midmarch Arts Press from her 1996 collection *Whirling round the Sun.*

I am very grateful for the canny editorial guidance of Judith McCulloh at University of Illinois Press. Her patience, support, good humor, wit, and clarity of judgment have been enormously valuable to me. She kept me going, and she kept me honest. Copy editor Matt Mitchell saved me from numerous stylistic infelicities and errors of fact without ever intruding on my voice or trying to alter my ideas. I am delighted with his work on my manuscript and thank him for his many graceful suggestions.

I am indebted to Richard Schroeder for his unflagging support of all my endeavors. Thanks, Rich, for the extraordinary gift of always thinking well of me.

Robert Johnson, Mythmaking, and Contemporary American Culture

Introduction: Mythologies of Robert Johnson

> But to be an American (unlike being English or French or whatever) is precisely to *imagine* a destiny rather than to inherit one; since we have always been, insofar as we are Americans at all, inhabitants of myth rather than history—and have now come to know it.
>
> —Leslie Fiedler, *Cross the Border—Close the Gap*

Since you have picked up this book, you probably know who Robert Johnson was: a traveling Mississippi Delta bluesman who recorded twenty-nine songs in the 1930s, influenced the growth of the blues and the development of rock and roll, died young, and fueled various myths and legends, most notably that he sold his soul to the devil in exchange for his musical prowess. This is a book about those stories and legends, about how they have been represented in literature and popular culture in the 1990s and beyond. It is not a biography of Robert Johnson the man. A number of dedicated scholars and writers, notably Peter Guralnick, Stephen C. LaVere, Mack McCormick, and Gayle Dean Wardlow, have done exhaustive research into Johnson's short life. Collectively, they have unearthed documents that record some of the main events of Johnson's life and interviewed people who knew him or saw him perform. But despite the excellent fieldwork done by such researchers, much about Robert Johnson's life seems destined to remain cloaked in mystery.

Part of this mystery results from the time lag between Johnson's death in 1938 and broad popular interest in his music. Johnson did not receive much recognition until 1961, when Columbia Records released an album of his music called *King of the Delta Blues Singers.* Not until his *Complete Recordings* appeared in 1990 did he receive widespread public acclaim. By that time he had been dead for over half a century, survived only by a few sketchy documents, the fading memories of aging people who knew him or claimed to have known him decades ago, and twenty-nine recorded songs. At this point, it seems that the more we probe into the past searching for the demographic details of Robert Johnson's life, the more we hear conflicting versions of events. The waters become increasingly muddy with the passage of time.

In this book I don't have anything new to say about Robert Johnson the man. I am interested instead in the myths that have been generated about him by those conflicting recollections and varied interpretations and in the many imaginative uses contemporary artists have made of those myths. Suddenly Robert Johnson is everywhere. In the mid 1990s, after I had read two excellent novels featuring Robert Johnson as a character and had begun conducting research for this project, I searched the World Wide Web for "Robert+Johnson+blues" and got three hits. In the spring of 2001, I got 123,000 hits. Admittedly, search engines have improved. In addition, not all of my thousands of hits are devoted to the Delta Johnson (the Robert Wood Johnson Foundation and the founder of the Black Entertainment Television Network, also named Robert Johnson, confuse the search), but ninety-nine of the first hundred hits do refer to Johnson the bluesman and include Web sites in English, Spanish, French, Italian, and Korean—enough of a change to illustrate the extent of the R.J. explosion. Robert Johnson is showing up in novels, plays, poems, films, short stories, and art installations; on T-shirts, posters, and calendars; in college syllabi; and on Web sites with startling frequency. He has become so familiar to us that the character of Tommy Johnson in the Coen brothers' 2000 film *O Brother, Where Art Thou?,* likely based on the historical Tommy Johnson who, before Robert, claimed to have sold his soul for his music, is frequently misidentified by film critics as a thinly disguised version of Robert Johnson (Newby; Wells). While no one claims to have seen Robert Johnson alive recently, he may yet become the Elvis Presley of the new millennium.

When figures enter into the popular imagination in this way, represented in both "highbrow" cultural artifacts like serious poetry as well as popular forms like Hollywood movies and casual clothing, they become cultural icons, symbols of what we as consumers value. They lose something of their individuality and their historical specificity as we recycle their images, reflecting instead what we think is important about them and thus important about ourselves and our own era. In her provocative study of Marilyn Monroe as a cultural icon, S. Paige Baty discusses this process. To define contemporary icons, she borrows the term "representative character" from Ralph Waldo Emerson, himself an iconic figure in American literary history. For Emerson, representative characters are model citizens who embody cultural ideals. Baty adapts Emerson's term to the postmodern era by noting that today representative characters cannot embody a single, unified cultural ideal because Americans no longer share one—if they ever truly did. Instead, today's representative characters personify "a multiplicity of values" and "a plurality of . . . competing discourses" that reflect the increasing diversity of the people who comprise contemporary American culture (10).[1] A cultural icon for the twenty-first century thus reflects the infinite variety of Americans today.

In this book I plan to examine the multiplicity of values that Robert Johnson has come to represent at the turn of the twenty-first century. Robert Johnson exists today at the center of many competing sets of ideas. My aim is to present the most provocative of those ideas and to explore them from a range of contemporary perspectives. Starting with the gaps in Johnson's biography, I will look at the various interpretations of his life story, focusing on what they reveal about the individual storyteller and about our increasingly diverse culture. These varied biographical interpretations exemplify our struggles to redefine ourselves in a newly inclusive way and reveal the different theoretical frames of reference that characterize contemporary thought and scholarship. Moving beyond biography, I will examine the ways that contemporary artists have recirculated Robert Johnson's life and legends. His image has been used in contexts that vary from the re-creation of history to the celebration of a pluralistic society, thereby revealing the intriguing processes by which history gets constructed and diverse cultures mingle. No discussion of contemporary American society would be complete without attention to technology, a force that has achieved a status formerly reserved for religion, at least in some circles. The various electronic uses of Robert Johnson offer insights into key facets of our burgeoning Internet culture. Finally, in the last chapter I myself will participate in the reexamination of Johnson's meaning. The fact that we know so little about Robert Johnson the man but have generated so much discourse about him parallels the social applications of chaos theory that are currently in vogue. Robert Johnson at the turn of the century is an empty center around which multiple interpretations, assorted viewpoints, and a variety of discourses swirl. Throughout this book I will examine that swirl in all its glorious diversity, hoping to illustrate how it reflects the complexities of contemporary American culture.

As a starting point, let me offer a case study of how my process works: a discussion of the extreme and varied reactions to the infamous 1994 Robert Johnson postage stamp.

Stamping the Image

In 1994 the United States Postal Service honored Robert Johnson by putting his picture on a twenty-nine-cent stamp. Johnson appeared as one of eight jazz and blues singers highlighted in a 1994 collection, the others being Bessie Smith, Muddy Waters, Billie Holiday, Jimmy Rushing, Ma Rainey, Mildred Bailey, and Howlin' Wolf. This commemorative collection was issued as part of the Post Office's Legends of American Music series, which began in 1993 with an Elvis Presley stamp and ended in 1999 with six Broadway songwriters, finally totaling ninety-three stamps—the largest commemorative stamp series in U.S. history. Enshrined amid ninety-two other American musical stars ranging from Eugene Ormandy to the Gershwins, Johnson instantly acquired official, governmental recognition as a great artist in his field and an icon of American musical history.

How did he get there? To be represented on a U.S. postage stamp, a figure needs to go through a rather elaborate vetting process. According to a U.S. Postal Service Web site, any citizen can nominate a potential subject for a stamp. The nominations are reviewed by the Citizens' Stamp Advisory Committee, formed in 1957 to consider the eligibility of nominees and to recommend subjects and designs. Noteworthy among the twelve major criteria used for selection are that the subjects must be American or "American related," that no living person will be honored, and that no stamps will be issued "to honor commercial enterprise or products." The committee suggests submitting nominations at least three years in advance of the proposed date of issue so that the Post Office has time to approve the subject and oversee the design.

This process has attracted the notice of the American public throughout the 1990s and early 2000s. The selection of stamp subjects, once a mysterious government process—what popular culture critic John Fiske would call the action of "power-bloc" authority—has become an arena for "the people," or average citizens, to exert localized power of their own (*Power Plays* 9–12). The Elvis Presley stamp design, for example, was chosen by voters throughout the country, who were offered two images to choose from: the young, slim Elvis and the older, bloated one (Roach 70). Their overwhelming choice of the young, slim version reflects the American cultural obsessions with youth and slenderness—but those are other stories. My point here is that stamp selection reveals the workings of popular culture within a dominating power and thus encodes popular values. An episode of the Emmy Award–winning television show "The West Wing" from November 2000 also illustrates the recent popular interest in commemorative stamp selection. The episode featured a subplot in which the assistant to the White House deputy chief of staff exerts enough influence to have a Puerto Rican revolutionary chosen for stamp honors. Her actions show that postage stamp selection has entered the public imagination as both a source of entertainment (a TV show's subplot) and also as a place for average citizens—"the little guy" (in this case, the assistant)—to affect the course of American recorded history. The Johnson stamp, too, reveals the impact of media on popular culture and government: given the three-year-in-advance requirement for nominating stamp subjects, the Johnson stamp was likely proposed shortly after the release of his Grammy-winning *Complete Recordings* in 1990. The stamp selection process thus illustrates the intertwining of the officially sanctioned and the popular, the governmental and the grassroots, the real and the media revision and recirculation of the real that will form much of my analysis throughout this book.

Robert Johnson on a postage stamp also illustrates two often conflicting forces at work: a dominant power (in this case, the government) and the people—although the stamp selection process suggests that the government would like citizens to see no difference between the two groups or forces, and in this case the two groups did agree on Johnson's noteworthy artistry. But perhaps because of the different workings of these two groups, and perhaps because, as Baty reminds us, our late-capitalist culture is becoming increasingly diverse and thus less willing to accept power-bloc operations uncritically, the 1994 Jazz and Blues Singers stamp series became immediately controversial. Much of the contention centered on the selection of the musicians depicted. The inclusion of lesser-known figures like Mildred Bailey and Jimmy Rushing over more celebrated artists like Louis Armstrong and Ella Fitzgerald caused much of the stir (Broomer), and the omission of the increasingly ubiquitous B. B. King, even though he is a living artist and therefore technically ineligible, was the subject of heated debate on online blues discussion lists like Blues-L and Harp-L. But the largest outcry centered on the Robert Johnson stamp because the Post Office altered the image.

Only two photographs of Robert Johnson are known to exist: a full-length studio portrait of Johnson wearing an elegant suit and hat and holding his guitar on his lap (see the frontispiece), and a photo-booth headshot with one hand beside his face, gripping a guitar neck (see figure 1). Julian Allen, the artist enlisted to create the Johnson stamp image (see figure 2), used the headshot as his model, a good choice for a small stamp in its lack of clutter (no hat) and its inclusion of a segment of Johnson's trademark guitar. But in the original photograph, Johnson also has a cigarette dangling from his mouth, and while Allen's first version of the stamp design included the cigarette, the Post Office ordered him to delete it.

Allen is a New York–based illustrator who now asserts that his greatest claim to fame is being the man who got Robert Johnson to quit smoking (Vickers 36). He did delete the cigarette, but he complained mildly that he thought the government action was "a little bit petty" and noted that he would have preferred to include the historically accurate cigarette in the picture. He told an interviewer that the Post Office had also rejected his initial design for the Muddy Waters stamp because, Allen suspected, the subject "looked too black," his surmise based on the Post Office's subsequent acceptance of a lighter-skinned version (Vickers 37). Allen's remarks suggest his discomfort with the operations of the power-bloc authority and raise the ugly specter of racism as a factor in stamp-design approval.

Figure 1. Robert Johnson. Photo-booth self-portrait, early 1930s. © 1986 Delta Haze Corporation. All rights reserved. Used by permission.

Figure 2. Robert Johnson 1994 Commemorative Postage Stamp. Stamp Designs © 1994 United States Postal Service. Displayed with permission. All rights reserved. Written authorization from the Postal Service is required to use, reproduce, post, transmit, distribute, or publicly diplay these images. Based on Robert Johnson photo-booth self-portrait. © 1986 Delta Haze Corporation. All rights reserved. Used by permission.

Smokers across the country were also quick to voice their dismay at the Post Office's decision to remove Johnson's trademark cigarette. Thomas Humber, then president of the National Smokers Alliance (with over one million members at the time), issued several protests on behalf of his organization. In a letter to the postmaster general, Marvin Runyon, Humber called the stamp revision "'an affront to the more than 50 million Americans who choose to smoke'" (qtd. in "Absent Cigarette"). And in a statement released on 15 September 1994, two days before the stamp was issued, Humber questioned the government's role in altering Johnson's image: "The issue here is, 'What is the job of the Post Office?' Their job should not be to corrupt history, no matter what anyone thinks about smoking." For Humber, an embattled libertarian in a culture that increasingly relegates smokers to porches and alleyways, "'Life is magnificent in its diversity. Why can't we just let it be?'" (qtd. in "Nicotine Fit").

The Post Office justified its action by citing historical precedents and health issues. Post Office representative Monica Hand explained, "'It's been an ongoing practice not to include cigarettes'" in stamp design, offering the Edward R. Murrow and George Meany stamps as examples where a cigarette in the model photograph was deleted in the stamp design (qtd. in "Nicotine Fit"). Cigarettes have been removed from stamp designs in cases before and after the Johnson flap, including those honoring Thornton Wilder, James Dean, and Jackson Pollock (Cash). Hand further explained that the Post Office "'didn't want the stamps to be perceived as promoting cigarettes'" (qtd. in "Absent Cigarette"). While most nonsmokers might concur that official government publications should not endorse an activity that is known to be deadly, the Post Office policy—which has been viewed as everything from censorship to a public health issue—does tell us something about our culture. In the words of Jean Baudrillard, a French cultural critic who has written extensively about America, we are an "obsessional society" that often operates on the principles "[p]rotect everything, detect everything, contain everything" (*America* 40).

In fact, while the Post Office may justly contend that its policy of not including cigarettes on stamps is designed to promote the public welfare, stamp historians note that stamps always serve multiple purposes of the regime in power. "'They've always been used as propaganda,'" claims Michael F. Schreiber, a senior editor at *Linn's Stamp News* (qtd. in Zane). One such governmental purpose is, of course, to make money. Commemorative stamps like those in the Jazz and Blues series are especially good for business, since, according to Post Office spokesperson Valoree Vargo, about 20 percent of them will never be used to pay for postage but will be saved by philatelists and music lovers, netting pure profit for the Post Office ("Absent Cigarette"). And while encouraging public health may be one purpose of deleting cigarettes from stamps, a number of commentators have observed the incongruity of claiming to promote wholesome and patriotic values while celebrating jazz and blues singers, who frequently led "vice-ridden" lives ("Nicotine Fit"). J. Peder Zane has noted, perhaps with tongue in cheek, that the proposed and sanctioned "old Elvis" stamp "glamorized the dangerously overweight singer" and could be interpreted as promoting poor nutrition. The Robert Johnson stamp offers an even clearer case in point: hard drinking, given to hitching rides on trains and messing with married women (both unsafe practices), and claiming to have done business with Satan himself, Johnson seems less a "representative citizen" than someone destined to be killed long before cigarettes could get to him. The stamp thus represents something of a double-edged sword for blues lovers, as music critic Stuart Broomer notes: Johnson is finally getting public recognition, but his image must be revised "lest the official culture seem to sanction any destructive habit that he practiced."

But the controversy over altering Johnson's photograph goes beyond the issues of smokers' rights or promoting wholesome values. Stamp historian Laura Heron describes stamps as "official visual statements of the state that issues them" (44), and in choosing to commemorate eight figures from jazz and blues history, the Post Office was also choosing to celebrate a specifically African American contribution to American culture. One irony of this choice is that Robert Johnson could not have seen an African American on a postage stamp during his lifetime, since the first African American so honored was Booker T. Washington in 1940, two years after Johnson's death. Before any African American appeared on a U.S. postage stamp, the Post Office had commemorated a number of Native Americans (Pocahontas in 1907, the Sioux chief Hollow Horn Bear in 1923, and the generic "Indian Hunting Buffalo" in 1898); inventions like the locomotive engine (1869), the electric automobile (1901), and Thomas Edison's first lamp (1929); a Viking ship (1925), the family of Virginia Dare (1937), and in 1938, the year of Johnson's death, the tercentennial of a Swedish/Finnish colony that survived in America for only twelve years. If, as historian Donald M. Reid asserts, stamps reveal "symbolic messages which governments seek to convey to their citizens and to the world" (223), the omission of African Americans from this system of communication speaks volumes about American culture in the pre–Civil Rights era. The development of the Black Heritage series, begun in 1978 with a Harriet

Tubman stamp and continuing to honor one African American leader yearly, was long overdue.

This erasure of African Americans from the official history of the United States as recorded on stamps makes the deletion of the Robert Johnson cigarette particularly troubling to some critics. Choosing Johnson only to alter his image raises a host of questions about the nature of representation and about who owns a person's image. In this case, the simple answer to the second question is that music researcher Stephen C. LaVere does, since he entered into a contractual agreement with Johnson's sister over the execution of Johnson's estate and copyrighted the two photographs. However, even that simple answer is complicated by a lawsuit brought by Claud Johnson, apparently Robert Johnson's son, who has recently been awarded the share of Robert's estate that formerly belonged to Johnson's sister. Appeals are pending at this writing, admirably illustrating Americans' notorious litigiousness. But the question of who owns a representation has theoretical ramifications beyond the legal ones. As Vernon Chadwick notes in his study of the posthumous representations of Elvis Presley, the politics of representation often "works to secure dominant modes of authority through construction of history and identity" (xviii). In the case of Robert Johnson, the authoritarian revision of his image recalls the disturbing history of misrepresentation of blacks by whites—epitomized by blackface minstrelsy, the most popular form of public entertainment in the nineteenth century—that has always marked American culture.

Blackface minstrelsy arose during the early nineteenth century in the United States, a time when the overwhelming majority of African Americans were slaves who were forbidden to read or write and thus denied access to the culture's systems of communication and representation. The first images of African Americans to emerge in the popular imagination were fabricated and performed by whites in blackface (the power-bloc operators of the era), men such as T. D. Rice, who created the comic minstrel character of the foolish Jim Crow. The fact that white audiences took these representations of a silenced people as realistic renderings forever complicates the representation of black people in America. As Eric Lott notes in his groundbreaking study of blackface minstrelsy, popular blackface actors like Rice created "an iconography of racial difference, clearly graphing difference as inferiority" (101). Even when African Americans began performing in minstrel shows themselves, they were often required to darken their already dark skin with cork or lampblack and to continue performing in the patterns set down by their white predecessors; black performers found themselves demonstrating their "authentic" blackness by emulating whites who had caricatured blacks. Given this history of African Americans being depicted primarily through demeaning stereotypes created by white Americans, the Post Office's insistence on refashioning Johnson's image can be seen as a contemporary example of the dominant (largely white) culture controlling how African Americans look to the world. We saw earlier that smokers' rights activist Thomas Humber complained about the Post Office's corruption of history. Seen in the context of blackface performance, the Post Office may have unwittingly recapitulated it instead.

One can argue conversely that *not* deleting the cigarette would also have been tantamount to racism. The U.S. Postal Service had already deleted the cigarette from images of white subjects like Murrow and Meany. As Adam Gussow has noted, the deletion of Johnson's cigarette might actually have been an attempt to treat all subjects equally, regardless of race. Since cigarettes had been deleted from stamp images of white hands, not deleting them from black hands might foster the impression that the Post Office "sees nicotine—and, by extension, other addictive, vice-accompanying substances—[as] somehow more 'natural' in black hands, more inevitably and indissolubly a part of black life" (Letter). Gussow makes a defensible point, based on principles of equality and fairness, in comments sensitive to the challenges inherent in representing African Americans. But the furor over altering Johnson's image suggests that the history of tampering with black images has created deep and permanent resentments that rational appeals to equality will not appease. Dr. Charles Snyder, the CEO of Central Virginia Educational Telecommunications Corporation, offers this scathing indictment of "the bold move of censorship" made in removing Johnson's cigarette: "'This is the stuff of great political farce—at once tragic and ludicrous. By altering the photo, the Postal Service has placed itself in the distinguished company of Stalin and Mao'" (qtd. in "News and Notes"). An action that provokes such extreme reactions is not likely to be explained away on the basis of symmetrical representational practices.

Adding to the myriad problems of representation is the Post Office's money-making motive in creating all commemorative stamps. Viewed again in a long-term historical context, the Post Office's Jazz and Blues series could look like another example of the cultural appropriation of black artistry for the profit of the dominant majority. Cultural critic George Lipsitz charges that white Americans have always demonstrated a "pathological need to control, contain, and even take credit for black culture"

(*Dangerous* 54). This charge—that white agents take over black art forms and reap the monetary rewards, denying black artists any control over or profit from them—recurs throughout American history and literature and certainly pertains to blues and jazz artists, past and present, like those celebrated on the 1994 stamps. In his 1941 autobiography *Father of the Blues,* W. C. Handy explains in some detail how he was cheated out of sheet music royalties on "Memphis Blues" (usually considered the first blues song to be published) by agents who lied about the number of copies printed, misrepresented the number of sales, and so coerced an unwitting Handy into selling his valuable music plates for a mere fifty dollars to cover his expenses (106–14). Big Bill Broonzy reports that he "'never got a penny'" for the three commercially successful songs he recorded in 1926 (qtd. in Lomax 444). Even today, one self-appointed task of the Blues Heaven Foundation, founded by the late Willie Dixon in 1981 and continuing under the leadership of his wife and daughter, is the recovery of royalties for living musicians who have been defrauded of their rights to their moneymaking songs. As Langston Hughes sums up this process in "Notes on the Commercial Theatre," white artists have "taken [his] blues and gone," transporting them to Broadway and Hollywood, and interweaving them with other musical forms until "they don't sound like [him]" (215–16). Seen as part of this historical situation, removing Robert Johnson's cigarette appears vexingly similar to the process Hughes describes, as the Post Office modified the historical image of Robert Johnson for laudable ends—to honor his musicianship—but also reaped a profit from it. Ironically, while refusing to consider stamp subjects that "honor commercial enterprise or products," the Post Office creates its own commercial product using images of artists who themselves had few opportunities to benefit from their own creations.

One might look at the above analysis of the Robert Johnson postage stamp and justifiably complain that the government—specifically the U.S. Post Office—is damned if it does and damned if it doesn't. It is criticized for not including African American subjects before 1940 and then criticized anew for the way it depicts them when it finally does. My aim in this case study of the Robert Johnson stamp is neither to evaluate Post Office procedures nor to impute nefarious motives to their decision to honor Robert Johnson. Rather, my summary of the various reactions to the apparently innocent Robert Johnson postage stamp is meant to demonstrate that cultural practices and the discourse about them can never be entirely neutral. The story of the Robert Johnson stamp reveals much about the storytellers and more about the values and myths of contemporary culture—from smokers' rights to African American cultural criticism—than it does about Post Office policies or about Robert Johnson himself.

But how did Robert Johnson, once an actual person bounded by the historical contexts of the rural South and the early twentieth century, become a disembodied presence, a myth? Much recent scholarship has explored this mythmaking process as it applies to contemporary figures, and excellent studies of human icons like Elvis Presley and Marilyn Monroe, or fictional ones like Batman and Superman, have helped me develop my premises.[2] Underlying a number of these studies as well as my own project are the theories of several influential critics, notably Roland Barthes, John Fiske, and Cornel West. In the next section I will briefly explain their theories of mythmaking, power relations, and multiculturalism and suggest how they can help us understand the postmodern emanations of Robert Johnson. In chapter 1 I will turn to Johnson's life story and explore how the many points of contestation within it function inside the mythmaking systems of twenty-first-century America.

Theoretical Foundations: Mythmaking, Power Relations, and Race

Writing about the Elvis Presley phenomenon in 1991, music critic Greil Marcus asked a provocative question: "It's easy enough to understand a dead but evanescent Elvis Presley as a cultural symbol, but what if he—it—is nothing so limited, but a sort of cultural epistemology, a skeleton key to a lock we've yet to find?" (*Dead Elvis* xv–xvi). This question intrigues me on several levels, but primarily for its shifting of Elvis from person to icon—"he" to "it"—and for the notion that this dead being, this "skeleton key," may be not a mere symbol but the indicator of entire ways of knowing, of a mythology that we may not yet recognize as such. In order to explore the ways of knowing that Robert Johnson, like Elvis, may represent and how we create icons from historical people and then myths from the icons, I turn to Roland Barthes's influential theory of how myth works in contemporary society.

Barthes based his work in semiotics, a method of determining meaning based on viewing virtually everything as a text, susceptible to multiple interpretations. In semiotic terms, anything—a book, a baseball cap, a hair style, a pair of jeans—can be a sign, a carrier of meaning that varies with time and context. Semiotics posits a relationship between two items, a signifier (usually an object) and a signified (a concept), and this relationship is made explicit in the "sign," which is the combination of the two. In Barthes's famous example, a rose is just a rose, devoid of meaning, but when he gives it to his beloved as a symbol of his passion it becomes a sign of something beyond itself—his feelings—while retaining its primary identity as a rose (112–13).

Myth, according to Barthes, operates on this same tridimensional relationship between a signifier, a signified, and the sign that is produced by their union. However, myth is a "second-order semiological system"; it begins by taking the sign produced by a primary semiotic equation (such as the rose that has been made to signify passion) and using it as the empty, devoid-of-meaning signifier of the next level of interpretation. In doing so, it differs from a basic semiotic equation, in which the first signifier (the rose) retains its original status as a rose even as it becomes a symbol of passion. When that symbol is used as a signifier in a second-order system, it loses its original meaning; it is no longer an actual rose but already a sign of something other than itself. As Barthes explains it, the signifier in a second-level system "empties itself, it becomes impoverished, history evaporates, only the letter [or outward form] remains" (117).

We have already seen these signs and myths operate in the case of the Robert Johnson postage stamp. The process of producing the stamp began with a historical person, a man, a signifier without semiotic significance. When the Postal Service decided to use his image to celebrate jazz and blues singers, Robert Johnson the signifier became Robert Johnson the sign, the signified being Americans' appreciation of their musical history. But the stamp itself then became a signifier, used by various interest groups as a sign of smokers' rights, cultural appropriation, censorship, or public health, depending on the signified as each group conceived it. In this process, Robert Johnson the artist was all but erased, his image used to create cultural myths that reveal the ideologies of different interest groups. The truth about Robert Johnson hardly matters. We invest the images of and stories about Johnson with our own values, leaving Johnson as another "evanescent presence" (like Marcus's Elvis), drained of his own history as he comes to signify something about ours. Throughout this book I will repeatedly explore the way Johnson the man and artist disappears into Johnson the image or Johnson the sign, and from there into myths that reflect current political and ideological formations. Barthes's semiotic method allows us to see the variable meanings of signs, to understand that myths are formed from signs, not objective "reality," and to recognize the ideologies inherent in what may seem to be "innocent" representations.

The work of John Fiske is also helpful in learning to recognize unexamined or unacknowledged ideologies. Like Barthes, Fiske uses semiotics to analyze popular culture, but he combines the insights of semiotics with two important and interrelated poststructuralist ideas: first, that identity and group relationships are not fixed but subject to change; second, that the meaning of popular culture emerges when we observe the operations of power in creating and consuming it.[3] For Fiske, neither the official power brokers with the money and authority to create cultural artifacts nor the people, the consumers of those artifacts, constitute a stable social category. Rather, both groups are "alliances of social interests formed strategically or tactically to advance the interests of those who form them" (*Power Plays* 10). In using the term "power-bloc" to describe top-down power (as I have used it in discussing the postage stamp), Fiske suggests a melding of different parts—a temporary alliance of forces—and not a solid object nor a permanent social class. Likewise, Fiske uses the term "the people" to indicate that the consumers of popular culture are not a monolithic group (that is, not a "mass culture") nor a social category bound by allegiances of class, gender, race, religion, age, or other identity positions. Rather, the term "the people" encompasses shifting coalitions of individuals united temporarily for a common interest (*Power Plays* 7–10). These alliances may coincide with other social categories—as, for example, one might find mostly women (a social category) at a feminist conference—but such alliances are not determined by social categories nor limited to them: there may be men at the feminist meeting, many women are not feminists, and feminist women may belong to other kinds of organizations. Combining Barthes's articulation of mythmaking with Fiske's understanding of mutable coalitions of power helps us understand the shifting significance of signs in a consumer culture that is constantly metamorphosing.

The study of popular culture has not always taken this approach. As Fiske describes its history in *Understanding Popular Culture,* before 1990 there were two prominent trends in the field. The first recognized that popular culture (everything from designer clothes to Disneyland to, say, Robert Johnson paraphernalia) had meaning, deemed it worthy of study, and celebrated it, without necessarily exploring its place in the context of the power relations developed by creation, consumption, and desire. The second trend placed popular culture within a model of power inequities but overemphasized the ability of dominating powers (that is, mainstream culture, the wealthy, the government, or, say, the Post Office) to force its authority on "the masses," who thus appear to be helpless dupes of the dominant culture. Fiske notes with enthusiasm the development of a third trend, which his work has done much to promote: it recognizes popular culture as a site of struggle, accepts the power of dominating forces, but emphasizes the alternative power wielded by the people in managing, adapting, or even resisting those power-bloc forces (*Understanding* 20). Using the example of blue jeans, which have shifted in significance over time from a sign of manual labor to a token of designer fashion, Fiske reads the 1980s style of wearing intentionally ripped jeans as consumer resistance to being commodified. Torn jeans reflect the people's power to reshape the significance of an item by their iconoclastic use of it; what once was a sign of poverty (torn clothing) becomes a statement, a challenge to existing norms and stereotypes (13–14). Fiske claims, "Popular culture is made by the people, not imposed upon them. . . . Popular culture is the art of making do with what the system provides" (25).

In the Fiskean worldview, operations of power can act from the top down or from the bottom up (*Power Plays* 9–12). These twin processes are illustrated in the example of the Robert Johnson postage stamp, where the power-bloc consisted of a governmental agency (the Post Office) as well as its Citizens Advisory Committee, which may include and was certainly influenced by average citizens like the fictional assistant on "The West Wing." The final decision on stamp design was certainly a power-bloc operation, but the process of stamp selection encourages input from the people. The reactions to the stamp by the people also illustrate the diversity within mass culture, as opinions varied sharply from one group of consumers to the next, from smokers to blues fans to champions of historical accuracy (and note that any protester could belong to all or some of these categories at various times).

Given this instability of groups and social categories, Fiske may be right in his assessment that the consensus model of understanding American culture is outdated; the melting pot of ideas has cracked. Like S. Paige Baty, who sees the contemporary United States as an amalgam of local interests, or a variety of competing discourses reflecting "a multiplicity of values" (10), Fiske argues that when there is no dominating overview opinion at the center of our thinking, it is time to replace our universalizing worldview with a newer paradigm, focused more on locally based "cultures of practice" than on an imperializing "culture of control" (*Power Plays* 19). He thus sees current multicultural initiatives (in education and in politics) as offering an important corrective to social inequities: multiculturalism acknowledges the bottom-up power of diverse groups of people and challenges the imperializing mindset of the power-bloc (281). While

Fiske has been criticized for his optimism in predicting that multiculturalism portends the end of traditional power hierarchies, his basic vision of the present and future as based on local, shifting, and diverse group interests is shared by a number of contemporary cultural critics, particularly those who focus on race and its relationships to power. Given the troubled history of race relations in U.S. history, one cannot ignore the influence of race—the way it intersects with both mythology and power relations—when discussing representations of an African American artist like Robert Johnson.

In a 1990 essay on new cultural criticism, philosopher Cornel West discusses power relations and the creativity of "the people," especially African Americans, in responding to them. Like Fiske and Baty, West acknowledges the recent trends among cultural studies scholars to criticize homogeneity and the monolithic in favor of the diverse and multicultural and offers some explanations for these trends ("New Cultural" 19). According to West, Europe had long been the model and arbiter of high culture, but this status has been challenged, if not displaced, as the United States has emerged as a center of global culture. As a result of the ascendance of the United States as a world power, the definition of "culture" itself has shifted. In addition to the products of European classical aesthetics, "culture" now includes the mass-mediated, technologically based popular culture objects that Americans so exuberantly produce, consume, and export. At the same time as this shift in the definition of "culture" began to occur, the so-called Third World became decolonized, and the sensibilities of its people emerged with some force in world culture (20–25). As a result of these shifts, the best critical method for examining this "culture of difference" would be one that identified and challenged power dynamics. In short, the best cultural criticism would "demystify" myths about the stability of power and the neutrality of representation, focusing on the ways human agency, "always enacted under circumstances not of one's choosing," constructs creative responses to conditions imposed upon it (31).

As I have described him so far, West may seem merely a globally focused parallel to Fiske, a champion of worldwide local powers that resist power-bloc operations. What West adds to the discussion, however, is an emphasis on race as culturally defined and crucially enmeshed in power relations, representations, and the creation of culture. Just as Fiske uses poststructuralist ideas to analyze the concept of culture, West uses them to complicate notions of race. Arguing that "blackness is a political and ethical construct" ("Black Leadership" 393–94), West calls for new networks of discourse that would deconstruct fixed notions of black identity, expose the racial bases of power imbalances, and create more complex articulations of black identities and black practices ("New Cultural" 29). In short, he advocates dismantling the entire cultural mythology surrounding race and its representation and then developing new ones.

A number of important scholars have recently been practicing a variant of this highly race-conscious cultural criticism. In an attempt to create definitions of black identity that focus on agency, they emphasize the "bottom-up" power operations practiced by African Americans. George Lipsitz, for example, emphasizes "the genius of African American culture in nurturing and sustaining moral and cultural alternatives to dominant values" (*Dangerous* 54)—a genius apparent in the development of the blues. Musicologist John Cowley has written persuasively about the tendency of rural African American bluesmen to gloss over the social protest embedded in their songs when interpreting the lyrics for white field researchers (135). Finally, and perhaps most appropriate to a discussion of Robert Johnson and his era, historian Clyde Woods describes early twentieth-century blues musicians as professors in a working-class, unwalled university in the Delta ("Opening Remarks"), where they preserved and spread African Americans' own "epistemology, their own theory of social change, and their own theories of class and depravity" (*Development* 103).

The influence of such scholars will be apparent in the pages that follow. Throughout this study of Robert Johnson's life, the legends about him, and contemporary artistic uses of him, I emphasize the different ways he has come to signify as a myth within the contexts of power relations and racial disparities. Robert Johnson himself was caught up in these practices, as he negotiated his way through the segregated, often violent, Depression-era South and through a recording industry controlled by white executives. The stories of people who knew him as well as the information found by researchers who have studied his life all need to be examined through these lenses. And the contemporary literary and popular uses of his legend need to be seen not only as myths (in the Barthesian sense) but also as reflections of the power imbalances and racial tensions that define American culture at the start of the twenty-first century. My discussion of the Robert Johnson stamp in the contexts of minstrelsy and cultural appropriation offers one example of this "demystifying" approach. I will continue to use it throughout this book in an attempt to expose some of the complex workings of myth, power, and race in our culture as illustrated in the Robert Johnson legacy.

Chapter 1 focuses on how Robert Johnson the man became Robert Johnson the sign and how Robert Johnson the sign became Robert Johnson the myth. The subsequent chapters leave behind the historical Robert Johnson and move on to a discussion of how contemporary artists (in literature, film, and other popular constructions) have used the myths about Robert Johnson to create further myths. In chapter 2 I look at texts that retell some aspects of the Robert Johnson story in its original historical context—in his own life and times. This chapter focuses on the creation of history, how it is used in artistic works like fiction, and how it intersects with the construction of myth. Chapter 3 and chapter 4 examine texts in which Robert Johnson is removed from his historical context and in which his life story is not the central tale. Rather, he functions as a catalyst for the actions and insights of other characters in other settings, ranging from a Spokane Indian reservation in the 1990s, to the memory of a homeless New Yorker, to a hellmouth eruption in New Orleans, to the quests undertaken by several young men in search of a hypothetical thirtieth Robert Johnson song. Imported into these new arenas, Robert Johnson circulates as a sign of contemporary cultural exchanges, offering inspiration to individuals and the promise of enriched intercultural understanding to American society as a whole. Chapter 5 focuses on the use of his image in various Web sites and explores what his presence on the Internet tells us about cyberculture. It also examines the metacommentary about the commentary on a silent film clip of what was once, for a short time, thought to be Robert Johnson. In the conclusion I briefly introduce chaos theory, an important contemporary scientific model, as a metaphor for all the different meanings that the image of Robert Johnson has accrued, for like the strange attractors of chaos theory, Robert Johnson has become an absent center around which comment and controversy revolve. Throughout this book I will be asking—and attempting to answer—the following question: what cultural purposes do these various re-visionings of Robert Johnson serve?

Peter Guralnick has written that Robert Johnson "never really died; he simply became an idea" (63). I would amend this statement to reflect the variety of contemporary American cultural practices and discourses and say that he became not one idea but a shifting complex or web of ideas. Let's look at some of the ideas that Robert Johnson became in the work of his biographers and his fellow artists near the start of the twenty-first century; let's listen for the resonances of his life and his uncanny guitar in the work of the turn-of-the-century researchers and artists whom he has inspired.

1
Robert Johnson as Contested Space

Robert Leroy Johnson was born in Hazelhurst, Mississippi, on 8 May 1911. Probably. Well, maybe. That's the date provided by his half-sister Carrie Harris Thompson, who recalled that their mother always cited it as Robert's birthday. It is also the date usually listed in the most thoroughly researched studies of his life, such as those by Stephen C. LaVere (7), Jas Obrecht (2), and Peter Guralnick (who gives the date as "probable" [10]), although David Evans offers "around 1912" (*Big Road* 195), and Stephen Calt and Gayle Dean Wardlow propose "between September, 1911, and August, 1912" (42). However, in the dispute over Johnson's estate brought by Claud Johnson, Robert's putative son, new documents and stories have cast doubt on 1911 as the year of Johnson's birth, as *Living Blues* writer Tom Freeland has summarized. The records from Indian Creek School, which Johnson attended, list his age as fourteen in 1924, which would make his birth year 1910; in 1927 the same school lists his age as eighteen, making 1909 the year of his birth. His first marriage license lists his age as twenty-one in February 1929 (therefore, born 1907); his second marriage license lists him as twenty-three on 4 May 1931 (also 1907); but his death certificate lists him as twenty-six in August 1938 (born, therefore, in 1912). Census records from 1910 do not list Robert among his mother's children, making a birth date before that year unlikely (Freeland, "Some Witnesses" 49). The recollections of Johnson's acquaintances vary, too, on the year of his birth. Honeyboy Edwards, Johnson's sometime musical partner, claims, "'Robert was about three years older than me. Think Robert born in about '12, or something like that'" (qtd. in Johnson 20). Johnny Shines, a frequent traveling companion of Johnson's, also puts his birth somewhat later than the usually agreed-upon 1911: "When Robert and I first met [in 1935] . . . he was about twenty-two or twenty-three"—and therefore born in 1912 or 1913 (31).

I recite these conflicting certificates and opinions to illustrate something fundamental about studying Robert Johnson: even the simplest, most apparently factual details are open to dispute. I don't care much whether he was born in 1911 or 1912, and I suspect that you don't, either. But if we decide to figure it out, we can consult legal documents (in Fiske's terms, the tracks of power-bloc operations in his life), or we can ask some of the people who knew him, and we will find that in all cases the "facts" vary. Before we can even get started documenting Johnson's life—before we can even ascertain a birth date and so bring him into the story—we become enmeshed in speculation. We must navigate the slipshod record keeping of black American life by white southern functionaries, and so immediately brush up against the racial tensions of the era. In the official documents about Robert Johnson we find not only discrepancies about birth year but also confusions over parentage and race: his two marriage licenses list his father's name as "Nora" and "Nola," respectively (rather than the correct Noah), and the first license lists Johnson's "color" as "man" (Freeland, "Some Witnesses" 49). This tendency of white officials to disfigure black records is a recurring theme in African American literature. In Richard Wright's autobiographical novel *Black Boy,* the narrator's grandfather is cheated out of his Civil War pension by a white officer who misspells his name, possibly because of the grandfather's accent and illiteracy, possibly because the officer was Swedish and had poor English skills, or possibly because the officer was a southerner who deliberately falsified the paper (161–62). And in Toni Morrison's fictional *Song of Solomon,* a drunken Confederate soldier puts information about newly freed slaves in the wrong boxes on a form, so that a man with Georgia roots whose father is deceased is inadvertently renamed "Macon Dead" (18). While this latter story, created for novelistic purposes, has its humorous aspects, both examples illustrate the perception that white officials in the late nineteenth-century South had little interest in compiling accurate records of African American lives. The truth of this perception is born out in Robert Johnson's history.

If we decide to forego official documentation and stick to eyewitnesses, we face conflicting memories of aging observers who may never have known Johnson's exact age in the first place. And then we must ask in each case whose interests are being served by the information and misinformation circulated: Was the court clerk mischievous, careless, partially illiterate, or perhaps intoxicated like Morrison's soldier? Do Johnson's acquaintances have personal agendas in telling stories about him? Did Johnson himself have occasional reason to lie about his age? And when so much inconsistent information emerges from a court squabble over who controls Johnson's sizable estate—a fortune that has accumulated mostly since 1990, when the *Complete Recordings* went platinum in sales—one also wonders if other documents might have been suppressed or memories refurbished. In short, every aspect of Robert Johnson's life represents a contested space, a gap that various people have filled in various ways and possibly to promote idiosyncratic agendas. Each version has its own submerged tale to tell.

These tales-within-tales—the myths about Robert Johnson—are the focus of this chapter. Any blues fan will know the basics about Johnson's life, and for those who don't, I will provide a thumbnail sketch before turning to an exploration of the myths that fill the gaps. For those seeking more biographical detail, I recommend Guralnick, the routinely updated Delta Haze web site, or Pearson and McCulloch's *Robert Johnson: Lost and Found.* In the meantime, here is an outline of the things we know—or think we know—about Robert Johnson's life.

The only thing we know for sure about Robert Johnson is that he was born into a world circumscribed by psychological uncertainties, social injustice, and racism. His mother, Julia, and her husband, Charles Dodds, had owned a successful farm and were raising a large family before an altercation with a white man forced Charles Dodds to flee to Memphis, where he changed his name to Spencer. Julia and some of the children stayed behind, and Robert was born some years later, the product of Julia's affair with a local farmer, Noah Johnson. His first few years were spent with his mother and sister in migrant labor camps, until Julia took the children to rejoin Dodds/Spencer (and his new wife) in Memphis, where she left Robert for a few years until Dodds tired of the responsibility. In 1918 Robert rejoined his mother in Robinsonville, Mississippi, where he grew to manhood under the care of Julia and her new husband, Dusty Willis, a demanding stepfather who apparently beat Robert. He endured a difficult childhood, with "three different fathers before he was seven, a series of sudden uprootings, and a succession of name changes" (Palmer 112). Tack onto the disruptions of that early life the 1930 childbed deaths of his beloved wife Virginia (at age sixteen) and their baby, and the sensibility that created song lyrics about hellhounds on his trail and Satanic visits is not difficult to imagine.

In the years after Virginia's death, castigated by her family and friends who believed that his playing "the devil's music" had brought on the disaster (Obrecht 4), Robert seems to have abandoned his attempts at a stable, settled existence and embraced the impermanence that had always defined his life. As he told his neighbor Elizabeth Moore, "'I don't wanna work; I'm tryin' to learn how to make my livin' *without* pickin' cotton'" (qtd. in Calt and Wardlow 43). He allegedly used a series of different last names, including Spencer, Dodds, Moore, James, Barstow, Dusty, Saunders, and Saxton or "Sax,"[1] sometimes to evade the law, according to Moore. However, one can also imagine his trying on a variety of identities as an exercise in self-definition. He traveled widely, learning what he could from local musicians like Son House and Willie Brown before disappearing into southern Mississippi to learn from Ike Zinermon and others,[2] eventually roaming as far as Ontario and New York. He married again, abandoned his wife, and developed a network of women friends with homes he could stay in wherever he went. Something of a chameleon, Johnson showed contradictory aspects of himself and his personality to the different people who knew him. Johnny Shines once remembered him as "'a bum who was always getting drunk and pissing in his pants'" (qtd. in Calt and Wardlow 42), yet Honeyboy Edwards describes him as always looking dapper, noting that no matter how dusty the work or how many nights he'd slept in his clothes, "'I'd catch my breath and see myself looking like a *dog,* there'd be Robert, all clean as can be, looking like he's just stepping out of a church'" (qtd. in Palmer 121). Some remember him as a loner, "A quiet type of guy [who] didn't associate with too many people" (Edwards 102), while others recall him as "'proud as a peafowl and terribly nervy'" (Son House qtd. in Lomax 16), "'a natural showman'" (Johnny Shines qtd. in Welding 76), a gregarious ladies' man able to charm an audience or a woman at a moment's notice. While some of the variations in his personality probably came from his heavy drinking—both Memphis Slim ("Death" 15) and Johnny Shines (Obrecht 8) report that he was a different person sober than when drunk—it is probably fair to say that Johnson's most consistent characteristic was inconsistency.

One constant running through his life, however, was his dedication to music. As a child he fashioned a diddley bow (a single string fastened to a wall) that he played with a bottle slide, as a teenager he played harmonica, and in 1927 he acquired his first guitar (Obrecht 4). When local musicians like House and Brown discouraged the unskilled youth from playing guitar publicly, he traveled south to hone his craft by listening obsessively to radio and records as well as to other master players. As his genius emerged and he made a name for himself throughout the juke joint circuit in the Delta, Johnson actively sought recording opportunities. He took the initiative to find H. C. Speir, a local music store owner with an informal recording studio and contacts in the recording industry, who recognized Johnson's talent and put him in touch with talent scout Ernie Oertle. This connection led to two recording sessions for Vocalion Records, one in San Antonio in 1936 and another in Dallas in 1937, from which emerged all the haunting Johnson music we have today.[3] Fourteen months later Robert Johnson was dead, apparently at the hands of a jealous husband, finally (if the stories are true) a victim of the violence of his culture and of his own promiscuity.

The music that he left, albeit enhanced by the mysteries of his life and death, is the primary reason that Robert Johnson is remembered, even revered, today. After the release of his posthumous 1961 record, an entire generation of music lovers was profoundly affected. Writer Russell Banks claims that "blues fans of my age like to tell about the first time they heard Robert Johnson. It resembles our compulsion to say where we were when the Kennedys were killed" (27). Banks's observation about the mythologizing impulse generated by first hearing Johnson's music is corroborated by numerous writers and musicians of his generation. Greil Marcus alleges that "Johnson's music changed the way the world looked to me" (*Mystery* 31); Peter Guralnick describes "the breathless rush of feeling that I experienced the first time I ever really heard Robert Johnson's music" (3); guitar great Eric Clapton recalls the "'shock . . . that there could be anything that powerful'" (qtd. in LaVere 22). The lyrics, full of harrowing images of loss, loneliness, longing, and entrapment, are one obvious source of the music's appeal. This often devastating imagery is compounded by the raw power and emotional intensity of the vocals, which are underscored by Johnson's compelling guitar mastery. Rolling Stones guitarist Keith Richards reports hearing the music and assuming that he was listening to Johnson and an accompanist—to two separate guitars (LaVere 21). Musicologist James Bennighof sums up Johnson's appeal well when he proposes that the whole package—the tightly integrated combination of lyric, vocals, and guitar rather than any individual component—is the source of the extraordinary emotional power of Robert Johnson's songs, a power readily apparent to blues aficionados and untrained listeners alike (155).

It is not only the intensely felt reactions to Robert Johnson's music, however, that have made him an American icon, the subject of countless books, films, plays, documentaries, and poems as well as a postage stamp. And while the intriguing gaps in his life story account for much of his current fame and will be the central focus of this study, they are not the whole source of his legendary stature. Even without the competing stories that have emerged to fill those biographical gaps, the simple outline of Robert Johnson's life conforms to archetypal patterns of western culture. Note Joseph Campbell's description of the mythic hero's life: "The usual hero adventure begins with someone from whom something has been taken, or who feels there's something lacking in the normal experiences available or permitted to the members of his society. This person then takes off on a series of adventures beyond the ordinary, either to recover what has been lost or to discover some life-giving elixir. It's usually a cycle, a going and a returning" (123). While this pattern is intended to suggest epic characters like Odysseus, Sir Galahad, or, in our contemporary culture, Luke Skywalker, Campbell could also be describing the life of Robert Johnson. Born into a society restricted by race and poverty, deprived of a stable family unit and even a stable identity, shattered by the deaths of his young wife and child, and resistant to the difficult but socially sanctioned sharecropper's life, Robert Johnson struck out on a quest to develop his musicianship, traveling farther than most of his contemporaries and returning with legendary skill and tales of supernatural intervention. Within this context of western mythic patterns, Robert Johnson would be the stuff of legend based on what we do know about him as well as on what we don't.

If we place the historical Robert Johnson within the context of specifically American mythology—such as the quest for the elusive "American Dream"—he also fits some well-established patterns. Gary Engle has observed that Superman is the quintessential American hero because, as an immigrant and an orphan, he recapitulates in his personal story the national story of origins, a story of displacement, rootlessness, and a resulting ability to reinvent oneself (677–81). While not exactly orphaned, Robert Johnson did face a series of abandonments by parents (or by those he believed to be parents) and undertook a journey to search (probably unsuccessfully) for his biological father. His reported habit of frequent name changes suggests the perpetual self-invention that Engle sees as characteristic of Americans. Finally, his migratory habits recapitulate the individual freedom to move, which Engle sees as "an integral part of America's dreamwork" (679), as well as the migration of African Americans from South to North (and sometimes back again) that has formed a historical and literary pattern in African American—and therefore American—culture.[4] And like so many other characters who have captured the American imagination (Marilyn Monroe, James Dean, John F. Kennedy), Robert Johnson died young, thus preserving the image of eternal promise in our collective consciousness. Greil Marcus sees this image of unfulfilled promise as a crucial element of the American Dream, part of the American "struggle to set oneself free from the limits one is born to, and then to learn something of the value of those limits. . . . To be an American is to feel the promise [of American life] as a birthright, and to feel alone and haunted when the promise fails" (*Mystery* 22). Struggling against limits, mobility, hauntedness, and promise only partially fulfilled—these are key elements of the life of the American mythic hero and also key elements in Robert Johnson's life story. Even without the gaps in his life that allow so much room for semiotic mythmaking, Robert Johnson's life has legendary proportions.

With the basics of his biography in mind, we can move on to those looming gaps in the story, to the different ways they have been filled in, and to what those interpolated stories reveal about American mythmaking and power relations in the twenty-first century.

The Legends, Part 1: Facing the Wall

The major myths surrounding Robert Johnson concern his astonishing musical development, whether or not he sold his soul to the devil to acquire it, and the exact cause of his death. But even less significant events in his life have taken on lives of their own, as eyewitnesses of the time and recent commentators offer competing explanations for even the small details of Johnson's life. One such small mystery: Robert Johnson was notorious for sometimes turning his back to an audience and facing the wall while he played his guitar. Why?

The account that may best reveal the workings of the culture that produced it comes from Don Law, the record company executive in charge of Johnson's two Texas recording sessions. When a record company set up a temporary field studio in the 1930s, they often brought in a series of artists or groups to record in a single day, all of whom waited on the sidelines while recording was in progress. Johnson's first recording session was thus attended by a group of Mexican musicians, to whom he turned his back while playing. To Law, who mistakenly saw Johnson as a shy country boy who "had never been off the plantation on which he was born" (Guralnick 35), turning his back to the Mexican musicians indicated that Johnson was "'[e]mbarrassed and suffering from a bad case of stage fright. . . . Eventually he calmed down enough to play, but he never faced his audience'" (qtd. in Obrecht 12). These comments from a white record producer clearly reflect the racial misunderstandings common to the period, the blinders created by white-controlled power-bloc operations like the recording industry. Law evidently misinterpreted Johnson's strategic guardedness around strangers—and especially around white strangers like Law—as shyness. Johnny Shines notes that in the 1930s "[i]t was open season on black folks in Mississippi" (Hunt), and the Mississippi-bred Johnson would no doubt have been reserved in a strange place and in the company of a strange white man who had power over his future. And as Francis Davis has pointed out, Law also failed to realize that Johnson was a widely traveled and highly experienced performer. Having made his living for years solely by playing music, he would hardly have been too shy to entertain an audience (126).

Johnson's fellow musicians from the era as well as other African Americans who knew him have a rather different explanation for his concealing his guitar playing from view. Johnny Shines describes him as an unwilling teacher of those who would imitate his style and suggests that he turned his back on other musicians to prevent them from copying his elaborate and often original picking patterns (Calt and Wardlow 46–48). When asked how he played something, Johnson would reply "just like you" instead of providing details or an illustration; if someone was watching closely he would even leave the room, sometimes mid-song, and could disappear for months (LaVere 13–14). Musician Robert Lockwood Jr., sometimes described as Johnson's "stepson" because Johnson lived with Lockwood's mother and taught Lockwood to play the guitar, believes that Johnson may have been guarding a method of tuning his guitar that he wanted kept secret, even from his own student (Delta Haze 12). Even Johnson's women friends reported waking up in the night to find him picking silently at his guitar and then stopping instantly when he saw their eyes upon him (Guralnick 56). As Stephen LaVere sums it up, according to his acquaintances Johnson "'was very protective of his playing because he was doing things on the guitar that nobody else was doing at the time'" (qtd. in Obrecht 12). In these explanations from his peers, one sees respect for Johnson's musicianship and a possible impulse to exaggerate the originality of his work (much of which was actually based on that of earlier musicians), perhaps to preserve Johnson's reputation and perhaps to bolster their own through association with the master. In no case, however, do his musical contemporaries or associates attribute this habit to shyness or stage fright.

Today's musicians have yet another explanation, based on acoustic principles rather than personality traits like timidity or secretiveness. Commenting specifically on Johnson's recording sessions, Ry Cooder notes that when facing a plaster corner, "'you get something called "corner loading." It's an acoustic principle that eliminates most of the top and most of the bottom and amplifies the middle, the same thing that a metal guitar or an electric guitar does. The midrange is where that metallic, kind of piercing sound is'" (qtd. in Obrecht 12). Keith Richards agrees, claiming, "'He [Johnson] was after a sound'" (qtd. in Obrecht 12). Like Johnson's contemporaries, these recent commentators attribute his habit of facing the wall to extraordinary technique, but of a sort more consistent with our technology-obsessed society. They may be correct, of course; there are oft-reported rumors that Johnson was playing an electric guitar in the months before his death, and the value of amplified sound would have been apparent to him from his exposure to resonator guitars like the National and the Dobro that were commonly available in the 1930s. Nonetheless, their explanation attributes unusual originality as well as experiential understanding of physics to Johnson and so participates in the romanticizing we have seen in the first-encounter-with-Robert-Johnson stories described above. While Don Law's obvious misperceptions stem from the *place* in which he met Johnson, the interpretations by turn-of-the-century musicians are probably influenced more by the *time* in which we live, a time when technology rules our lives, when much music is amplified, and when cyberpunk literature, *Star Wars* (both the movie and the missile defense system), and films like *The Matrix* dominate the public imagination.

This brief investigation into why Robert Johnson faced the wall is not intended to be conclusive. Rather, it is meant as a teaser, a promotional glimpse at competing mythologies, where they might come from and what they might mean, before we delve into the deeper mysteries about his life and legacy and the more complex mythologies surrounding them.

The Legends, Part 2: The Devil at the Crossroads

When Robert Johnson was a young man, hanging around the local Robinsonville juke joints and listening to Son House and Willie Brown play guitar, his own musical skills were relatively modest. In fact, the hired musicians had to keep him away from their guitars when they took a break because his bad playing drove away the customers. So when he disappeared into southern Mississippi for a time (reports of the length of his absence vary from six months to two years) and returned with an amazing mastery of the guitar, his old acquaintances were so startled that, according to Son House, "'all our mouths were standing open'" (qtd. in Guralnick 17). Rumors quickly started that Johnson had gone to a crossroads where he had sold his soul to the devil for his talent. This sequence of events leads to two questions, both of which are hotly debated among scholars, blues fans, and those who knew Robert Johnson: Did Robert Johnson sell his soul to the devil? And if not, how did he acquire his astonishing guitar prowess?

Blues musicians and scholars offer several explanations other than a deal with the devil to explain how Johnson's guitar playing improved so dramatically in so short a time. Foremost among these reasons is simply Johnson's broadened experience. As he traveled through the Delta, he became acquainted with guitar styles and methods of tuning that were unfamiliar to his more stationary Robinsonville associates. We know he lived and studied with Hazelhurst guitarist Ike Zinermon for a while (Freeland, "Some Witnesses" 47), and he may have had other mentors. His recordings reveal traces of influence from a wide assortment of musicians of the era, suggesting that he also listened avidly to radio and phonograph records, using the new recording technology to research and learn music beyond that from his immediate home area. This project was aided by his uncanny ability to learn music by ear. Johnny Shines reported that after hearing a piece one time from another musician, on the radio, or on a phonograph, Johnson could play it note for note—even if the music had just been playing in the background of a conversation, with Johnson apparently paying little attention (Meyer, *Can't*). And, of course, he must have practiced. And practiced. And then practiced some more. Some musicians take offense at the idea that a pact with the devil has replaced talent, dedication, and hard work in Johnson's life story (Herman, "Re: Hawkeye"). But other commentators believe that all these factors—knowledge of new musical forms, the free time to work hard, and talent—cannot fully explain the change in Johnson's playing on his return to Robinsonville. Robert Palmer, for instance, observes, "It is tempting to ascribe Johnson's rapid evolution to his broad listening tastes, but no list of influences can explain what happened to his music and his personality during that year or so in Hazelhurst and the next few years he spent rambling around the Delta" (117).

Enter the devil. The story about Johnson's making a pact with the devil may have started with Son House, who told interviewer Pete Welding in 1966 that Johnson "'sold his soul to the devil in exchange for learning to play like that'" (qtd. in Welding 76). Several of Johnson's relatives also appear to have believed this explanation, since they told researcher Mack McCormick about the pact with the devil and claimed to know the location of the specific crossroads where the meeting took place (Palmer 113). According to musician and researcher Paul Trynka, however, Johnson himself was the original source of the legend, having "told Son House that his newly-acquired guitar skills came from a meeting with 'a black man'—the Devil—who tuned his guitar for him" (39).

That Johnson or anybody else would spread such rumors is not as surprising as it might appear to us today. The blues and blues musicians were often associated with the devil in the Delta of Johnson's era. Churchgoing folks in the area often called blues "the devil's music," possibly because it encouraged face-to-face dancing, which some Calvinist religions denounced as extremely sinful (Lomax 365). The Reverend Booker Miller, a Greenwood, Mississippi, musician who later became a Baptist minister, told Gayle Dean Wardlow, "'Them old folks did believe the devil would get you for playin' the blues and livin' like that'" and claimed that the idea of selling one's soul to the devil came from "'those old slavery times'" (qtd. in Wardlow, *Chasin'* 197).

Thus labeled as devil's minions within their communities, some musicians actively embraced the image, notably the popular Peetie Wheatstraw, who billed himself as "The Devil's Son-in-Law." But the specific story of selling one's soul to the devil for musical proficiency was most commonly associated with Tommy Johnson (probably no relation to Robert), who lived in Hazelhurst, Mississippi, where Robert Johnson also lived for a time during his absence from Robinsonville. According to LeDell Johnson, Tommy's brother, Tommy told this story:

> "If you want to learn how to play anything you want to play and learn how to make songs yourself, you take your guitar and you go to where a road crosses that way, where a crossroad is. Get there, be sure to get there just a little 'fore twelve so you'll know you'll be there. You have your guitar and be playing a piece sitting there by yourself. You have to go by yourself and be sitting there playing a piece. A big black man will walk up there and take your guitar, and he'll tune it. And then he'll play a piece and hand it back to you. That's the way I learned how to play anything I want." (qtd. in Evans, *Tommy Johnson* 22–23)

Robert no doubt heard this account during his Hazelhurst residency. Hazelhurst is also the town where Johnson studied guitar with Ike Zinermon, about whom little is known other than his claim "that he had learned to play guitar in a graveyard at midnight while sitting atop tombstones" (LaVere 11)—an image with unsettling supernatural implications of its own. Given the Hazelhurst context in which Johnson's skills matured, it is not surprising that he returned to Robinsonville with his talent fully developed and his story firmly in place. Many blues critics today see the spreading of this tale as a marketing ploy on Johnson's part. Wardlow sardonically comments, "Today we would call such devilment 'hype'" (*Chasin'* 197).

Historians have offered a variety of explanations for why blues musicians like Wheatstraw and Johnson would foster this "hype." Most obviously, affiliation with the devil may have been adopted to titillate the juke joint crowd, much as rock artists have used it in recent decades; think of the group Black Sabbath, or the Rolling Stones in their *Sympathy for the Devil* album. Francis Davis suggests that being associated with Satan might also offer a traveling bluesman some protection from rough juke joint crowds, where local men might resent their women's admiration for the flirtatious out-of-town musician (129–30). Philosopher Jon Michael Spencer postulates that Delta bluesmen may have felt some divine justification for their lifestyles, living as they did under serious oppression and daring to sing songs that told the truth. In this case, as bluesman Henry Townsend put it, they were simply not "hell-scared" (31–32).

Given this common association of bluesmen with the devil, it is somewhat curious that the legend of selling his soul stuck so tenaciously and so particularly to one artist—Robert Johnson. According to Wardlow, interest in Johnson's alleged deal with the devil is a fairly recent phenomenon. It was not mentioned at all in the liner notes to the 1961 Columbia record. Evidently contemporary interest in the myth started with Pete Welding's 1966 interview with Son House. The legend grew when David Evans interviewed LeDell Johnson for his 1971 biography of LeDell's brother, Tommy Johnson, and heard the formula for how one makes such a crossroads pact. From there the story traveled through the work of Greil Marcus, Robert Palmer, and Peter Guralnick, all of whom use Evans and/or Welding as a source, and finally made it into the popular imagination in the 1988 film *Crossroads* (Wardlow, presentation). But if blues was the devil's music, then Robert Johnson was no more the devil's spawn than were his peers. Why has this legend clung so closely to Robert Johnson? We can begin to answer this question by looking at who believes the story, who doesn't, and why.

Interviews with Johnson's contemporaries—in terms of my Fiskean discussion, "the people" who knew him—vary somewhat on whether or not Johnson had sold his soul for his talent. As noted above, Son House (at least as recorded in his interview with Pete Welding) and Johnson's family (at least as reported to Mac McCormick, and repeated by Robert Palmer) apparently believed the tale. But the jury of Johnson's peers is not unanimous. A single subject sometimes contradicts him- or herself from interview to interview, possibly depending on who is asking the questions and what those questions are. In 1979, when noted folklorist Barry Lee Pearson conducted a series of interviews with Honeyboy Edwards, Johnny Shines, and Robert Lockwood Jr., they all spoke at length about Robert Johnson "but never offered any comment about a deal with the devil." In Pearson's 1991 interviews with the same three subjects, all three denied Johnson's having made a deal with the devil, asking such pragmatic questions as, "'I want to know how you do that [sell your soul]'" (Lockwood) and "'I want anybody that believes in that, bring me your soul up here and lay it on the stage'" (Shines; qtd. in Pearson 222). Pearson's research suggests that Johnson's contemporaries did not mention the story of a crossroads pact unless asked, leaving one to wonder if they believed the legend and were trying to keep it secret, trying to give the inquiring interviewer what he or she wanted to hear, or purposely misleading the interviewer in what Stuart Hall would call a "globally contrary" response (103). In any case, different interviewers clearly elicit quite different responses from some subjects.

Honeyboy Edwards provides a good case in point. Pearson's interviews from 1979 and 1991 indicate that Edwards did not put much stock in Johnson's having dealt with the devil. In a 1996 essay, however, Paul Trynka published this story, told to him by Edwards:

> "He [Robert Johnson] told me about going to the crossroads. Matter of fact he spoke that he went to the crossroads, and I didn't know exactly at that time what he mean, and what he'd done. But from then on, when I go to the country I went to the crossroads. I come there, sit at the crossroads, get me a bottle of whiskey, half a pint, and I sit there play the blues at night, until the sun shine. I went to the crossroads and played and it turned out I got to be a pretty good guitar player. . . . [Robert] maybe did talk about the crossroads just to frighten people—he said he went down to the crossroads and went down on his knees and met a man, but I never met a man! Robert was a big bullshitter." (qtd. in Trynka 38)

Within this account, Edwards describes his own vacillation between belief in the crossroads legend (even trying it out himself, unsuccessfully) and hearty skepticism—"Robert was a big bullshitter." Of course, he may have simply been describing the difference between his gullible young self emulating Robert Johnson and his mature self, a recognized musician in his own right, wise to marketing tricks. Possibly he was catering to the interviewer or toying with him, an experience Trynka had encountered on occasion with other subjects. Trynka recalls showing up for a planned interview with Robert Lockwood Jr., who claimed never to have heard of

Trynka or agreed to the interview. In Trynka's words, "He tells me I don't exist. The meeting we'd arranged didn't exist, the letters I had written hadn't arrived . . . as far as Lockwood and family are concerned, they've never heard of me." With commendable respect and humility, Trynka decides to leave Lockwood alone for the time being: "Reflecting on the implication that I'm both a figment of my own imagination, and an asshole, I decide that now might be a good time to leave" (29). Trynka's deference was rewarded when Lockwood agreed to an interview some months later.

Other blues artists who knew or knew of Robert Johnson aren't always lucky enough (or perhaps adamant enough) to avoid being pestered by interviewers with one-track agendas. In a 1990 interview with bluesman Lonnie Pitchford, for example, David Nelson and Lauri Lawson ask Pitchford to list his influences, which he does without mentioning Robert Johnson. They ask no follow-up questions about any of the artists Pitchford mentions. Later, they ask if Pitchford ever listened to Johnson's records, to which Pitchford replies that he has, but only recently. Nonetheless, they ask him seven further questions about Robert Johnson (Nelson and Lawson 45–47), obviously looking for specific answers even when Pitchford is disinclined to oblige them. Evidently the Johnson industry has become so-intense that artists from his era have no choice but to speak about him—even if they have nothing firsthand to say. This context helps explain the response of Son House, after John Hammond, ignoring House's own contributions to the blues, had called Johnson his "absolute favorite" and pressed House to agree. Later sharing a drink with interviewer Dick Waterman, who had been present during this encounter, House wryly toasted Robert Johnson "'for being dead'" (qtd. in Waterman).

Whether Honeyboy Edwards was deliberately misleading Trynka or not, he later had more to say about Johnson and his alleged deal with the devil in his 1997 autobiography *The World Don't Owe Me Nothing*. Working with an interviewer, Janis Martinson, and Edwards's manager, Michael Robert Frank, who interviewed him for the book over a five-year period, Edwards revisits the crossroads legend and takes a decidedly nonliteral approach to it—an approach very different from the one he took in earlier interviews. He says: "It may be Robert could have sold himself to the devil. In the way he was, the way he played and acted, he could have felt that he sold his soul. A special feeling could have hit him like he done that and that feeling come out in his music" (105). Edwards suggests that whatever the literal truth of the situation, Johnson seemed to have believed himself a sinner, one who had at least metaphorically sold his soul; Johnson "the big bullshitter" is replaced by Johnson the soul searcher. Edwards here echoes Jon Michael Spencer, who suggests that some blues artists, as products of the culture that produced them, may have absorbed the widespread belief in their own sinfulness as blues musicians (55). Recall also that Johnson's neighbors blamed his young wife's death on his playing the devil's music; much of that guilt, deserved or not, possibly remained with him. Other neighbors and acquaintances of Johnson's share Edwards's psychological understanding of Johnson's relationship to the devil, reading the story of selling his soul as true, but not literally so. Johnson's onetime neighbor and girlfriend Queen Elizabeth Thomas, for example, commented that *of course* Robert Johnson sold his soul to the devil, that that was why he *had* to play. She went on to say that, in their compulsion to sing the blues, all blues singers have in some sense sold their souls to the devil (Hunt).

In these varied responses from Johnson's contemporaries, all of them African Americans from the Delta, we see a perfect illustration of John Fiske's point that the consumers of popular culture can be quite varied and creative in their uses of what the culture provides. Robert Johnson the man comes to signify very differently for different groups who knew him. For musicians like Lockwood and Shines, the story of selling one's soul for musical talent is an insult to Johnson's (and by implication, their own) dedication, hard work, and talent. For Edwards and Thomas, the literal truth may be (at least some of the time) superseded by the psychological and social realities of Robert Johnson's life and times. But what of the others, the ones like Johnson's family and (possibly) Son House, who reportedly believed that Robert literally sold his soul to the devil? In the case of Johnson's relatives, that stated belief may have simply been an attempt to promote their own welfare by enhancing Robert's most unusual claim to fame. While their remarks were made well before Johnson had a sizable estate to inherit, a brush with fame and a few royalties may have been enough motivation to enhance the legend. There is, however, another reason that African Americans from the Delta might be inclined to believe that Robert Johnson truly had sold his soul to the devil, a reason that emerges from the hybridity of African American culture.

As people of African descent living in the southern United States, Johnson and his contemporaries would have absorbed a variety of cultural beliefs from the dominant European-based culture, but they would also have retained spiritual and cultural practices passed down from their African ancestors, perhaps without knowing the origins of these practices. The belief that it is possible to traffic with the devil is common to both systems, but the nature of the "devil" is dramatically different. The western version of the devil would have come to blues artists through church institutions. Bertrum Barnes and Glen Wheeler note the similarities between Delta blues versions of a pact with the devil and the Faust legend of sixteenth-century Germany, which includes musical genius as one of the devil's gifts (26). Greil Marcus sees strong Puritan influence in the persistent association of the devil with the blues: "This side of the blues [its awareness of sin] did not come from Africa, but from the Puritan revival of the Great Awakening. . . . It was an explosion of dread and piety that Southern whites passed on to their slaves and that blacks ultimately fashioned into their own religion. The blues singers accepted the dread but refused the piety" (*Mystery* 25). The devil in this Puritan taxonomy becomes "a symbol of uncontrollable malevolence, of betrayal, of disaster, of punishment" (35). This is the devil of Christian iconography, the forked-tailed, silver-tongued, treacherous overlord of hell's fires, designed to strike terror into the breasts of the sinful and unrepentant.

But this devil is not the only one to roam the Delta, as many commentators have noted. Alongside this Christian version of Satan lives a much less threatening, African-based equivalent of "the devil" derived from the divine trickster figure of African mythology, Esu-Elegbara, or Legba. In the belief systems of many African communities, Legba functions as a mediator between humans and gods; significantly, he is guardian of the crossroads and master of the mysterious boundary between the human and the divine (Gates 5–6). He is also closely associated with music, often seen as the guardian of the interpretive arts, both musical and verbal. But because Legba is unpredictable, with a "mordant sense of humor" and a "delight in chaos and confusion," he became associated in the United States with the Christian devil, even though he has nothing to do with sin, torment, or eternal damnation (Palmer 61). Legba contains both good and evil, helpfulness and trickery, but when transplanted to the Christian system of binary oppositions, this combination of supernatural power and caprice—what Spencer calls "his synchronous duplicity" (33)—doomed him to the status of devil.

This spectrum of beliefs about human interaction with the devil can help us assess the responses to the legend of Robert Johnson's selling his soul. The crossroads story would have resonated for his friends and family, who would have interpreted it both as Americans and as heirs of African spiritual traditions. While many of Johnson's contemporaries were Christian, churchgoing people, some of them (and sometimes the same ones) would have looked to African practices—bottle borders, spirit writing, hoodoo charms—for guidance in everyday living.

At least one blues scholar, Julio Finn, interprets the story of Johnson's selling his soul primarily within this context of African spiritual retentions in the West. In his passionate, idiosyncratic, and fascinating book *The Bluesman,* Finn traces the evolution of African-based religious traditions throughout the western hemisphere, as African Vodun mingled with elements of imposed Christianity to become voodoo in Haiti, Obeah in Jamaica, Santeria in Cuba, Candomblé in Brazil, and hoodoo in the United States. According to Finn, one reason the black Church in the Delta castigated the blues was for its strong association with hoodoo, which they saw as an anti-Christian throwback to "primitive," unsaved Africa (*Bluesman* 178–79). The connections between blues singers and hoodoo are well established, both by scholars (Ferris, Finn) and by virtue of the hoochie coochie men, goopher dust, black cat bones, mojo hands, John the Conqueror roots, and bad signs that pervade blues lyrics. Finn observes that in some voodoo-based religions, charms can be made by taking earth from a crossroads and singing a song that invokes Legba's aid in "opening the gate" between the physical and spiritual realms of existence. Furthermore, in these African-based religions it is also quite common for a supplicant to offer him- or herself to the gods for possession by them. In these ceremonies, the supplicants allow themselves to become "riding-horses" for the *orisha* (minor gods) (Floyd 141). If you have read Chinua Achebe's powerful novel *Things Fall Apart,* you may recall a similar "riding horse" rite, which Achebe's Ibo people call an "egwugwu" ceremony. Finn believes that during his lengthy absence from Robinsonville, Johnson went south to the bayous to seek out a Root Doctor, someone deeply versed in hoodoo practice, to whom he then pledged himself, and that his initiation into and intimate knowledge of hoodoo are evident in his lyrics.[5] Finn contends that Robert Johnson's famous "pact with the devil" may have actually been a hoodoo ceremony in which he sought Legba's assistance in "opening the gate" to his musical powers (*Bluesman* 214–21).

Finn's discussion is interesting to me because it emerges from an Afrocentric position. Finn strongly identifies himself as African American, sees fundamental cultural similarities between Africans, African Americans, and other circum-Atlantic black peoples, applies these insights to Robert Johnson's story, and gets irate with what he sees as white critical blunders. As a result, he offers an alternative perspective on Johnson's possible pact with the devil that many other scholars overlook or downplay.

Yet in his pique at what white scholars have to say about Johnson's contract with the devil, Finn himself oversimplifies some issues. For example, he makes the following claim about Johnson scholars: "His biographers are divided into two camps: the bluesmen who knew him and believe that he made a pact with the Devil at the crossroads; and the folklorists, who don't. The former are black, the latter white; and this division has no small weight in determining the manner in which this story has come down to us" (*Bluesman* 210). This statement offers a laudable attempt to demystify (as Cornel West would say) the power relations between black artists and white scholars and the ways the two groups interpret culture differently. But he also reduces some complex issues into a facile binary opposition, replicating the Manichean logic of black/white antitheses that has contributed so much to the colonization of Africans and the oppression of African Americans. As we have seen, not all of Johnson's black contemporaries believed the devil story; conversely, many of the white scholars who delve into the story do mention Legba and Yoruba mythology. In fairness, some of this work done by white scholars was published after Finn's book appeared in 1992. However, in dividing scholars sharply along racial lines, Finn presents race as a stable and unified trait and overlooks the shifting coalitions that form both the people and the power-bloc. Finn presents all Johnson's African American contemporaries as like-minded believers in African spiritual practices. Likewise, he depicts white academics as a homogeneous group, the dominating producers of culture, rather than as an assortment of musicologists, historians, folklorists, and cultural critics from all parts of the globe and from various social classes, joined only by their shared interest in the blues. Finn's assertion that these scholars deal "not with what Johnson believed but with what they themselves believe" (222) has merit; he is directing attention to the thorny racial issues inherent in the study of the blues and its reception and asking hard questions about who owns the culture. But he creates his own monolithic racial categories that are belied by careful study of the myriad responses to Robert Johnson.

Despite this tendency to oversimplify racial attitudes, Finn's work offers a valuable look at what Robert Johnson's story of a pact with the devil may have signified to different groups, both during and after Johnson's life. Like any potent signifier, Johnson at the crossroads becomes a multivalent sign, depending upon the sign system—racial, religious, historical, and so forth—in which it is interpreted. Signs, as we have seen, mean different things in different contexts, through time, through use, and in the minds of different people who interpret them in distinctive ways. But

Finn's irritation with the many white academics who have tried to understand Robert Johnson's life and his pact with the devil brings up another issue. To Finn, these white male scholars constitute the equivalent of a power-bloc, a group of people with the means—education, financial assets, access to mass media—to produce and interpret culture for "the people's" consumption. I imagine that most academics would be astonished to think of themselves as powerful, or as a "bloc," but in this context Finn's division between black Delta residents and white outsider scholars, while oversimplified, echoes Fiske's useful strategy for examining popular culture. And connecting Finn with Fiske leads to yet another question: Why has so much attention from the white power-bloc (if such it be) been focused on Johnson's pact with the devil, since, as Finn notes, most of these scholars don't believe the story anyway?

Part of the answer lies in the lyrics to Johnson's songs. Most of his twenty-nine songs concern sexual relationships or traveling rather than Satanic influences. Johnson sings about kind-hearted women, no-good women, sweet women, brown-skinned women, unkind women, pretty mamas; Ida Belle, Beatrice, and Willie Mae; women with spark plugs, Elgin movements, and hot tamales; and about walking, rambling, hitching a ride, and dusting his broom (slang for leaving in a hurry). Two of his songs, however—"Hellhound on My Trail" and "Me and the Devil Blues"—do specifically describe denizens of hell who have been loosed in this world; a third, "Preaching Blues (Up Jumped the Devil)" has a devilish subtitle; and some listeners interpret "Cross Road Blues" as a reference to selling one's soul at the crossroads. It is from the imagery of these songs that much of the legend has been perpetuated.[6] In "Hellhound on My Trail," for example, which also includes a chilling vocal performance, the singer repeatedly laments that he's got to keep moving because he's being chased by hellhounds. "Me and the Devil Blues" describes the singer's awakening one morning to a knock on the door, only to find Satan standing there, warning him that "it's time to go" and then walking by his side and encouraging his evil thoughts. "Preaching Blues," while it does not specifically mention an inhabitant of the underworld, does personify the blues, which come "walkin' like a man," perhaps reminiscent of the devil in "Me and the Devil Blues."

But it is in "Cross Road Blues" that many commentators see the most explicit connotations of Johnson's deal with the devil. As we have seen, the association of a crossroads with devil pacts was widespread in southern folklore. In Johnson's song, the singer goes to a crossroads specifically to ask God's mercy; once there, he drops to his knees and asks the Lord to save him. After calling on God, he tries to flag a ride, but he is denied by all passersby; nightfall is quickly approaching; and he is alone, fearful of "sinking down." One could interpret these lines as describing the mental state of a persona fearful of losing his soul to an approaching evil (such as the temptation to sell one's soul for musical talent), or as a veiled version of a singer's seeking Legba's help in "opening the gate." Giles Oakley has noted, with some justification, that Johnson's lyrics in songs like this create "visions of a restless, self-destructive interior world filled with secret fears and anxieties. At times he seems . . . on the edge of an abyss of complete psychic disintegration" (199).

In contrast to those who view Johnson's lyrics as evidence of his contact with the devil, however, other blues historians have persistently warned against reading too much into Johnson's lyrics. The lyrics from "Cross Road Blues," for example, say nothing explicit about meeting the devil. They could refer to any number of issues, such as the difficulty of making correct choices, or loneliness, or the literal fear a black man would experience alone after dark in night-rider territory. It is likewise open to question whether these lyrics and Johnson's harrowing vocals reflect the emotional scars of a turbulent childhood, the anxieties of living in a violently racist society, or a pact with the devil. Other than Finn, Robert Palmer is perhaps the most sympathetic toward those who seek evidence of the supernatural in Johnson's songs, noting, "it's undeniable that Johnson was fascinated with and probably obsessed by supernatural imagery." But even Palmer cautions against excess, warning that the "school of thought that sees voodoo symbolism in almost every line Robert Johnson ever sang . . . has rightly been ridiculed by blues scholars" (127).

Scholars more commonly view Johnson's lyrics as images and metaphors rather than literal descriptions of life events. Jon Michael Spencer, for example, sees "Me and the Devil Blues" not as about making a deal with the devil but as a an expression of "a genuine consciousness of sin" (55). Russell Banks offers a psychosexual rather than a spiritual interpretation. Citing the persona's desire to beat his woman in "Me and the Devil Blues," Banks suggests that for Johnson, "the devil and other myths of damnation often signify and dramatize the complex forms of social and sexual pathology, especially toward women, that lie just beneath the surface of our civilization" (28). The clearest condemnation of this tendency to read the lyrics too literally may come from folklorist Barry Lee Pearson, who laments the critical tendency to "construct biography from repertoire" (222).

The lyrics provide some clues as to the persistence of the crossroads story, but as we have seen, they offer only innuendo and subtext about a deal with the devil. They remind me of the 1969 Beatles song that, when played backwards, allegedly revealed that Paul was dead: thrilling, but inconclusive. So given this insubstantial evidence, why has the legend hung on? The answer may lie less in the lyrics, or in the facts about Johnson as we know them, than in the culture and disposition—including the race, class, and gender—of those who are hearing the music.

When Robert Johnson was first rediscovered after the 1961 record release, people who heard the music tended to romanticize the long-forgotten artist, that ghost from the past come back to haunt us with his wrenching music. Peter Guralnick sums up this romantic impulse (in which he partakes) this way: "What could be more appropriate to our sense of romantic mystery than an 'emotionally disturbed' poet scarcely able to contain his 'brooding sense of torment and despair'? . . . Robert Johnson became the personification of the existential blues singer, unencumbered by corporeality or history, a fiercely incandescent spirit who had escaped the bonds of tradition by the sheer thrust of genius" (2). Anyone who has tried to teach the works of a romantic poet like Edgar Allan Poe to undergraduates will recognize this syndrome. Attracted to the psychological complexity of Poe's neurotic narrators and to his spooky imagery, students fixate on nineteenth-century misinformation about his various addictions, reading "repertoire as biography." After enjoying the hallucinatory poetry and fiction, they actually become angry at Poe's logically constructed, almost hyperrational essays designed to demystify the artistic process and replace the image of a frenzied poet with that of a serious craftsman—which Poe was. It is no surprise that the romantic vision of Robert Johnson started with a group of disaffected, artistic, college-aged men during the turbulent 1960s—British rock stars like Eric Clapton and Keith Richards who heard Johnson's recordings in 1961, covered a number of his songs (including "Cross Road Blues"), and so made a cult figure of a Robert Johnson with preternatural skills and supernatural connections.

A number of scholars from a variety of fields have written powerful critiques of this tendency to romanticize Robert Johnson. Musicologist Susan McClary is especially persuasive in connecting our romantic view of a haunted Johnson with the 1960s musicians who rediscovered him. Noting the longing for "authentic" emotional experience that formed much of the 1960s rebellion against the perceived sterility of postwar culture, McClary claims that for British rockers of the period, "African Americans were thought to have access to real (i.e., preindustrialized) feelings and community—qualities hard to find in a society that had so long stressed individuality and the mind/body split." Furthermore, in British culture, where (according to McClary) musicians had long been perceived as effeminate, "blues seemed to offer an experience of sexuality that was unambiguously masculine" (55). So these young British men displaced the irony in much of the blues' explicit sexual references, embraced an embarrassing image of African Americans as emotional and expressive, perhaps even "primitive" (here seen as something positive, but a reductive stereotype nonetheless), and so found images of themselves as they wished themselves to be. Barry Lee Pearson concurs in this analysis. He writes that Johnson's songs "obviously spoke to an alienated '60s youth culture, providing strangers to the blues tradition the opportunity to filter Johnson's potent lyrics through their own imaginations" (221). It could be that the story of Johnson's pact with the devil (which, as we have seen, was not widespread until the mid 1960s) burgeoned because of the alienated sensibilities of the generation that resurrected him: it is a product of the Age of Aquarius. Seen in this light, the idea that Robert Johnson sold his soul to the devil reflects the youth, the threatened masculinity, and the countercultural attitudes of the musicians who recognized his musical genius and are largely responsible for popularizing his music. Feeling emotionally dispossessed by their culture, they appropriated Johnson's literal dispossession and elevated it to mythic status. Their response was shared by the music critics of the era, other young white men who continue to wax rhapsodic on how Robert Johnson's music reshaped the world for them. Through their published work, the romanticized legend of Robert Johnson entered the media and from there circulated into popular culture.

This romantic vision of Robert Johnson, created from 1960s rebelliousness and nostalgia, fueled the development of the Robert Johnson mythology that I have been tracing. As part of this process, the signifier that was Robert Johnson, like all signifiers elevated to the status of myth, loses its connection to time and place—its "history evaporates" (Barthes 117). The transformation from historical figure to mythic icon strips Robert Johnson of his identity as an accomplished musician who honed his craft and pursued professional opportunities. Likewise, his music loses its connections to the historical circumstances (such as brushes with the law, Depression-era poverty, and violence—all subjects mentioned specifically in the lyrics) that informed it. It is this loss of social and temporal setting that recent commentators (from the 1990s onward) object to most strongly; the Age of Aquarius is over, at least in literary and cultural studies. Their protests reflect the current imperative in interpretive studies to ground artifacts in their historical contexts.

Cultural critic George Lipsitz's work on Johnson offers one example of such historicized analysis. Lipsitz argues that contemporary romanticism, with its emphasis on self-expression and tortured genius, "imagines an art immune to commercial considerations" (*Possessive* 121). Yet as we have seen, Robert Johnson actively sought out recording opportunities and was thus hardly "immune" to the commercial aspects of his art. In fact, he is often credited as being one of the first blues artists consciously to craft his songs to the length and format most appropriate for the recording studio (Palmer 125; Guralnick 57). He can reasonably be called "a typical walking musician who stuck to the road and hung out with other musicians until the end of his life" (Pearson and McCulloch 111). For Lipsitz, the romantic obsession with Johnson's pact with the devil reveals a major shift in values between his time and ours and suggests the problems in taking a story out of context:

> The current commercial value of the crossroads story depends in no small measure on the ways it erases its cultural origins and suppresses its original social intentions. Derived from diasporic African legends and trickster tales intended to teach the importance of human agency, the crossroads story here functions instead as a register of Western culture's enduring attachment to romanticism, to separating life and art, to elevating individual emotions over collective conditions, and to making an aesthetic of social pain. (*Possessive* 119–20)

In ignoring historical circumstances and romanticizing our artistic icons in this way, we hide our "unquestioned assumptions about artistic expression in our own time" (120). This same set of romantic assumptions leads my students to glorify Poe's imagined creative frenzy, ignoring the fact that he carefully tailored his work for publication and profit because his family was starving. And on that somber, antiromantic note, exit the devil.

Comparing these different responses to Johnson's selling his soul reveals many of the "hidden assumptions" Lipsitz mentions. It shows that the conflicting interpretations of this legend emerge from differences in age, gender, race, generation, religious predisposition, geographic area of origin, educational level, and occupation. It also suggests that the "plurality of competing discourses" and "multiplicity of values" that Baty and others see as central to postmodern culture are indeed operating in the Johnson mythologies. Looking at the different interpretations currently in circulation can thus unmask many important facets of the Robert Johnson myth industry and move us a bit closer to unlocking that cultural epistemology to which Robert Johnson may yet be the skeleton key.

The Legends, Part 3: Dying Young

There is one fact about Robert Johnson that everyone agrees on: he died on 16 August 1938, just outside Greenwood, Mississippi. This information is recorded on his death certificate and confirmed by people who knew him. What we don't know for sure, however, is *how* he died—who or what killed him. For that information we must once again sift through layers of contradictory stories that disclose some of the unquestioned assumptions of our time and illuminate the society from which Johnson departed so young.

Let's begin with the story most commonly presumed to be true, since it was told by Honeyboy Edwards, an eyewitness to some of the events. On Saturday, 13 August 1938, Robert Johnson was performing at a juke joint in Three Forks, Mississippi, near Greenwood. He had been playing guitar in the Greenwood area for several weeks and, according to Edwards, having an affair with the juke owner's wife. When Edwards arrived at the juke late on Saturday the thirteenth, Johnson, who had been playing all evening and accepting free drinks, had become too sick to play and was taken back to his room in Greenwood. After several days of serious illness, with symptoms including bleeding from the mouth, vomiting, and "crawling around like a dog, and howling" (Edwards 104), Robert Johnson died, possibly the victim of a jealous husband's poisoned whiskey.

Johnson's death certificate, a document that contains the authorized, governmental version of events, confirms much of Edwards's account. Gayle Dean Wardlow spent over three years searching for the death certificate, finally unearthed it in 1968, and published it in *Blues Unlimited* in 1971. The certificate fills in some factual gaps that Edwards didn't remember, such as the exact date of Johnson's death, but it also contains the errors and omissions that mar so many official records of African American lives. Once again his father's name is erroneously listed, this time as "Norah." In addition, the section on cause of death simply states "No Doctor" even though Mississippi state law required that a cause be listed, and Johnson's age is given as twenty-six, although he was probably (maybe) twenty-seven. In 1996, however, Wardlow found evidence that an official (if haphazard) investigation of Johnson's death had been made. On the back of the death certificate was this previously unseen report by the LeFlore county registrar, Cornelia J. Jordan:

"I talked with the white man on whose place this negro died and I also talked with a negro woman on the place. The plantation owner said that this negro man, seemingly about 26 years old, came from Tunica two or three weeks before he died to play a banjo at a negro dance given there on the plantation. He staid [*sic*] in the house with some of the negroes saying he wanted to pick cotton. The white man did not have a doctor for this negro as he had not worked for him. He was buried in a homemade coffin furnished by the county. The plantation owner said it was his opinion that the negro died of syphilis." (qtd. in Wardlow, *Chasin'* 91–92)

This report reveals the interesting mixture of fact, opinion, and supposition that can metamorphose into an official record. Johnson's age, listed at twenty-six on the front of the certificate, was evidently just a guess, and Johnson was not known to have played a banjo. Furthermore, picking cotton was simply not his style; *avoiding* such farm work had been a major impetus in Johnson's developing his musical gifts and adopting a traveling lifestyle. These discrepancies make me sympathize with the columnist for *Blues Access* magazine, who read this official report of Johnson's death and wondered "how many blacks in 1930s Mississippi were pronounced dead of syphilis . . . with bullet holes in the backs of their heads?" ("New Information" 108). A white landowner had seen Johnson around for a few weeks, did not know him, and was obviously trying to avoid culpability, yet his opinion on the cause of death is the only one we have, his voice ringing across the decades, loud and clear.

The unnamed "negro woman," in contrast, remains voiceless for the record, silenced by race and probably gender. Whatever information she may have had (whoever she was) was not considered worth recording when the authoritative testimony of a white plantation owner was available. One wonders about her: What was her relationship to Johnson? Did she know anything about his death? Whoever she was and whatever she knew, her thoughts and interpretations were not considered worth preserving for the record.

The various scholarly reactions to the information in this report indicate the intermediary position of academics and researchers today within the power relations of popular culture: we are interested in studying the lives and culture of "the people," yet we often rely primarily on official documents, authoritarian "proof," in interpreting what we see and hear. No one (to my knowledge) has commented on the faceless, voiceless woman and what she might have had to tell us. Instead, scholars typically consult other "authorities" in various professions. Wardlow, for example, conferred with a Dr. Walter Holladay, "who headed a state charity hospital for more than 20 years," to determine the plausibility of the recorded cause of death. A scientist, administrator, and thus a good source of official information, Dr. Holladay opined that if Johnson had been born with congenital syphilis, he could have died at age twenty-six from an aneurism of the blood vessels, a problem that would have been exacerbated by his heavy drinking. Given the three-day gap between Johnson's sudden illness and his death, however, Holladay suggested that a combination of "poison, moonshine, and liver damage could have caused pneumonia," which was incurable in 1938. The doctor concluded that without an autopsy, the cause of death would be impossible to determine (Wardlow, *Chasin'* 92).

Wardlow typifies today's scholars and researchers in using apparently scientific information to interpret Johnson's unsettling death throes. Filmmaker Robert Mugge, for example, sees the poison story as "romantic nonsense," believing instead that Johnson died of congenital syphilis, as stated on the back of the death certificate (Asakawa 25). Wardlow comes to an opposite conclusion about the poisoning, but like Mugge he takes a medical approach, explaining that "'[w]hen you're poisoned, you bleed internally, so that story about him barking was probably a description of him gagging or vomiting. He obviously died of internal bleeding'" (qtd. in Obrecht 14). LaVere also engages in medical speculation, casting his vote for poisoning *and* pneumonia: "He [Johnson] was young and virile enough to withstand the poisoning; . . . he made it through the night. He lay deathly ill at the home of a friend, and in his weakened condition, he apparently contracted pneumonia (for which there was no cure prior to 1946), eventually succumbing on Tuesday, August 16" (18). In each of these cases, well-educated researchers reveal themselves as products of a technological age in which science is seen as the best and final arbiter of truth. Their explanations may be correct, of course; I do not mean to dismiss the value of scientific evidence and factual testimony. About Robert Johnson's death, however, we have neither, so appeals to general medical information to explain it can be no more true than speculations based on other sorts of information. Perhaps the ultimate example of relying on partial factual evidence to explain the unexplainable comes from blues archivist Edward Komara. In response to the cynical query of the *Blues Access* columnist noted above, Komara complains that "'such a casual dismissal . . . should not be made until individual details are verified'" (qtd. in Wardlow, *Chasin'* 93). While it is true, as Komara contends, that verifying the identity of the white plantation owner could help pinpoint "the vicinity of Greenwood where Johnson died and was buried" (93), such facts will not reveal the cause of Robert Johnson's death. In his search for accurate detail, Komara misses the key implication that racial stereotyping inevitably distorted the official investigation into Johnson's death.

Not surprisingly, these scholarly intermediaries between the power-bloc and the people look at very different factors than do the individuals who knew Robert Johnson—people usually without formal education but with deep connections to the mores, conventions, institutions, and lore of African Americans and Mississippi Delta society. Some Delta locals, as one may have predicted from previous sections of this chapter, concluded that Johnson's early death was his payoff to the devil, part of the price of his talent. According to Robert Palmer, when folklorists Alan Lomax and John Work tried to get answers from Johnson's neighbors and acquaintances in 1941, "Nobody who was willing to discuss the incident was very clear about the details. It was widely rumored that Johnson had been the victim of powerful, malignant conjury, that he'd spent his last hours crawling around on his hands and knees and barking like a dog. Most of the folks who repeated these tales didn't know whether they believed them or not, and most of them didn't really care very much" (Palmer 3). While this statement suggests some of the usual difficulties white researchers have found in interviewing black Delta residents, the devil-payback story reported by Lomax and Work is corroborated by others who knew Johnson. Johnson's relatives, for instance, told Mack McCormick that the deal with the devil had left Johnson only eight years to live (Palmer 113). Honeyboy Edwards likewise reports that "some people" believed that Johnson's painful death, including the crawling and barking, "had something to do with Robert selling himself to the devil" (Edwards 104). Johnny Shines also "'heard that it had something to do with the black arts'" (qtd. in Welding 103).

Others in the area disagreed, believing instead that Johnson was murdered. The method of murder and the identity of the murderer, however, vary widely within these community versions. A number of local residents subscribe to the poison theory, although they differ on the details. As we have seen, Honeyboy Edwards (who was present during some of the events of Johnson's last few days) tells the story of poisoning at the hands of a jealous juke owner, a story corroborated by Johnny Shines (who probably heard it from Edwards in the first place). Note that death by poison does not preclude death as the devil's due; Edwards repeats both versions on the same page of his autobiography, although he personally attributes Johnson's death to poison, not conjury. In a more detailed variant of the story, Sonny Boy Williamson, a noted harmonica player who may have been performing with Johnson earlier on the evening of 13 August, allegedly told musician Houston Stackhouse the following version of events. During a break in the music, someone sent Johnson an open bottle of whiskey. Williamson, an older and more experienced musician who apparently knew about Johnson's affair and the juke owner's resentment, knocked the bottle from Johnson's hand, saying, "Man, don't never take a drink from a open bottle. You don't know what could be in it." The gesture evidently angered Johnson, who retorted, "Man, don't never knock a bottle of whiskey outta my hand." When a second open bottle arrived, Williamson stood watching helplessly as Johnson drank from it. Shortly thereafter Johnson took sick with what would be his fatal illness (LaVere 17–18). This version of events adds titillating notes of melodrama, dramatic irony, and suspense, but it may well be apocryphal. Musician Scott Ainslie, while noting that the dialogue and the foreknowledge of Sonny Boy Williamson "make a great story," also observes that Mississippi was a dry state in the 1930s, and bootleg whiskey was almost never sealed (Ainslie 10).

Other versions of Johnson's poisoning also circulated through the Delta, with differences in detail and attribution. In some versions a woman brought him the poisoned bottle. CeDell Davis, who was a child when he knew Robert Johnson in the late 1930s, claims that a woman known as "Craphouse Bea" gave the poisoned whiskey to Johnson, possibly without her knowledge, since Robert and Bea were "'kind of monkeying around a little bit'" (qtd. in "Death" 15). In an interview with Tom Freeland, Johnson's neighbor, Sadie Wyndham Brazley, reported that an unknown jealous woman in "Greenville" poisoned Johnson: "'she got jealous at the party, everybody was drinking, they put something wrong in it. They killed Robert, killed Robert'" (qtd. in Freeland, "Some Witnesses" 48). Others claim that an out-of-town woman poisoned Johnson. Alan Lomax heard two similar versions: according to Son House, a woman in Louisiana gave him poison in his coffee (16), and according to Big Bill Broonzy, "a dark girl" down in Bogalusa, Louisiana, poisoned him (449). James Banister, a self-proclaimed "personal friend" of Johnson's, offers the most bizarre of all the poisoning stories: he claims that Johnson was poisoned by a woman from Detroit who gave him a beer with a "douche tablet" in it. "'And he drank that bottle of beer and fell from the bar, it dried up his blood just that quick. In five minutes you couldn't stick a pin all over him and couldn't get a drop of blood'" (qtd. in "Death" 16).

In all these variations, whether based on eyewitness accounts like that of Honeyboy Edwards (and possibly Sonny Boy Williamson) or rumor, the central recurring element is sexual jealousy, sometimes accompanied by female treachery. This may be what led Robert Mugge to deem the whole story "romantic nonsense." The romantic aspect of the poisoning legend has been expressed succinctly by Keith Richards, one of those once-youthful rebels who idolized Johnson in the 1960s. Comparing Johnson's music to that of Calvin Frazier, a Johnson contemporary, Richards asserts that Johnson "'put more sting in it because he was more manic. I mean, that's why he died so young. The man was asking for trouble and didn't mind saying so. In all of his records, the man's asking for trouble all the way down the line. All his deals with hellhounds and the bitches—one of them will get you'" (qtd. in Obrecht 8). For Richards, supernatural agency and women were the enemies, recalling McClary's description of the exoticism and virility that early British rockers projected onto Johnson and the blues.

Not all Delta residents subscribe to the poison theory of Robert Johnson's death, however. A number of parallel stories exist, also involving a woman, in which Johnson came to a more immediately violent end. One variant of the story involves Johnson's one-time girlfriend Queen Elizabeth "Bet" Thomas. In an interview with *Living Blues* magazine that is marred by her inconsistencies, hesitations, and failing memory, Thomas recalls hearing that Robert Johnson had been stabbed on "'Quito bridge . . . he was comin' from, no he was fixin' to go to a dance to play. Somebody walked up behind him and stabbed him'" (qtd. in "Death" 13). (And let me note for the record here that *Living Blues* does not report Thomas's last name; she is the only woman interviewed for this special story on Johnson's death and the only one addressed and described by first name only, leaving her potentially as nameless as the "negro woman" who didn't make it into the county report on Johnson's death.) Her story is corroborated and expanded by Miller Carter, a neighbor of Thomas, who claims that Bet's father, Jonas Thomas, killed Robert Johnson with a shotgun after Johnson had beaten Bet—a beating that she confirms (Obrecht 14). Similarly, Willie Moore, Johnson's sometime musical partner, told Wardlow a rumor that Robert Johnson had been shot to death near Eudora, Mississippi, again over a woman ("Searching" 6). Bob Scott, a longtime Greenwood resident, complicates the story even further with his report that "'I don't remember how he died. Stabbed sounds reasonable to me'" (qtd. in "Death" 15).

Reading over all these interviews, often based on innuendo and gossip, with subjects asked to remember events and rumors from fifty years ago and maybe enjoying their own small, belated brush with fame, I suspect that it's just too late to get a factual account of Robert Johnson's death.

And rather than seek official endorsements from governments, scientists, and other expert witnesses, perhaps we should follow John Fiske's lead. Fiske argues against constructing dominating overview opinions about cultural events, opting instead to center our thinking around a nexus of smaller, localized opinions, around local "cultures of practice" rather than top-down "cultures of control" (*Power Plays* 19). In the case of Robert Johnson's death, this nexus of local viewpoints does not give us the ultimate answer that some researchers seek, but it does illuminate many other important aspects of the Robert Johnson story.

Look back, for example, at the different stories about Johnson's death. The white researchers focus on disease and illness—pneumonia, syphilis, liver damage—while the black Delta residents focus on violence—poison, stabbing, shooting. Julio Finn makes an important point about researchers dealing "not with what Johnson [or, in this case, his counterparts] believed but with what *they* themselves believe" (*Bluesman* 222). As we saw earlier, the romanticism of the 1960s Johnson revival obscured Johnson's historical context. The different versions of his death story suggest that this veiling of history includes underestimating the violence of the Depression-era Jim Crow South, violence that (as the Delta residents' stories indicate) was pervasive and profound, stemmed from a variety of sources, and becomes visible in Johnson's life once we resituate it in its original time and place.

Some recent scholars, recovering from or never having been infected by the 1960s Robert Johnson idolatry, have tried to restore him to his original historical context. Many emphasize the economic hardships that bedeviled African Americans of the era. The primary opportunity for subsistence was farming, with sharecropping (an exploitative system) and migrant picking (a difficult life based on enforced homelessness) the only options for those who owned no land. In central Mississippi some WPA road-building projects offered a chance for employment, although the work was backbreaking and often involved long absences from home. These were the "opportunities" available to Robert Johnson and his peers, options that persuaded him to pursue a life as a professional musician. As Francis Davis writes, it was a world of "lumber and levee camps, . . . prison farms, and plantations," where "the hounds Johnson was trying to stay one step ahead of may not always have been metaphorical" (132).

As Davis's image of bloodhounds suggests, this widespread poverty among African Americans in the South was sharply exacerbated by racism. We have seen one institutionalized form of racism in the distorted official records of Robert Johnson's life, but beyond shoddy record keeping lay the ever-present threat of racially motivated violence. Itinerant blues musicians were especially vulnerable, since many white people found strange black men more threatening than familiar ones. In his account of traveling through the South with a touring company of black minstrels, W. C. Handy explains that the company Pullman train car was equipped with a "get-away," a hidden compartment under the floor, which Handy himself once used to escape a sheriff's search posse after an altercation with a white man (45–46). Sometimes the violence took less overt forms than the threat of a posse or an angry mob. Robert Lockwood Jr. tells an appalling story about being jailed for vagrancy, along with harmonica player Rice Miller. The pair played music out the jailhouse window and attracted a large crowd who tossed them coins. Seeing this, the sheriff detained them for twenty-one days, renting them out to play at white picnics and parties and pocketing their money for himself. The musicians did relatively easy time—they were supplied with good food, women, and whiskey and were allowed to keep part of their earnings. But in Lockwood's words, "'it was terrible 'cause it was against our will. . . . As soon as we got out, we hit the highway'" (qtd. in Palmer 182–83). We know that Robert Johnson was arrested at least once, with his companion guitar player Willie Moore, for singing an unflattering song about the local sheriff in Robinsonville (Obrecht 6). The cumulative effect of living with such day-to-day risks is hard for a cultural outsider to comprehend. As Fiske notes, violent acts by police or others may seem to an outsider to be isolated events, but "the African American way of knowing it understands it not as a series of individual incidents but as a power-bloc strategy in the war against them: each incident is thus part of a much larger picture" (*Power Plays* 237).

Given this cultural climate, African Americans of the era expected nothing positive from the white power structures, whether governmental or societal, and these limited expectations also affected the way Robert Johnson died and the way his death was investigated. As to his death, Honeyboy Edwards notes, "People couldn't call the doctor. What black person had any money then? Doctors charged them and there wasn't no money. So he just died for attention" (104). On the investigation, Queen Elizabeth Thomas told a *Living Blues* interviewer, "'You know if anybody kill you down here you ain't goin' to find out much'" (qtd. in "Death" 13). Unless white interests were at stake, black lives and deaths meant little to the prevailing powers. As Memphis Slim asserted, "'If you were a good worker, you could kill anyone down there, so long as he's colored. [Just] don't kill a good worker'" (qtd. in Davis 132).

In the face of a dominant culture at best unconcerned about their welfare and at worst openly violent, African Americans in the Delta carved out an alternative world of their own, a localized culture that recognized but also resisted the powers that restricted their lives. In response to limited opportunity, omnipresent danger, and uncertain outcomes, they created a subculture, a carnival world of juke joints and beer halls where inhibitions could be released and tensions discharged. Novelist Stanley Crouch describes it this way: after dark in the segregated South, "black men and women could act as wildly as they wished as long as they didn't harm the lives or ownings of whites. Where the blues was invented, refined and danced to, people who usually did hard, mindless and boring work in the cotton fields, sawmills, on turpentine farms . . . put on the dog," creating a world of "homemade glamour and glory" (xii). For historian Clyde Woods, the "blues culture" that developed in this setting was more than just a response to outside forces; it was "the law for African Americans living in a lawless environment" (*Development* 83). Seen in this context, Robert Johnson's death may have been an almost inevitable by-product of the forces that constrained his life: within the dominant culture, he was menaced by powerful whites if he overstepped the arbitrary boundaries they set for him; within the African American alternative culture, he was in danger from hard-drinking juke-joint men who were intent on escaping outside pressures and often resentful of a traveling musician who flirted with their women.

George Lipsitz is especially eloquent on how placing Robert Johnson's death in its historical setting helps us understand more—or at least differently—than we would from factual details like the exact cause of his death. To disaffected youths in the 1960s, Johnson was a sign, a signifier divorced from context, who represented rebellion against convention, the romance of life on the road, unfettered freedom, and the epitome of artistic self-expression. Lipsitz points out that although Johnson "turned homelessness into an art," he was not escaping the banality of middle-class culture, as were many of his 1960s fans. He was a man of his time and place "whose pursuit of pleasure and emotional intensity compensated for his systematic disenfranchisement as a worker, citizen, and racial subject" (*Possessive* 127–28). Johnson's death looks less romantic when viewed in this way. Rather than seeing him as a symbol of reckless passion, Lipsitz argues that his dangerous womanizing and lack of stable relationships must be viewed "in the context of the high female mortality [consider the early death of Virginia Travis, his first wife], inadequate male wages, and pressures that poverty and racism imposed upon family formation in his era" (128).

This discussion of the circumstances in which Robert Johnson lived and died indicates that a nexus of local viewpoints and the "plurality of competing discourses" (Baty 10) about his life contain much more valuable information than a doctor's death certificate or an eyewitness account of his death would tell us. While they do not clear up the mystery of who or what caused Robert Johnson's death, a mystery that is probably unsolvable, they do offer us a way to understand Depression-era economics in the South and the history of race relations in America, to estimate the changes in critical commentary (scholarly and popular) from the 1960s to the early twenty-first century, and to gauge how different critical strategies produce widely varying interpretations and results. To scholars with the money and time to travel throughout the Delta searching for documents and interviews, Robert Johnson's death is a tragic puzzle to be solved. Because they have access to media that will publish their findings, they also have power to create cultural artifacts and influence public opinion. To Johnson's few remaining contemporaries who lack these advantages, his death is simply another example of how the devil will get his due, how poverty and homelessness lead to early death, or how black lives have always meant little to white authorities.

It may be that future research into Johnson's death will reveal more of the facts. Mack McCormick claims to know who killed Robert Johnson and that the man is living in Florida, but since McCormick obtained the information by promising anonymity to his informants, his conclusions will not be published during their lifetimes ("Postscript" 27). This story recapitulates in miniature many of the ideas I have put forth in this section on Robert Johnson's death. On the one hand, McCormick, a researcher with media access, can be applauded for keeping his word to his sources. He evidently made the promise years ago, before the big nineties boom in the Johnson industry. Much of the work published by critics like Guralnick and Palmer is based on his research, yet McCormick himself refrains from breaking his promise and catching a ride on the Johnson gravy train. On the other hand, he apparently possesses information about a murderer who may still be alive, and such information might be important to Johnson's family, if not to the municipal authorities where Johnson died and where the alleged murderer has been living. In withholding such information, is he not abetting murder? The operations of the power-bloc and those of the people sometimes conflict and sometimes coalesce, with researchers and scholars trapped between our interest in this vibrant local culture and the official way we were trained to see the world.

Regardless of exactly how Robert Johnson died or how one interprets the competing discourses about his death, a final, central fact has helped perpetuate his myth and keep the controversy going: Robert Johnson died young. Like so many other American cultural icons—Marilyn Monroe, James Dean, Buddy Holly—Johnson tantalizes us with his perpetual youth. Not surprisingly, his early death, like everything else about him, has prompted a variety of telling responses. For Peter Guralnick, Johnson's early death adds to his legendary status: "like Housman's athlete, like Orpheus, Keats, and James Dean, [Robert Johnson] was kissed by the flame of youth and never lived to see the effects of the infatuation wear off" (61). For Guralnick, a lyrical prose stylist, Johnson resides in the company of mythic and poetic figures whose early promise was cut short, an association that helps insure his reception in the pantheon of great artists. Julio Finn responds in his typical Afrocentric fashion by describing Guralnick's imagery as "a blatant 'whitening' of black culture" and goes on to ask, "What, in the name of the Devil, has Robert Johnson got to do with Keats, James Dean, et al.? Surely the likes of Magic Sam, Jimi Hendrix, Minni Ripperton and Bob Marley are more apt comparisons" (*Bluesman* 210). For Finn, race consciousness always takes precedence over things like mythic resonance or status within western culture. And for Honeyboy Edwards, his friend's early death is viewed through a musician's experiences with contemporary music marketing: "Robert's more popular because he died, like everybody else who dies young" (105). Just as Robert Johnson's life seemed predesigned for mythic status (in traditional terms and in Barthes's semiotic reformulation), his early death perpetuates the legend.

Robert Johnson, Elvis Presley, and Postmodern Culture

In the introduction I suggested that Robert Johnson may be the Elvis Presley of the new millennium. While I have not yet heard rumors of Robert Johnson impersonators congregating in House of Blues clubs, one Web site trumpets this Elvisian disclaimer about Johnson's death certificate: "It says he's dead, but we know he still lives" ("Robert Johnson's Death Certificate"). In a similar vein, music writer Gary B. Patterson notes that Elvis Presley and Robert Johnson both died on the same day of the same month—August 16 (33). Such comparisons between Elvis Presley and Robert Johnson, whether implicit like the first or explicit like the second, don't say much about the artists, but they speak volumes about the formulation of American celebrity and about cultural shifts over the last few decades of the twentieth century.

Unlike Robert Johnson, Elvis Presley was already being studied as a cultural icon while he was alive. In 1975, two years before Presley's death, music critic Greil Marcus wrote a piece called "The Presliad," the title of which alone declares it as a paean to Presley's mythic status. Marcus's essay laments that Presley's revolutionary music and performance style had, by 1975, turned mainstream, and his concerts had become events "where no one is challenged and no one is threatened" (*Mystery* 140). The writer is saddened to see Elvis performing only his myth, not his talent. However, Marcus acknowledges and applauds Elvis's iconic status. Of all American icons, writes Marcus, Elvis Presley alone was adored by people from all walks of American life; he alone had the scope to encompass all of America (137–40).

This same quality that Marcus saw in 1975 (with some justification) as universal appeal looks rather different to Elvis scholars at the turn of the century. Instead of seeing something comprehensive and timeless in Presley's popularity, recent commentators (including Marcus, in *Dead Elvis*) see a series of disjunctive fragments in his life and legend, with different interest groups coalescing around the different fragments to honor very different aspects of Elvis Presley. An example of these varying responses to Elvis appears in the work of John Fiske, who discusses Presley's body as a contested space. During Presley's lifetime his body represented sexual liberation to youths but lewdness and immorality to power-bloc adults, like parents or the producers of "The Ed Sullivan Show." After his death, his corpse likewise became a source of controversy. The scientific view that Presley was dead conflicted with a nexus of localized views, which contended that the body in the coffin was a dummy or an impostor, two stories that contradicted each other less than they contested the official opinion that Elvis was dead. For Fiske, all the questions about Presley's death—was it suicide? an accidental overdose? is he really dead? was he really in the coffin?—reveal the potency of local cultures of practice to control popular knowledge and counteract authoritarian opinions (*Power Plays* 94–108).

Given Fiske's abiding focus on local networks as a primary source of cultural knowledge, one might be tempted to chalk up his interpretation of Elvis to his perhaps idiosyncratic method of reading popular culture. But many other Elvis scholars agree with him. Vernon Chadwick stresses that the very name Elvis represents an enormous variety of fans' passions:

"Elvis" means spiritual bonds and religious community but also celebrates earthly sexuality; "Elvis" champions the working classes and the self-taught but has long been a subject of academic discourse; "Elvis" represents the segregated South yet helped integrate music (xiv-xxv). Erika Doss's reading of "Elvis culture" in the 1990s likewise emphasizes Elvis's hybridity, the way he means differently to different admirers. For her, Elvis's longevity as a cultural icon is due not to a universal appeal but to his shape-shifting ability, with the "narrative instability" of his image reflecting endemic conflicts in American attitudes and values (18–19).

These recent commentators illustrate a dramatic reversal in what Elvis Presley has come to signify, as his image has mutated from a symbol of uniform appeal to a sign of our increasingly multifaceted society. This particular shift in understanding Elvis reflects a major cultural change, as mid-century claims about the universal and timeless have been replaced in cultural and literary studies by an appreciation for changing contexts, variable identities, and diverse viewpoints. S. Paige Baty observes a similar process in the continual repackaging of Marilyn Monroe who, like Presley, was a mid-century icon with widespread popularity both during and after her lifetime. For Baty, the current celebrity of Monroe represents nostalgia for the era in which she lived (a time when people supposedly believed in universal appeal) but also contains traces of all the intervening eras that have turned her into calendar art and a marketing symbol and that have reformulated her life through revisionist history (the Kennedy scandals), best-selling novels (*Blonde*), and made-for-TV movies (22).

A shorthand way to describe this shift is to say that we have moved from a modern to a postmodern way of reading the world. As Cornel West reminds us, the totalizing worldview held by many westerners at mid-century has been effectively challenged, politically and philosophically, by the international marketing of American popular culture and the simultaneous emergence of Third World cultures: think Coca-Cola and Afro-pop music. And once we recognize the late twentieth century as a time when gaps, narrative omissions, unstable identities, metamorphoses, multiple interpretations, and racial and ethnic differences are valued, it becomes glaringly obvious why Robert Johnson has lately become a subject of popular appeal and scholarly attention. Robert Johnson's story exudes postmodern possibilities.

It is not only Robert Johnson's highly contested life story, however, that makes him an exemplary postmodern mythic figure. Uncannily, his music itself shares some qualities with postmodern cultural productions. Postmodern art tends to be constructed out of the bits and pieces of previous art rather than copied from nature. Just as postmodern culture is characterized by fractures and discontinuities, postmodern artifacts bear traces of past and present, of borrowed images recirculated in a new context, of resituated signs: consider sampling, collage, mixed-media installations, hypertext. Whether we refer to these techniques as pastiche (Jameson), simulacra (Baudrillard, "Simulacra"), or bricolage (Levi-Strauss), it is clear that postmodern artifacts revel in their own constructedness. In music, such interests have led many composers since the 1960s to believe "that music should be 'com-posed'—literally, put together—from elements recognizable to a substantial community of listeners" (McClary 141). Postmodern art enhances accessibility by placing what is novel in a familiar context. Because such art is sometimes seen as mere copying, its detractors denounce it as parasitic and cynical. Its champions, in contrast, contend that postmodernism's "flaunted artificiality . . . can register confidence in the power of human signs to shape social reality. And it has the effect of unmasking anything that tries to present itself as natural, centered, or authentic" (McClary 153). Postmodern artifacts thus celebrate the human ability to construct our own cultural realities while also revealing some of the unquestioned assumptions upon which those realities are built.

One final controversy about Robert Johnson pertains in this context of postmodernism, and it concerns whether his music is original or derivative. For some, Robert Johnson was important to music history because he was a supreme innovator. Johnny Shines claimed that "'Robert came along with the walking bass, the boogie bass, and using diminished chords that were not built in one form. He'd do rundowns and turnbacks, going down to the sixth and seventh. He'd do repeats. None of this was being done'" (qtd. in Banks 30). Shines also maintained that "'[t]he things he was doing [on guitar] was things that I'd never heard nobody else do. . . . Robert changed everything, you might say'" (qtd. in Guralnick 19). Others comment on the originality of Johnson's lyrics (Davis 129), on his unprecedented use of a moving bass riff (Rubin, "Robert Johnson" 38), on the novel thematic unity of his verses (Guralnick 38–39), and on his unusual guitar tunings (Delta Haze Corporation). Robert Palmer, noting repeated rumors that Robert Johnson was playing an electric guitar with a small band shortly before his death, predicts that had Johnson lived, he would have invented Chicago blues (131). In 1991 *Musician* magazine went so far as to proclaim Johnson the "Father of Rock and Roll."

Recently—and not surprisingly, given the shift in critical interest from romantic originality to historical context—critics have looked more closely at Johnson's musical heritage and concluded that he was working in a well-established tradition. Some sneer at the whole notion of originality. LeLand Rucker, for instance, argues that "Johnson was no innovator, no pioneer of the particular guitar style that Southern bluesmen adopted. There were many before him that plowed the same musical turf" (3). For Scott Ainslie, "Johnson was a singular musician of extraordinary talent, but he came out of somewhere. And he had good company" (127). Seen in this context, Johnson's vaunted ability to copy records and performances can look more like borrowing than creating, and many critics have traced the influence of earlier musicians like Kokomo Arnold, Son House, Skip James, Charley Patton, and Peetie Wheatstraw in specific Johnson tunes. A case in point is blues historian Stephen Calt, whose liner notes to *The Roots of Robert Johnson* present nearly every Johnson song as an appropriation of an earlier one.

A few notable commentators, however, take a middle ground and see Johnson's real innovation in his revising, adapting, and reconfiguring of the tunes and techniques he had inherited. Barry Lee Pearson describes him as both a synthesizer and an innovator, "a creative individual working within a tradition yet able to mold it into his own personal vehicle" (223). Ray Templeton describes Johnson's best work as catalytic, creating "a unique kind of synergy, in which the various elements of his roots were brought together to create something that was really very special" (33). And in a wonderful *New York Times* piece from 1998, Tony Scherman elegantly navigates this narrow strait, arguing that Johnson was neither the first rock and roller nor the mere sum of his influences but a unique and powerful genius who both built on the music around him and transcended it in magnificent ways. "Woody Guthrie built his songs on earlier ones too," writes Scherman, "but nobody would call 'This Land Is Your Land' a rendition of 'You Are My Sunshine'" (38). What these recent—and to my mind, sensible—reactions collectively suggest is that Robert Johnson anticipated postmodern art: he took pieces of existing music, placed them in different contexts, different keys, and different combinations, added his imaginative and technical powers, and so created something gloriously new yet still familiar and accessible out of inherited bits. Johnson was not alone in this practice, of course, which is fundamental to the cultural transmission of folk music. But because Johnson today towers above his peers in popular recognition and media representation, this discussion of the wellsprings of his art is revealing. The debate over self-created versus inherited forms shows us to be a culture in transition, as romantic notions of originality contend with the more recent, postmodern appreciation of art recycled and resituated from the past. Just as the competing discourses about his life reveal contemporary cultural fissures, so the reception of his music illustrates the intertextual nature of much contemporary art and the current popularity of these unabashedly constructed forms.

× × ×

Writing about novels, theorist Mikhail Bakhtin describes the process by which a text takes on additional meanings over time, a process that he calls "re-accentuation." He writes:

> Every age re-accentuates in its own way the works of its most immediate past. The historical life of classic works is in fact the uninterrupted process of their social and ideological re-accentuation. Thanks to the intentional potential embedded in them, such works have proved capable of uncovering in each era and against ever new dialogizing backgrounds ever newer aspects of meaning; their semantic content literally continues to grow, to further create out of itself. Likewise their influence on subsequent creative works inevitably includes re-accentuation. (421)

Throughout my discussion of the legends about Robert Johnson, I have been attempting to read Johnson as "a classic text" and to show how our culture has "re-accentuated" his life and music through our various responses to them. We all take the incomplete text of his life and fill in the gaps in the ways that make most sense to us, bearing in mind that "we" are neither monolithic nor static. Because we as a culture have elevated Johnson to mythic status, he has been removed from his history. While this process can lead to misreadings of his life and work, it also reveals important cultural ideologies as we re-accent his story to reflect what we (variously) believe to be true and important.

2

The Invention of the Past

> I stick to the facts as I imagine them.
> —Alan Greenberg

In chapter 1, we saw how Robert Johnson the man became Robert Johnson the sign, how the sign became Robert Johnson the myths, and how the myths reveal some unquestioned assumptions of our culture. Along the way, we discovered the romanticizing tendencies of the rock musicians and critics who rediscovered Robert Johnson in the 1960s. For these early fans, Johnson lived an artistic life unfettered by convention; he was a genius without precedent or obligation. More recent studies have revised this interpretation by rereading his life and work within their original historical contexts, noting the hardships that contributed to his sensibility and the influences he drew upon in creating his masterpieces of song. In this corrective view, Robert Johnson loses perhaps a bit of his sui generis status but becomes a more complete artist and human being, one who was shaped by his culture and who created important music from the pieces that came to hand.

Roland Barthes, whose work on myth I discussed in chapter 1, explains such corrective processes in semiotic terms. For Barthes, a myth is created when a sign is used as the signifier in a second-level semiotic equation and so becomes divorced from its original historical reality. Such was the case, for example, when Robert Johnson the man became Robert Johnson the postage stamp, a sign of American musical heritage, and then that sign (the stamp) came to signify smokers' rights, censorship, government efforts to promote the health of its citizens—all things quite distant from the historical figure that was Robert Johnson. Myth was created, and it removed "determinism and free will" from Johnson's story. With this "miraculous evaporation of history" (Barthes 151), the material Robert Johnson was lost.

One could assume from this analysis that the way to demythologize a sign would be to restore it to its original historical context, as many recent writers have done with Robert Johnson. A good example of this process appears in the work of George Lipsitz. To illustrate how myth is constructed, Lipsitz compares Robert Johnson to rock legend Eric Clapton, who frequently cites Johnson as a major influence. Remarking that "on his best day Robert Johnson caught more hell than Eric Clapton has ever imagined," Lipsitz emphasizes the hardships of Delta life for African Americans in the 1930s. He also highlights the long musical tradition—another social context—from which Johnson emerged, noting that "the musical forms that Clapton has explored as a form of personal self-discovery came to Johnson as part of a shared social language honed under historically specific circumstances for eminently practical purposes" (*Possessive* 121). In Barthes's terms, such a reinsertion into history functions as an "artificial myth," a process that undermines myth by revealing it as a human construct, the inevitable product of ideology (here, Clapton's romanticism) rather than something "natural." By thus restoring Robert Johnson to his original place and time, Lipsitz "vanquishes myth" (Barthes 135); he replaces the idyllic wandering troubadour with a Depression-era, Jim Crow–era, African American musician, a man with extraordinary talent, troubles aplenty, and a rich musical heritage.

Critics who focus on historical context, such as Lipsitz, offer an important revision of Robert Johnson. But does restoration to history always and inevitably vanquish myth? It seems to me that such an assumption rests upon shaky theoretical grounds. In semiotic terms, there is always some "slippage" in an image; theorists from Jacques Lacan (a psychoanalytic critic) to Jacques Derrida (the father of deconstruction) have pointed out that signs can never fully represent what was originally signified. Thus, Robert Johnson as we see him today can only approximate the Robert Johnson who lived and breathed. And since most of what we know of that living, breathing Robert Johnson has been filtered even further through myth, it is doubtful that we can ever view Robert Johnson in an unmediated way. He will always be partly what he has been made to signify—partly composed of the legends that have surrounded him—even if we take great pains to strip away those legends and replace them with his history as we understand it. As novelist Ralph Ellison has phrased it, a writer using a historical figure must be aware that he or she operates in a field "dense with prior assumptions" (74).

Compounding this problem of accrued meanings through time is the nature of history itself. History is not entirely factual, verifiable, nor agreed-upon; it is the product of human interpreters with ideologies and agendas, conscious or otherwise. Historian Robert Rosenstone lists this instability of history as one of the things historians like to forget. Those things include: "That all history, including written history, is a construction, not a reflection. That history (as we practice it) is an ideological and cultural product of the Western World at a particular time in its development. That history is a series of conventions for thinking about the past" (11). Other contemporary historians agree, noting that no history "'mirrors' all or even the greater part of the events or scenes of which it purports to be an account" (White 1193) and that to "address history from the point of view of 'accuracy' alone is to accept that such a condition exists and that it is disinterested rather than ideologically motivated" (Custen 27). This postmodern understanding of history's constructedness, with its foregone gaps and omissions, casts a long shadow over what reinsertion in historical context can tell us. While serious historians (like those cited above) look carefully at what is known about the past through documents and factual records, instead of reading them selectively (or not at all) as mythologists tend to do, documents (such as Robert Johnson's birth, marriage, and death certificates) and other such historical artifacts can be missing, incomplete, or erroneous. When interpreting those potentially flawed artifacts, historians create individual narratives of the past that are shaped by their own assumptions as well as by any "facts" they have discovered.

One final problem further complicates this process of restoring Robert Johnson to his historical context. Since even scholarly history cannot completely reflect the past as it was, what happens when that historical context is also an artistic construct—a fictional, cinematic, or dramatic vision of historical reality? A number of contemporary artists have attempted to retell Johnson's life story in its original setting, as it apparently happened: Chris Hunt and Peter Meyer in film documentaries, T. Coraghessan Boyle in a short story, Bill Harris in a stage play, and Alan Greenberg in a screenplay. Many of them directly state that they are attempting to recover the historical Robert Johnson, the man behind the myth. But does this process of reinsertion in *imagined* history, presented in the formulas of inherited artistic genres, vanquish myth? The aesthetic structures through which history is expressed inevitably shape our understanding of it. Furthermore, as Alan Greenberg reminds us in the epigraph to this chapter, artists adhere to creative imagination as well as to the facts and legends they choose to portray. The use of artistic conventions and the vision of the individual artist unavoidably intervene in any attempt to create accurate pictures of the past in fictional frames.

In this chapter I explore late twentieth-century artistic re-creations of

Robert Johnson in his original historical setting. I will ask and attempt to answer the following questions: What are the uses of history? How does the re-creation of history intersect with the construction of myth? And most importantly, what does this repositioning of Johnson in artistic versions of the past reveal about our cultural assumptions today? In these historical re-creations of Robert Johnson's life and times, we can see how contemporary artists use Robert Johnson to make "the past meaningful to the present" (Rosenstone 49) and in so doing reveal contemporary methods of constructing meaning.

Documentary and Its Discontents

Documentary film is probably the closest artistic neighbor to written, scholarly history. The noted "historian of consciousness" Hayden White, in an essay on "Historiography and Historiophoty"—that is, on written history and filmed history—sees similar value in the two processes, commenting that "[e]ven written history is a product of processes of condensation, displacement, symbolization, and qualification exactly like those used in the production of a filmed representation. It is only the medium that differs, not the way in which messages are produced" (1194). Given this endorsement from a respected scholar, one might assume that a documentary film about a historical figure would be as close to "accurate" as history can be.

Documenting the life of Robert Johnson on film, however, poses particular problems. Most obviously, there is no documentary footage of Johnson (despite the 1998 furor over the now-discredited silent film clip, once thought to be Robert Johnson, which I discuss in chapter 5). As of today there are only two published photographs of the bluesman. Few people still alive ever saw Robert Johnson perform, travel, drink, or flirt, the four activities for which he is best known. Furthermore, the facts of Johnson's life, as we saw in chapter 1, are all debatable. If historians of the written word cannot agree on an accurate portrayal of Robert Johnson's life, what can a documentary filmmaker do?

Chris Hunt, in *The Search for Robert Johnson* (1992), and Peter Meyer, In *Can't You Hear the Wind Howl?* (1997), have both attempted to uncover the "real" Robert Johnson, to extricate the man from his myth. The two films have many techniques in common, such as interviews with Johnson's surviving contemporaries, footage of the area in which he lived and died, a soundtrack featuring Johnson's music, and even some of the same film clips of rock stars (Eric Clapton, Keith Richards) waxing rhapsodic over

Johnson's musical genius. Both films present the outlines of Johnson's life in chronological sequence interrupted by relevant interviews, and both examine the stories about him as the myths that they are, seeking factual explanations for why he played facing the wall, or if he believed he had sold his soul to the devil, or how he died. But in this process of restoring Robert Johnson to historical context, do these films vanquish myth?

Hunt's film would seem the likeliest candidate to do so, since he uses a fairly traditional documentary format. Meyer, in contrast, includes some dramatic reenactments of scenes from Johnson's life, moving the film closer to something like docudrama than straight documentary. One might expect a more "factual" representation from the documentary form, and indeed, historical accuracy does seem to be one of the goals of *The Search for Robert Johnson.* In addition to the interviews with Johnson's associates, the film is rich with information uncovered by serious Johnson researchers like Mack McCormick and Gayle Dean Wardlow, who discovered many of the records and documents we now have about Johnson's life. Interviews with these scholars are enhanced by the presentation of the few documents they and others have found, such as Johnson's marriage license to Virginia Travis, a photo of talent scout H. C. Speir, and the playbill from the Spirituals to Swing concert at Carnegie Hall where Johnson would likely have appeared, had he lived. The film also includes some important information that was previously unknown. We see the first interview with Claud Johnson (who has since been legally declared Robert Johnson's son) and meet Claud's son and grandson, thus witnessing possibly three generations of Johnson's descendants. And we watch the emotion on the face of Willie Mae Powell, once a girlfriend of Johnson's, as she hears "Love in Vain" for the first time and learns that in this famous song he called her name.

The film also goes to some lengths to help us understand the historical reality in which Johnson lived. In addition to the documents that specifically pertain to Johnson's life, the film offers myriad photographs of the era in general, taking us to cotton farms and juke joints, on cars and trains of the 1930s. The interviews with Johnson's contemporaries also provide important historical commentary, particularly about the degradation and violence blacks often faced during Johnson's lifetime. Johnny Shines declares that in Mississippi at that time, "it was open season on black folks"; Honeyboy Edwards explains that Robert Johnson may have died simply because black folks had no money for doctors; a local minister reports that few black people owned cars in the 1930s, so it is likely that Johnson (whose grave site, like everything else, is contested) was buried close to where he died. Johnny Shines describes himself and Johnson staging "headcutting contests," in which they would play guitar simultaneously on rival street corners, trying to steal each other's audiences and so best each other's take of money. Hunt's film, in short, offers factual documentation as well as rich textural background to Robert Johnson's life and times.

There are moments, however, that undercut this recaptured history. Filmmaker Leslie Woodhead has argued that even creators of straight news programs acknowledge the "'inescapable subjective content in every camera movement and edit,'" that "'the manipulative presence of the director'" is unavoidable and significant in both daily news reporting and in documentaries (qtd. in Edgar 180). This directorial subjectivity is certainly true of *The Search for Robert Johnson,* as romanticism creeps in to fill the cracks in the historical narrative.

Hunt's documentary begins with brief interviews with Keith Richards and Eric Clapton, both of whom were instrumental in reviving Johnson's reputation in the 1960s, and both of whom idolize Johnson. According to Richards, Johnson's music is as intricate as Bach's. Clapton asserts that Johnson was simply the best—the best guitarist, the best singer, the best songwriter—in folk-blues history. A documentary interested in authenticity thus begins with hyperbole, which sets the scene for the introduction of the film's narrator, John Hammond Jr. For decades Hammond has made his living playing the blues, much of it Robert Johnson's blues, which he does with great skill and passion. Hammond acts as our tour guide through the Mississippi Delta, driving us from town to town, following the trail of the original Johnson researchers on their search for facts about Robert Johnson. But Hammond, like Clapton and Richards, reveres Johnson, and the film follows the rock stars' adulation with Hammond's own description of his trip as "the quest of a lifetime." Structured as a journey, described as a "quest," the film thus undercuts its own historical impulses with the romantic/mythic framework it erects at the start, partaking as much in hagiography (that is, idealized biography, as of a saint) as in historical recovery. Eventually the documentary becomes something of a star vehicle for Hammond, as the interviews and photographs are increasingly interspersed with John Hammond Jr. (in train cars, at a crossroads, in a graveyard) performing Robert Johnson songs. At one point, after Johnny Shines describes himself and Johnson in the headcutting contests of their youth, Shines and Hammond reenact a headcutting scene, with Hammond inhabiting the Robert Johnson position and the staged crowd eventually leaving Shines's corner to hear Hammond play Johnson.

The Search for Robert Johnson is a well-researched attempt to recover what is knowable about the historical Robert Johnson. It was well received by critics, as Emmy-winner Chris Hunt's documentaries on musical figures typically are. As one admiring critic describes it, the film "encompasses a detective story overlaid with folk memory, its interviews succinctly to the point, containing humor, superstition and contextual information in equal parts" (Slaven 22). But the reanimation of Robert Johnson in the form of John Hammond Jr., a white artist, is troubling throughout, especially in the staged scene where Hammond draws the listeners (all black) away from Shines's corner to hear his own cover of a Robert Johnson song. In this scene, a white artist functions as a surrogate for Robert Johnson, as the film attempts to illustrate what a headcutting contest would look like. But in using a white artist to perform Johnson's stealing away Shines's listeners, the scene also and equally enacts the white cultural appropriation of black art. I am reminded uncomfortably of the Langston Hughes poem cited in the introduction: "You done taken my blues and gone."

John Hammond Jr. is a talented musician with impressive credentials and has every right to perform Robert Johnson's songs. I can attest from experience that his concert renditions of those songs are powerful and moving. Likewise, his interviews with African American informants in *The Search for Robert Johnson* are handled with sensitivity and grace. He asks open-ended questions that allow people to tell their own stories, quite unlike the leading questions (described in chapter 1) that some white interviewers pose. But in the context of this film, I find myself once again thinking of John Fiske and the thorny issues of access to discourse, media, and therefore power. Creating discourse about history, whether written or filmed, produces a knowledge of the world and therefore exerts power over it. Fiske writes: "There is a physical reality outside of discourse, but discourse is the only means we have of gaining access to it. . . . [W]hat is accepted as reality in any social formation is the product of discourse. . . . Putting into discourse is a negotiating procedure which involves the selection of certain features of the real (and thus the repression of others), and its circulation in the interests of some social formations (and thus the repression of others)" (*Power Plays* 15). *The Search for Robert Johnson* "puts into discourse" a well-informed version of Robert Johnson's life and times. But by repressing the racial difference between Robert Johnson and John Hammond Jr. in the headcutting scene, even while the interviews with Johnson's contemporaries emphasize the racial oppressions of the 1930s, Hunt and Hammond "create a discourse" about Robert Johnson's life in which race doesn't matter. By naively using John Hammond Jr. as a surrogate for Robert Johnson and thereby repressing the issue of race, this often laudable film distorts the picture of Johnson's social reality that it purports to portray and instead enacts a number of current cultural assumptions. For one thing, the scene performs the assurance of white people that they can claim title to all American cultural productions—a right not usually extended to minority groups. For another, it depicts the black listeners at the headcutting contest as a monolithic and subservient group, as they cross and recross the street, herdlike, at the obvious bidding of the white director. Finally, the scene positions Johnny Shines, an important bluesman in his own right, as an also-ran in his own life story, thus completing the cultural appropriation of black art and life suggested by the repeated use of Hammond as a Johnson surrogate.

If a traditional documentary can have such difficulties in presenting the "truth" of Robert Johnson's life, can a docudrama—or a dramatized documentary—fare any better? Peter Meyer's film *Can't You Hear the Wind Howl?* covers the same thematic and geographical territory as Hunt's film but in a somewhat different format. Interspersed among the interviews with musicians past and present who have been influenced by Johnson (including John Hammond Jr.), Meyer stages reenactments of scenes from Johnson's life, using African American blues musician Kevin Moore (better known by his stage name, Keb' Mo') as the stand-in for Johnson. Before any interviews take place, the film opens with a dramatized scene of Moore as Johnson entering a photo booth, putting a cigarette to his lips, grabbing his guitar, and posing for the camera, much as Johnson must have done in creating the "photo booth" picture that became the basis for the infamous postage stamp. This reenactment technique continues throughout the film, as we witness scenes of Johnson as a boy playing harmonica and making a diddley bow; then as an adult, played by Moore, courting his wives; playing his guitar at the crossroads, in juke joints, in recording studios, and on street corners; hitching rides, catching trains, and walking highways; and being rousted by police in various locales. In none of these scenes do we get a distinct look at his face, nor do we hear Moore/Johnson speak. Instead, the action is shot from a distance and played out under Johnson's music or under a relevant interview. Linking these dramatic scenes with the interviews is the narrator, Danny Glover, who provides the necessary context and background stories to unify the film.

Given these reenactment scenes, Meyer's film may be something closer to docudrama, a "nonfictional drama" that "claims to provide a fairly accurate interpretation of real historical events" (Staiger), than to documentary.[1] But regardless of the term we apply to Meyer's film (and Meyer himself consistently calls it a documentary [Meyer, "Mystery"]), the approach of mixing documentary realism with dramatic reenactments is risky, as Meyer himself has acknowledged. Critics and audiences wonder how much of the information presented is factual, whether or not an audience can tell the fictional from the factual, whether or not characters and situations have been oversimplified for dramatic effect, and whether or not the film espouses "official" positions or counterarguments (Corner 45). And while the reaction to Meyer's film was largely positive, controversy did occur around the dramatic reenactment scenes. Matt Ashare, a film critic for the *Boston Phoenix,* for example, after complaining that Glover's narrative is too simplistic, claims that the docudrama sequences are the film's "most egregious" weakness: "It's not the inherent inaccuracy of the re-enactments that's so troubling as the way they make you feel you're watching an episode of *America's Most Wanted.* Which is too bad: Robert Johnson would be a great subject for a straight documentary treatment *or* a feature film, but not both." Ashare's response illustrates several of the recurring concerns about docudrama: Ashare worries about the relationship between fact and fiction in the reenactments and fears that dramatization will reduce the historical life of a cultural icon to the level of cheap television entertainment.

Luckily for Meyer, most other critics saw positive value in his mixed-genre film. Sam Sutherland, for example, while remarking that the film "sometimes drifts too far into biopic territory," also recognizes that "the ambitious mixture of dramatic reconstruction with traditional documentary affords excellent insight" into Johnson's life and music. Commenting specifically on the effectiveness of the dramatic scenes, Sutherland continues: "The film's strength is its power of suggestion: we never see the Johnson character up close, never hear him talk. As if in a dream, he flits in and out of scenes, whether courting his girlfriend or stirring a juke joint to mayhem. . . . We never see him such that we can know him, which is an accurate representation of the elusive musician." Sutherland sums up Meyer's hybrid film this way: "*Can't You Hear the Wind Howl* transcends its genre of 'docudrama,' providing the well-researched information we'd expect from a conventional documentary with the dramatic impact we could hope for in a Hollywood film" ("Review of *Can't You Hear the Wind Howl?*"). Howard Reich, a film critic for the *Chicago Tribune,* concurs, observing that the mixed form of *Can't You Hear the Wind Howl?* is "a risky approach for any documentary. . . . [But the dramatized scenes] never intrude on the documentary tone of the film or its veracity. Instead, they give the story a flesh-and-blood quality it would not otherwise have" (*Can't You Hear*). This mixture of factual context with dramatic reenactment in Meyer's film helps us know the historical Robert Johnson in ways not permitted by the more traditional documentary, by fictional re-creation alone, or by myth.

Peter Meyer himself was obviously aiming for historical accuracy despite the minidramas in his documentary, an intention apparent from the film itself and from Meyer's comments in interviews. In fact, he claims that the film was designed to be not only a biography of a music genius but a reclamation of overlooked history, especially African American history. Distancing himself, perhaps, from the hagiography of Hunt's film, Meyer says that *Can't You Hear the Wind Howl?* is "a story about Robert and his music, but it's also a story about that particular time in black history and the music that comes from the land. . . . I could have done a documentary that praised his music up and down and said what a genius and brilliant man he was (which is in the documentary), but I also wanted to show the setting where he created this music" (Meyer, "Mystery"). Meyer is aware of the dangers of intermingling drama and documentary. Believing that "when you do a documentary, everything in it needs to be accurate and true," he nonetheless struggled with one of the "limitations" that John Corner sees as a reason to mix drama and documentary: the absence of images. With only two photographs and no moving footage, Meyer decided that using someone to portray Johnson would allow the audience "to hear his songs as well as visualize, perhaps, what it was like back in that time" (Meyer, "Mystery").

The film itself emphasizes this attempt to recover history, despite offering no commentary from Johnson scholars or traditional historians. Instead, the film presents interviews with numerous people who knew Johnson, from fellow musicians to childhood friends. And despite the fictionalized photo-booth scene with which the film begins, it is clear from the outset that exploring historical context is a primary goal of the film. In contrast to *The Search for Robert Johnson,* in which the first spoken words were paeans to Johnson by Keith Richards and Eric Clapton, the first spoken words in Meyer's film come from the contemporary bluesman Robert Cray, who says: "Whenever I listen to Robert Johnson's music, I think he's probably the prime example of how America was back in those times." This opening sequence supports Meyer's contention that the film is not simply an homage to Robert Johnson but an attempt to place him in history, and this attempt to recover history occurs repeatedly throughout the film. Like Hunt, Meyer uses numerous interviews and photographs to help an audience understand conditions in Johnson's time, but Meyer's tend to focus on the difficulties of Delta life. Many of the photographs depict harsh social conditions, such as "Colored Only" signs and migrant workers in the cotton fields, and the dramatized scenes enact the itinerant Johnson repeatedly being harassed by white law enforcement officials. In case an audience has missed the point, Robert Cray returns to remind us that Robert Johnson is "the perfect example of what anybody should listen to if they want to get an understanding of blues and just plain old American history." And at the end of the film, bluesman and Johnson acquaintance Henry Townsend claims that "Robert Johnson is a parable. He was getting to be a very famous guy . . . and why is he dead? His fame killed him." In these views, Robert Johnson was not necessarily "the greatest bluesman" that ever lived but a gifted musician who lived in a violent era, the voice of an almost forgotten time and place, and an object lesson for those who would seek to follow in his footsteps.

Do either of these films—Hunt's *The Search for Robert Johnson* or Meyer's *Can't You Hear the Wind Howl?*—provide enough historical context to demythologize Robert Johnson? Yes and no. Both films do an admirable job of presenting the known facts about Robert Johnson's life. Both also directly address the myths that have accrued to Robert Johnson's story and offer commentary by Johnson's contemporaries (Shines in the Hunt film; Shines, Lockwood, Edwards, and Townsend in the Meyer film), all of whom flatly deny the possibility of selling one's soul to the devil. But both films pose problems as recontextualizations of Robert Johnson. Hunt's film, despite its traditional documentary format, is perhaps the more troubled as a historical record because it engages in hero-worship and downplays race. Meyer's film is controversial because of the dramatized scenes, although I would argue that their congruence with the facts as we know them and the accuracy with which they depict the settings may, in fact, bring history more fully alive than a traditional documentary can do. The scene of Johnson/Moore playing his guitar for his young wife outside an isolated sharecropper's shack, for example, lingers in my mind, forcefully imprinting both the dashed hopes of Johnson's youth and the hardships of the life he attempted to escape through music. And as Ralph Ellison has noted, fiction can be more truthful than history if it chooses to talk about the things historians omit (70). It may be that no biography can entirely recapture history and that no reinsertion into history can rescue the historical Robert Johnson from the accumulated legends about him. Perhaps the best we can do is join Alan Greenberg and "stick to the facts as we imagine them."

Cultural Bifurcations 1: Uses of History

Since the format in which history is presented seems to affect its accuracy less than other factors, it may be that fictionalized versions of Robert Johnson's life can recapture his history at least as well as documentary. But when examining fiction, one enters a field of literary discourse with a history of its own. Later in this section I will discuss some pertinent elements of American literary traditions. For now, I will simply assert that many literary texts about Robert Johnson partake of the inevitable "duplicity" that British novelist D. H. Lawrence identified in 1923 as a defining element of American literature. For Lawrence, "the rhythm of American art-activity is dual" (65). This duality is apparent in stories about Robert Johnson that portray the material conditions of his life as well as the gothic or romantic elements of his legend. They offer both realism and romanticism and thus suggest much about the bifurcations of American culture from its beginnings and into the twenty-first century.

T. Coraghessan Boyle's short story "Stones in My Passway, Hellhound on My Trail" was published in *Greasy Lake and Other Stories* in 1979, before much information about Robert Johnson was available. Sam Charters's sketchy *Robert Johnson* had appeared in 1972, Greil Marcus's highly romantic *Mystery Train* in 1975, and a few articles in music journals had tackled the elusive subject in the late 1960s and early 1970s, but Boyle's story was written before the groundbreaking research of Gayle Dean Wardlow or Peter Guralnick was published. Much of what was written about Johnson in those days was speculation based on lyrics—the tendency to "construct biography from repertoire" (Pearson 222). Boyle's story inevitably shares this romantic vision, having been shaped by the legends then available about Johnson as well as by Boyle's own youthful interest in Robert Johnson's music. Born in 1948, heavily influenced by rock and roll and by the blues music that informed it, Boyle describes his younger self as a "proto-hippie," indicating his 1960s cultural roots and suggesting his investment in the wandering-troubadour image of Johnson (Boyle, Frequently Asked Questions).

Yet in writing this story, Boyle also reveals his abiding interest in history, his college major. In response to my query about the origins of this story about Robert Johnson and in an echo of Greenberg's epigraph to this chapter, Boyle wrote: "The story came from my love of the music and from my desire to tell the definitive story of his death (definitive in my universe, anyway)" (Message Board). This statement concurs with the view of history we saw above, since it implies that any history is partly the product of a writer's imagination, of his or her worldview. In Boyle's case, we see a worldview influenced by both historical fact and romantic disposition.

"Stones in My Passway, Hellhound on My Trail" recounts the events of Robert Johnson's last day—the poisoning in a juke house. Moving back and forth in time from this central scene, Boyle gets the outlines of Johnson's life right, although many of the details are incorrect or simply invented. Boyle places Johnson's recording session in New Orleans rather than San Antonio or Dallas, locates the fateful juke joint in Dallas rather than Greenwood, and creates fictitious names for the characters in the juke scene, such as the jealous Ida Mae Doss, who poisons Johnson's eggs and beans. But Boyle is also quite aware of the facts as they were then known about Robert Johnson. The story lists the names of some of Johnson's women friends and many of the towns through which he passed. It relates the episode of Johnson's triumphant return to the Robinsonville jukes as an accomplished guitar player. It also includes the story (which is true, according to Don Law Jr.) of Johnson's first recording trip to Dallas, during which he twice interrupted the producer, Don Law Sr. (Walter Fagen in Boyle's story), at dinner. The first call came from the police station, after Johnson had been arrested for vagrancy; the second came directly from Johnson, who asked for money to buy a woman's company because he was "lonesome." Finally, the oft repeated account of Johnson's being poisoned in a juke joint out of jealousy forms the spine of the story.

In addition to portraying known events of Johnson's life, Boyle takes pains to invoke the era in which Johnson lived and died. The juke scene is presented in rich detail, with dim lights swaying, field workers spitting tobacco juice, a makeshift bar, and frenzied dancers. Boyle also establishes the larger historical era, pulling the spotlight away from Johnson's death scene several times to report on world events. After establishing the juke setting in the first two paragraphs, Boyle provides this context: "It is 1938, dust bowl, New Deal. FDR is on the radio, and somebody in Robinsonville is naming a baby for Jesse Owens" (147). Later, as the juke characters become increasingly drunken and violent, Boyle steps back to note violent world events of 1937: "Franco laid siege to Madrid, the Japanese invaded Nanking, Amelia Earhardt lost herself in the Pacific, and Robert Johnson made a series of records" (150)—although he changes the name of the record company from Vocalion to Victrix. Clearly this story is fiction—the needless name changes indicate that—but it also attempts to "tell the definitive story" of Robert Johnson's death and to show its connections to its time.

Ultimately, however, the romantic view of Robert Johnson wins out. This is most apparent in Boyle's depiction of Johnson as a naif, a man strangely unmarked by world events.[2] At the end of the paragraph about current affairs in 1938, Boyle writes: Johnson "spent six weeks in Chicago and didn't know the World's Fair was going on. . . . He's never heard of Hitler" (147). This is a rather strange claim to make about someone who traveled widely, listened obsessively to the radio, and whose songs included references to places as far away as Ethiopia and the Philippines. The story also uses evocative sensual imagery to foreshadow Johnson's death. In the late-night juke, just before Johnson is poisoned, "the lemons are pulp, the rum decimated. . . . The final chord rings in the air, decapitated" (149). Such images of things used up and destroyed prefigure Johnson's own imminent demise, as does a flashback early in the story. In this scene, Robert as a child witnesses a dying, apparently poisoned dog trying to claw its own intestines out. This gruesome imagery of self-mutilation is repeated at the end of the story, when Robert, clutching his abdomen, his bowels "on fire," "snarls" (152). This connection to the self-mutilating dog suggests that Johnson was both victim and agent, a self-destructive seeker of his own death, and so echoes the "repertoire as biography" tendency of Johnson's earliest fans. Taken together, the depiction of an unsophisticated Johnson and the imagistic foreshadowing combine to present a vision of Johnson as a doomed, haunted singer—a figure of romance, detached from the historical setting Boyle carefully constructs around him.

This emphasis on foreshadowing suggests a further dimension to Boyle's work. He links the story directly to myth, although he superimposes an ancient Greek tragedy onto the story rather than the familiar deal with the devil to amplify the import of Robert Johnson's life and death. As Johnson orders the fateful eggs from the seething Ida Mae—whose kitchen counter unsafely includes rat poison alongside the salt and pepper—the following line appears in a paragraph by itself: "Agamemnon, watch out!" (151). And at the end, as the pain of the poison strikes him, we are told that he feels "a sword run through him" (152). These two brief references to the Greek hero Agamemnon, stabbed to death by his vengeful wife Clytemnestra, enlarge the parameters of the story. Instead of a simple narrative about one historical figure's death, the story becomes a universal tale of treachery, betrayal, and tragic fate. Rather than demythologizing Robert Johnson by restoring his historical context, Boyle actually extends the mythology, overlaying doomed poet with fated king and enlarging the mythic contexts in which Johnson's life resonates.

This analysis of the story's mythic elements is not meant to criticize it as a work of fiction. It is generally considered one of the most powerful of

Boyle's early works, noted for its "brooding, Pinteresque atmosphere of menace" (Kakutani 22), its "sensuous, evocative prose" (McCaffrey 16), and the "feelings generated [that] are not simply visceral" (Shepard). In its heavy use of foreshadowing and its insistent intermingling of myth with historical fact, the story predicts Boyle's 1987 historical novel *World's End,* arguably his biggest critical success to date. In an interview about *World's End,* a saga of his native Hudson River Valley, Boyle remarked: "'I wanted to re-invent history, to use it as a point of departure. . . . I think you can get bogged down with facts that people would be better off getting from history books. I'm interested in history as a setting for working out my feelings about contemporary society, and for making entertainment and seducing the reader into having the same fascination for the period as I do'" (qtd. in Kammen, "T. Coraghessan Boyle" 252–53). In similarly reinventing Robert Johnson, Boyle has created a powerful short story, grounded in historical fact, that nonetheless extends the mythology surrounding Robert Johnson more than it tells the "definitive story." For Boyle, there may not even be a defining line between history and myth. Speaking again about *World's End,* he says: "'I wanted to be a purveyor of myths about the [Hudson River Valley] myself. I wanted to invent myths and use [Washington Irving's] myths and play off them. And talk about history as myth, too, and weave it all together'" (qtd. in DeCurtis 55). "Stones in My Passway, Hellhound on My Trail" likewise "weaves together" history, classical myth, and contemporary legends about Robert Johnson.

If "Stones in My Passway" is any indication, incorporating historical facts into the story of Robert Johnson will not always reveal the constructedness of the legends nor restore Johnson to human proportions. It may be that "artificial myths" are best created in some other fashion, that reinsertion into historical context does not always suffice. Or it may be that the mixture of history and fiction is simply not factual enough to unpack the Robert Johnson mythology. But Boyle's comment about his use of history in *World's End*—that it was "a setting for working out [his] feelings about contemporary society"—implies that historical study reveals the present as much as the past. In this belief he concurs with theorist Frederic Jameson, who contends that historical fiction "can no longer set out to represent the historical past; it can only 'represent' our ideas and stereotypes about that past" (21). What might Boyle's story tell us about contemporary uses of Robert Johnson, about our "ideas about the past," and thus about contemporary American culture in general?

One important thing the story tells us is that American writers' search for a "usable past," first called for by Van Wyck Brooks, is still very much a part of the American cultural scene. Writing in 1918 and anticipating the postmodern historians mentioned earlier in this chapter, Brooks observes that the "past has no objective reality; it yields only what we are able to look for in it" (338). Seeing American literature in his time as lacking any sense of "inherited resources" (337), Brooks calls for the creation of a past that would yield what was needed: "The present is a void and the American writer floats in that void because the past that survives in the common mind is a past without living value. But is this the only possible past? If we need another past so badly, is it inconceivable that we might discover one, that we might even invent one?" (339). Much post–World War II literary history, as well as much history in general, documents this obsessive national search for and invention of a "usable past," and Boyle's story certainly reflects this long-standing tradition. Intrigued by a figure about whom little was known, Boyle intermingled fact, legend, and fancy to create a "usable" Robert Johnson. Having thus reinvented him, Boyle's Johnson becomes "a point of departure" from which the past can comment on the present. This connection becomes clear from the story's inclusion in Boyle's *Greasy Lake* collection, in which most of the stories take place in the 1960s and 1970s. Despite the difference in temporal setting, however, many of them involve instances of treachery and alienation like those found in "Stones in My Passway, Hellhound on My Trail." Boyle's Robert Johnson thus functions in part as an analogue to figures from Boyle's youth and from contemporary society in general. Boyle presents the universal pain of betrayal, captures a moment in American history, and develops the legend of a then-little-known musician into a usable icon.

Perhaps because it fulfills all these cultural functions at once, Boyle's story also partakes of the duality of American literature that Lawrence identified almost a century ago. Numerous American literary historians since World War II have studied this tendency to enact binary oppositions. Using terms like "the divided stream" of American literature (Walcutt), the "paradoxes" of American culture (Steinbeck), and the "biformities" of our "contrapuntal civilization" (Kammen, *People*), literary historians and theorists largely agree that American literature is characterized by contradiction.[3] While the perceived sources of these contrary impulses in American literature have been attributed to various historical circumstances (such as Puritanism, the diversity of immigrants, or the inherent conflict between individualism and conformity in a democracy), scholars largely agree that American literature is bifurcated. These literary bifurcations are evident in Boyle's "Stones in My Passway." While the theme of betrayal and the sense of inevitability unify the story's various elements, it nonetheless includes a dichotomous mixture of fact and fancy, history and myth—or, in literary terms, realism and romanticism. By mixing together factual historical content with the imaginative license of fiction and allusions to ancient myths, Boyle invents an emotional reality that seems commensurate with Johnson's life and senseless death.

This interest in the contradictions of American culture—what Jameson calls our "cultural schizophrenia" (26–29)—has marked recent popular culture studies as well. Bifurcations are not simply a literary phenomenon, and Boyle's story reflects cultural contradictions beyond the merely academic. This dialectic is seen everywhere from fashion trends to musical tastes, but it shows up especially in two arenas: Hollywood films and advertising. Film critic Robert B. Ray is helpful in uncovering the contradictions inherent in popular American movies. For Ray, Hollywood films consistently set up paradoxes and then solve them simplistically, "conceal[ing] the necessity for choice," fostering a "reconciliatory pattern" that refuses to resolve contradiction (57–58). This tendency is most evident in movie heroes, who tend to embody oppositional traits (a boxing violinist, a pigeon-raising boxer) or to fall into one of two categories: the "official" hero, who stands for commitment and the common good, and the "outlaw" hero, a self-determining loner, subject only to the demands of his own conscience. These parallel hero types, most commonly found in films about conflict between the individual and the community, represent "the general pattern of American mythology: the denial of the necessity for choice" (63). They also provide a clear analogy to the competing trends of realism and romanticism in American literature (and in Boyle's story). For Ray, "The American mythology's refusal to choose between its two heroes . . . not only overcame binary oppositions; it systematically mythologized the certainty of being able to do so" (63–64). In other words, Americans not only want it (whatever it is) both ways, we have created a national culture of refusing to believe that we cannot have it so.

The other arena where American binary oppositions reign supreme is in contemporary advertising, the most ubiquitous form of cultural production today. While ads reveal all sorts of cultural contradictions, the most obvious appears as the competing desires for status and equality. In magazine ads for cigarettes we see both the elegant Barclay gentleman in his tuxedo and the rugged Marlboro man. On television, we eavesdrop on chic thirtysomethings enjoying wine on their sunset-drenched deck, yet minutes later we share the fun of a cheap beer with loutish friends. Many commentators link this recurring conflict between elitism and populism to an inherent contradiction in the American Dream, that quintessential myth that anyone can succeed in America. In America we're all equal, but we can still try to be superior to everyone else.

Seen in the light of these conflicts, T. Coraghessan Boyle's story tells us much about the American mind in the late twentieth century. In its creation of Robert Johnson as tragic hero, the story suggests the importance of our search for a "usable" past that must inevitably reflect our present thinking. In its fusion of realistic historical detail with romantic legend, of material man with supernatural creature or fated king, it reveals our inherent doubleness—our desire to have things both ways at once. While "Stones in My Passway, Hellhound on My Trail" does not reclaim Robert Johnson from the mythic constructs that have accrued to his image, it nonetheless reflects some foundational assumptions of contemporary American culture.

Cultural Bifurcations 2: Double Consciousness

Bill Harris's award-winning 1992 play *Robert Johnson: Trick the Devil* has some similarities to Boyle's story. Like "Stones in My Passway," *Trick the Devil* takes place in a southern juke joint on the day Robert Johnson is poisoned, and it echoes the story's themes of jealousy and treachery. It realistically invokes its historical era, both in the juke setting and in a wider social context, while including enough romanticism to reflect some of the same cultural bifurcations as Boyle's story. Yet Harris, an African American playwright, adds some different, specifically African American dimensions to the tale. Director Woodie King Jr. notes that in all his work, Harris is particularly interested in "giving voice to the often unheard, ignored, or misunderstood independent and creative spirit of African American males" (2). Accordingly, in *Trick the Devil* we get to hear Robert Johnson's side of his own story (at least, as Harris envisions it). But in addition to re-creating Johnson and his historical context, Harris also shows how Johnson's story came to be mythologized by cultural outsiders who glamorized Johnson and so removed him from history. According to Harris: "'Every society has its indelible and embedded myths, and they're necessary to that society. One of the things that I've wanted to do is raise discussion about these myths as they apply to African-Americans, especially African-American men. The whole idea of Robert Johnson having to sell his soul in order to be able to play the way he did . . . that's where I start . . . and then examine the why of the myth, rather than just it itself. Why does America need to believe that?'" (qtd. in Tysh). Examining the "why" of the myth is a crucial element of *Trick the Devil.* In so doing, the play offers an artistic deconstruction of the Robert Johnson myth because it depicts the myth being created.

The key element in this exposure of mythology as a construct is the character of Kimbrough, a pretentious northern professor and the only white character in the play. He enters "Georgia Mayberry's Colored Jook Joint" early in the play, searching for Robert Johnson, much as researchers from John Hammond Sr. to Alan Lomax must have done. His outsider status is immediately apparent in his language. Unlike the lively vernacular spoken by Georgia Mayberry (the juke proprietor) and Stokes (the blind piano player), Kimbrough speaks in blank verse, his dialogue replete with allusions to Shakespeare, his research specialty. Kimbrough freely admits that he is out of his element and that he is afraid. He worries about being in the Delta environment, "a world / of shadows and smoke where nothing [is] solid," a world unlike his own realm "of reason, / order and certainty" (11). He is searching for Robert Johnson because the power of Johnson's recorded music has upset his preconceived assumptions about race and culture. Speaking directly to the audience, Kimbrough marvels that Johnson's songs remind him of the Bible and Shakespeare, that they resonate with themes of loss and atonement. He wonders: "How does he—this unschooled black Orpheus / produce songs as universal and complex / as the intellectual love of my life?" (24). Because Kimbrough accepts the stereotype that southern black people are primitive, "superstitious," "childlike perpetrators of unrepentant, / potluck violence" (11), he is unnerved that Johnson's songs echo "universal" themes. Kimbrough apparently regards the Mississippi Delta as part of some universe other than his own.

Kimbrough has also heard the legend that Johnson sold his soul for his talent, "traded something he didn't think he needed, / for what he couldn't get any other way" (13), but he doesn't know whether this or any other story about Johnson is true. Late in the play Robert Johnson himself tells the "true" story to Kimbrough. In this version, Johnson goes to the crossroads at midnight, but the devil is "just an ordinary white man in a suit and tie," some white power broker (a recording company executive, perhaps?) trying to exploit him. Because he is particular about other people touching his guitar, Johnson refuses to allow this white devil to tune it and instead plays as ferociously as he can. His impassioned playing eventually expresses not only his own life story but all of the misery in his racial memory: "the bondage, being bid for on the block, the lash, Jim Crow, the rope, the chain gang and the Klan. . . . And *that's* what got the Devil, because he couldn't call none of it a lie!" (40–41). Infuriated, the devil plays his own guitar in a sort of demonic headcutting contest, and by watching him, Johnson becomes a virtuoso. Harris's Robert Johnson thus beats the devil at his own game simply by telling—and playing—the truth.

Kimbrough, it turns out, is himself tortured by a secret: his family wealth originated from slaveholding ancestors. When Kimbrough confesses this, Robert Johnson gives him the following advice: "Face your devil, walk along with him, side by side, then go your separate ways. That's the only way. And just like me you ain't got no choice" (42). He encourages Kimbrough: "Go back and teach, professor. Go trick the Devil and tell the truth" (44). The truth, however, is too much for Kimbrough to face. Unwilling to give up his tainted fortune and unable to live with himself for keeping it, Kimbrough instead creates a legend about Robert Johnson that sidesteps all the issues. In the play's epilogue we see him lecturing, creating a myth about Robert Johnson that fits neatly into the worldview that Kimbrough held before his southern journey and before meeting Robert Johnson. Claiming that his "research proves that [Johnson] / was in league with Satan from the age of / seventeen" (45), Kimbrough describes Johnson in imagery more suitable for Macbeth's witches than a Delta bluesman. He depicts Johnson and Satan this way:

> They would consort during thunder, lightning
> and rain. And when they practiced their hurly
> burly the multiplying villainies
> of nature transmuted fair to foul
> and foul to fair. (45)

Kimbrough creates a myth about Robert Johnson that distances the truth-telling musician. He thereby preserves his "rational" worldview in the face of inexplicable musical genius and avoids acknowledging his own complicity with the hellhounds dogging Johnson and himself.

Kimbrough's willful misrepresentation is obviously an exaggeration of the ways white scholars have used the Robert Johnson story. No researcher that I know of came face to face with Johnson, heard his story firsthand, and then distorted it for personal aggrandizement. However, Harris's inclusion of Kimbrough in his reinvention of Robert Johnson—as well as his imagining the devil as a white man in a business suit—suggests that white privilege often rests upon black exploitation. In an artistic way, Harris is asking the question I asked throughout the introduction and chapter 1: whose interests are served in such a representation? Harris's answer is uncompromising. During Robert Johnson's lifetime, African Americans were commodities used to shore up the personal fortunes—whether monetary, academic, or otherwise—of white people with power and media access. And if Harris uses Johnson's story as Boyle did, as "a point of departure" to comment on the present, one might assume that he is commenting on white exploitation of black talent today as well as in Johnson's era. Harris uses the story of Robert Johnson to reveal the power imbalances within American race relations and to show that myth is constructed by human beings with assumptions and agendas. By performing the construction of myth, *Trick the Devil* successfully unmasks it.

But *Robert Johnson: Trick the Devil* does more than expose the underpinnings of myth. Like Boyle's story, Harris's play is the product of a bifurcated culture, although Harris's focus is primarily on a racial divide, made apparent in the differences between Kimbrough and the other characters. Unlike Boyle, who intermingles realism and romanticism within his own narrative prose, Harris ascribes a pragmatic view of the world to his rural black characters and a naive romanticism to his more powerful white one. The realistic worldview of the black characters is best embodied by Lem, Georgia's estranged husband, who returns in mid-play from building a levee for the government. In the absence of other paying work (a reference to the Depression setting) Lem felt he had no choice but to accept the levee job, which he then found "worse than slavery" (31). He describes long days of backbreaking labor under cruel white supervisors for small pay and with no time off. After enduring months of these conditions, Lem enters the juke enraged at Johnson's presence in Georgia's room and angry at the world: "I ain't the same as I was before I went up there moving that dirt," he warns Georgia, "so be careful, you don't know how much I can stand" (30). Eventually, Lem poisons Robert Johnson. Through Lem, Harris establishes the broader social context that can impel individual actions and shows the tragic psychological effects of limited opportunity.

Lem's life is most unlike the bucolic fantasies of the rural South that Kimbrough harbors, although Kimbrough soon learns that his idea of an idyllic South is a misconception. Expecting to find "the undisciplined world of soil tillers, / idlers, roaming song singers" (11), he discovers instead "a powder keg ready to explode" (28), his pastoral fantasy replaced by the harsh reality of a Depression-era, racist economy. His differences from the black characters are everywhere apparent, from his elevated language to his response to folk culture. When Georgia and Stokes talk about Brer Rabbit and Brer Fox—stories about betrayal and wiliness and thus relevant to the events at hand—Kimbrough dismisses them as "[n]onsense tales. . . . Diversionary, but little more" (24). Unaware that the man he is seeking will be killed that very day in the juke joint where he sits, Kimbrough recalls a juke joint dance he once witnessed as "[j]ust darkie fun" (23). Repeatedly the black characters observe that white people "can't see nothing but what they want to see" (19), and Kimbrough repeatedly proves them right. The contrast is sharply etched in a fragment of dialogue near the end, when Robert is trying to help Kimbrough face his personal devils. After an intense, climactic dialogue in which Kimbrough describes the demon that haunts his dreams, we hear:

> Kimbrough: It's a metaphor.
> Robert: Metaphor my ass, it's a hellhound, fool. (43)

In this brief exchange, Harris encapsulates the different worldviews of the two characters and emphasizes Kimbrough's dangerous romanticism. Robert faces the truth regardless of what it brings him; Kimbrough displaces it to the status of literary trope. Kimbrough's final retreat to the mythmaking lecture of the epilogue is the ultimate abandonment of what he has learned, a betrayal of both Robert and himself. While imagining Johnson in league with Satan may restore his ability to function in his rational world—where poor black singers cannot be Orpheus—one wonders who has really sold his soul in this play.

In addition to the cultural fissures between black and white, realism and romanticism, Harris's play goes one step further to explore the bifurcations within African American culture itself. The scene opens on a rainy afternoon in the juke, where Georgia and Stokes swap stories as they prepare for their evening clientele. Through their opening conversation, Harris reveals his grounding in what novelist Arthur Flowers calls the "literary hoodoo" tradition of African American literature. For Flowers, "literary hoodoo" writers are spiritually inclined heirs to a double literary tradition of western written forms and African American oral ones (75–77). Their works include elements of both western and African culture and arts and preserve the stories that are vital to "communal health and empowerment" (79). The opening dialogue between Georgia and Stokes offers a succinct example of such cultural hybridity. The blind Stokes can see the future, a gift he has inherited from his hoodoo-practicing grandmama. Yet African American culture was influenced by southern Christianity as well as by African spiritual practices, and Georgia, who knows firsthand that Stokes's predictions come true, nonetheless sees herself as someone who "went for Christian" rather than hoodoo (Harris 8). This double heritage is also reflected in the structure of Harris's play. Like most western dramas, the play proceeds in a linear, cause-and-effect manner, with characters' actions clearly motivated and plot complications leading to a climax and a denouement. The play itself thus reveals its roots in western literary traditions while it nonetheless celebrates African American oral ones.

And celebrate that oral culture it does. The play is not exactly a musical, but it includes performances of many Robert Johnson songs, and as one reviewer noted, "many of the play's speeches and sequences play like musical numbers" (Holman). The vibrancy of African American folk culture is highlighted once Kimbrough enters, his presence creating "an opportunity for the other players to reveal the ingenious language, signifying, and role-playing African Americans created to keep their real life separate from the life the white man saw" (Leonin). Georgia and Stokes invoke numerous African American folk figures, from Brer Rabbit and Brer Fox to the Signifying Monkey; they imitate black vaudevillians Butter Beans and Susie; they discuss cultural traditions like Stokes's grandmama's healing "tricks" or the significance of names to African Americans. Through their exuberant verbal facility they reveal the vitality and value of African American culture; for them, western traditions like Christianity coexist easily with African-derived cultural products and values.

Writing in *The Souls of Black Folk* in 1903, W. E. B. Du Bois famously described this duality of outlook among African Americans as "double-consciousness," or the ability of African Americans to see the world simultaneously from a majority viewpoint (as Americans) and from a marginalized one (as oppressed African Americans). He wrote:

> [T]he Negro is a sort of seventh son, born with a veil, and gifted with second-sight in this American world,—a world which yields him no true self-consciousness, but only lets him see himself through the revelation of the other world. It is a peculiar sensation, this double-consciousness, this sense of always looking at one's self through the eyes of others, of measuring one's soul by the tape of a world that looks on in amused contempt and pity. One ever feels his twoness,—an American, a Negro; two souls, two thoughts, two unreconciled strivings; two warring ideals in one dark body, whose dogged strength alone keeps it from being torn asunder. (102)

Most commentators on Du Bois's notion of double-consciousness focus on the pain of the condition, on the "twoness," the internal "war." Yet Du Bois's definition includes some decidedly positive aspects as well. He describes double-consciousness as a gift—as second sight, or the ability to see things others do not see. Elsewhere in *The Souls of Black Folk* Du Bois predicts that "the problem of the twentieth century will be the problem of the color line" (100), and one suspects that people able to assess this problem from two different viewpoints, majority and oppositional, might have some advantages in understanding the world around them. In the case of Harris's characters, at any rate, double-consciousness enables them to function smoothly in two worlds: they know how to avoid revealing themselves to Kimbrough, and they know how to survive the hardships of their own lives, often with grace and good humor. Their pragmatism is thus a result of their cultural heritage. They easily recognize and manipulate multiple frames of reference; they can see complexly in a world full of contradictions.

In this, the pragmatic African American characters contrast sharply with the bookish Kimbrough, the ivory-tower romantic with no appreciation of multiple perspectives. His worldview cannot accommodate the presence of another; all things must be shaped to fit within his singular ideas of validity and value. The poverty of this unitary vision within a bifurcated culture is emphasized in Harris's epilogue, where Stokes, not Kimbrough, has the last word. Immediately after Kimbrough's lecture on Johnson's traffic with the devil—a chilling moment, since the audience knows that Kimbrough knows better—Stokes offers a final comment. Emphasizing his own "second sight" and offering interpretive options Kimbrough could never imagine, the blind Stokes says: "Robert Johnson? He be back. He just going down to hell and ease some people's minds; maybe move some rocks around, even change the way the river run. Aw, he'll be back directly, don't you worry 'bout a thing. Just like he been here before he be back again. How I know? 'Cause it's happened before. And I seen it with my own eyes!" (45). With this comment, an amalgam of cultural images, the play ends. The picture of Robert Johnson that lingers is of a man with supernatural insights, prodigious talent, and an ability to rise again that links him to Christ, the phoenix, High John the Conqueror, or all three, depending on your cultural frame(s) of reference. What also lingers is the sad fact that Johnson's legend and legacy have been co-opted and distorted by the Kimbroughs of the world, purveyors of proscriptive "truth" who are unable to face truths about themselves and the sources of their privilege. Perhaps, suggests Harris, the very act of mythmaking is the inevitable product of our differences, of our misunderstandings and refusals to see—in short, of our quintessentially American cultural bifurcations.

Imagined Facts: "A Quasi-Alchemical Technique"

Two related points should be clear from my discussion of these written and filmed texts that portray Robert Johnson within some approximation of his historical context. One, reinserting an image into history, however one invents, re-creates, or imagines that history, does not insure that the historical figure will reemerge from the accumulated myths around it. However (and this is my second point), if that depiction of history also shows how the myth came to be constructed, as we see in Harris's play, an avenue opens up for recovering a more historically based image, or at least an alternative myth. Portraying or performing the actual construction of the myths may be the clearest path to recovering Robert Johnson.

Alan Greenberg's screenplay *Love in Vain: A Vision of Robert Johnson* takes this process a step further. Like the texts already examined in this chapter, *Love in Vain* is thoroughly grounded in historical fact: the published book includes a 198–page screenplay, with an additional forty-eight pages of research notes on everything from Depression-era economics to blues artists' biographies to African American folklore. *Love in Vain* also acknowledges the mythology surrounding Robert Johnson, including the pact with the devil, and like Harris, Greenberg finds a way to reinvent that myth. What is somewhat different is that Greenberg's text offers a much wider focus. Rather than zooming in on a specific juke joint on the day of Robert Johnson's poisoning, Greenberg depicts Johnson's life and times more expansively, ending with his death but building up to it with scenes of his life through his teenage years and into adulthood. Greenberg also establishes the social milieu in which Johnson lived, a world of jukes and cotton fields, family, competitive musicians, and racial and economic oppression. Most importantly, the material world that Greenberg creates is a place already imbued with myth and legend—a place where people act on myths as much as they do on "facts," where legend and fact are equally functioning components of reality. The bifurcations apparent in Greenberg's Delta world seem less cultural contradictions than multiple kinds of truth.

The opening two scenes encapsulate much of Greenberg's artistic vision. On the edge of a cotton field stands "a tiny clapboard church" from which emanates the sound of a choir. Above the choir we hear the preacher's sermon, warning his congregation that "the hounds of hell are . . fast on our trail." A woman steps out the back door of the church into the pouring rain, picks up an axe, and begins "chopping determinedly at the rain and the muddy ground" (1). The scene cuts to a gravel road after the same rain. Two sharecroppers push their broken jalopy, on which is tied the dead body of a young black man, while one recounts the story of some local slaves who escaped by flying back to Africa. The jalopy ends up parked at a juke joint.

These two opening scenes establish the culture Greenberg is trying to reproduce. They document the background into which Robert Johnson was born with their oblique references to slavery (the story), lynching (the dead young man), hellfire-and-brimstone religion (the preacher), and sharecropping (the cotton fields). They depict a world permeated with music, from the church choir to the rhythmic preaching of the minister to the dance music coming from the juke joint. They also reveal that in Greenberg's 1930s Delta, Christian hellhounds coexist with flying Africans, and the folk belief that an axe can "chop the storm in two" (199) shares the stage with cars. As one reviewer put it, "Greenberg re-creates a world where telephones, automobiles, and phonographs coexist with conjurers, devils, and mojo hands" (Sutherland, "Review of *Love in Vain*"). It is a world of seemingly impossible juxtapositions, all of which were nonetheless facts of life or commonly held beliefs of the time.

The epigraph to this chapter—Greenberg's comment that he sticks to the facts as he imagines them—suggests both the strange juxtapositions of the world he creates and his multiple purposes in creating it. On one level, Greenberg is clearly interested in historical accuracy. His emphasis on factual history explains the unusual presence of extensive research notes in a published screenplay. In an interview, Greenberg proudly mentions that Johnson's associate Johnny Shines applauded *Love in Vain,* saying that the screenplay "'has finally cleared up all the lies and crap about Robert and his life'" (qtd. in McGonigal). The text offers much detail about historical conditions—about the culture in general, about specific people like Charley Patton and Tommy Johnson, and about Robert Johnson's life. Greenberg notes that when he started his research for the screenplay, not much was known about Robert Johnson or his times. He claims that *Love in Vain* was "the first book ever written about him . . . [so] my goal in writing *LiV* was not to restore Robert Johnson to his historical context, but to create an historical context that was utterly absent" (Greenberg, "RJ").

The screenplay does an excellent job of supplying that context, as two types of scenes illustrate. First are the juke joint scenes, where the characters attempt to release tension. Almost phantasmagoric in their weird lighting, frenzied dancing, and sudden outbursts of violence, these surreal scenes nonetheless depict a real cultural milieu and specific historical events, such as the slicing of Charley Patton's throat by his jealous girlfriend. Even more imbued with historical fact are the scenes that take place in the cotton fields among the laboring sharecroppers. In one, Robert must use his hoe to kill a deadly cottonmouth snake; in another, a mule knocks down a woman as she attempts to bridle it; and in most of them, the laborers sing work songs and blues while they sweat and chop under a broiling sun, supervised by a foreman carrying a gun. As in the jukes, dangers abound.

What is especially compelling about the farming scenes is that Greenberg depicts sharecropping as both an individual misery and a systemic evil and then links it explicitly to another exploitative system that directly shaped Robert Johnson's life, the recording industry. In a series of early scenes (scenes 9 through 15), we see men, women, and children toiling in "the awful heat" of a cotton field (13). An armed foreman enters with Henry Speir, the real-life talent scout who discovered Johnson and who is here searching for Goat, a fictionalized version of the historical Tommy Johnson. Afraid of being caught playing guitar instead of picking cotton, Goat drops his guitar behind a wagon, where a mule steps on it. The symbolism is clear: life as a sharecropper countermands musical aspirations. When Speir approaches Goat to discuss some "record business," Goat asserts that he can no longer record, having sold the rights to his songs while he was drunk for much less than they were worth. Apparently the historical Tommy Johnson, having been similarly cheated, "somehow believed that he had sold his right to record ever again" (208).

Victimized by the sharecropping system and defrauded by the recording industry, Goat represents everything that Robert Johnson seemed destined by historical circumstances to be, and everything that he refused to become. Trapped between competing systems of oppression—one seemingly from the dark ages, the other a harbinger of the technological future—Greenberg's Johnson is determined to escape the crushing fate he sees embodied in the drunken, diminished Goat. But despite the overwhelming power structures designed to keep them down, Greenberg shows his characters as individuals with agency. They are like Fiske's "the people," who are circumscribed by "power-bloc" operations but who nonetheless respond to those forces in creative ways. This agency is abundantly clear later in the play when Goat, intoxicated as usual (this time on sterno, the "Canned Heat" of Tommy Johnson's most famous song), reiterates the mule's action and puts his foot through his own guitar. As this repeated image suggests, Goat's ruin is partly the result of exploitation and partly his own doing, a lesson Robert Johnson (in the Greenberg version) recognizes and acts to avoid. Greenberg thus takes a step toward "vanquishing myth" (in Barthes's terms) by restoring "determinism and free will" to the Robert Johnson story.

As we have seen in the opening sequence of *Love in Vain,* however, the historical reality that Greenberg constructs is already permeated with myth and legend, and his screenplay likewise partakes of this admixture. Even within the detailed realism of the cotton field scenes, Greenberg's imagination runs free. For example, Goat's mule-smashed guitar is more than an image of exploitation: "Goat's guitar has fallen beside a front wheel of the wooden wagon. The mule eyes the guitar, then puts its foot through it and laughs" (17). Is the mule laughing at Goat, at the sharecropping system that he himself symbolizes, at musical aspirations, at his own bizarre agency? Can mules laugh? Stanley Crouch has noted that Greenberg's screenplay is "grounded as much in myth, legend and tall tale as in research" and that "we can learn as much from good mythology as from fine documentation—if the mythology carries or transmits how a world may have *felt* to those participants, onlookers, and descendants" (ix). While Goat never sees the laughing mule, its chilling image can help convey to a modern audience the unspeakable injustices and disrespect that Robert Johnson and his contemporaries daily endured. It can transmit how the world must have felt to people continually confronted by incomprehensible acts of random and unthinking violence, whose dreams could be crushed by some jackass's laughing whim. Like Meyer, whose reenactment scenes within a documentary allow an audience to "visualize, perhaps, what it was like back in that time" (Meyer, "Mystery"), Greenberg's mythic components help us understand his characters' emotional responses to factual events. He explains: "My purpose in writing *LiV* was to create a reality so plausible and clear and rooted in fact that the end result would be closer to hallucination than history. To achieve this I had to develop a quasi-alchemical technique that blended historical fact with myth and personal vision. I never resorted to sheer imagination; everything in *LiV* didn't necessarily happen, or exist, but could have" ("RJ").

This last comment—that everything *could have happened* as depicted, even if it didn't—is apparent in the screenplay. Greenberg is conspicuously well informed on the available demographics of Johnson's life, but his screenplay plays fast and loose with them. Concerning Johnson's first wife, Virginia, for example, we see significant changes to the known events. This is most apparent in the scene dramatizing Virginia's death. Historically, Robert was on the road playing music when Virginia died in childbirth back home. In Greenberg's version, the two are in a car with Johnson's sister, here called Hercules, and brother-in-law, Granville Hines, when the car stalls, Virginia goes into labor, and the family tries to get her to the hospital. Panicked, Robert calls out, "GRANVILLE! VIRGINIA'S STARTIN' TO PERCOLATE! . . . HEAR ME, GRANVILLE? 'GINIA'S PERCOLATIN'! FAST NOW, GRANVILLE, FAST!" (85). As they attempt to restart the car, they are passed by a vehicle full of white passengers who laughingly shout "Nigger!" as they pass the desperate group. Once at the hospital, Robert is informed "coldly" by white hospital personnel, "It was a boy, Johnson" (87), and Virginia's corpse is relegated to a mop closet.

Greenberg modifies the facts as they were then known in two important ways. First, he transports an incident that actually happened to a different context. According to Stephen C. LaVere, on one occasion during Virginia's pregnancy she and Robert were riding in the country with the Hineses. Proud and protective, Robert playfully asked Granville to slow down on the bumpy road because his wife was "percolatin,'" or pregnant (9). In Greenberg's screenplay, "percolatin'" means that Virginia's labor has begun, and Johnson is fearful for her safety (85). Why the transposition? Throughout his handling of Virginia's death, Greenberg repositions facts and legends to express the emotional truths of the characters. Here, the alteration of a playful remark to a desperate one suggests Johnson's love for Virginia, his fears, the powerful effect of her loss, and his feeling of helplessness in the face of racism and tragic fate. It captures how the world must often have felt to Robert Johnson.

The second and more compelling modification is Greenberg's introduction of a hospital as the setting for Virginia's death. While the actual place of Virginia's death remains unknown, given Honeyboy Edwards's comment in Hunt's *The Search for Robert Johnson* that African Americans of the era didn't have money for doctors, one might reasonably assume that she died at home. In Greenberg's version, the hospital setting is partly an homage to the famed blues singer Bessie Smith, who was rumored to have died in a 1937 automobile accident outside Clarksdale, Mississippi, when a white hospital refused her admittance.[4] The story is apocryphal, but the myth persists. Greenberg explains that he fictionalized the circumstances of Virginia's death because he lacked factual information and used the Bessie Smith story "to create a plausible situation of my own making based on Delta realities" ("Re: Robert"). His inclusion of discrimination in the health-care industry developed from something he encountered during his research into Robert Johnson: "As late as 1978 I found old Delta hospitals still bearing their out-dated signs for separate 'White' and 'Colored' entrances and facilities, which gave me food for thought" ("Re: Robert").

By including this invented hospital scene, Greenberg is able to reflect the harsh realities of segregation and echo the truths, embedded in Bessie Smith's legend and relevant to Robert Johnson's life, that roadside assistance, health care, compassion, and basic respect were things black Americans in 1930s Mississippi could not expect from white ones. His "quasi-alchemical" blending of "fact, myth, and personal vision" creates a scene that *could have happened,* that expresses the systemic racism of the era, and that enables audiences to feel the shattering emotional reality of these recurring losses, fears, indignities, and frustrations.

Not surprisingly, the Robert Johnson that Greenberg places into this world of strange juxtapositions is himself a man of contradictions. An inhabitant of a world that is partly controlled by white authorities, partly sustained by local legend and myth, partly fated, and partly free, Greenberg's Johnson is a chameleon. As critic Luc Sante admiringly notes, Greenberg captures the elusive Robert Johnson by "not attempting to explain anything. His Johnson is a changeling, flesh-and-blood but mutable and secretive, and he dwells in a world of workaday magic" (50). We see an example of this mutability in his relationship with Callie Craft, his second wife, whom he seems to love but whom he nonetheless deserts, and whom he marries, but on condition that the marriage be kept secret. Most of all, we catch glimpses of his "changeling" qualities in the way Greenberg depicts his becoming a musician.

Greenberg the researcher knows that Robert Johnson must have spent countless hours honing his craft and developing his technique. He portrays Johnson as a devoted student of music, closely observing other performers at work, listening avidly to records, keeping a notebook of songs, and practicing on his guitar. As a product of a culturally diverse world, however, Johnson would have respected various otherworldly powers—Sante's "workaday magic"—as well as skill and discipline, so Greenberg also shows him visiting a conjurer, seeking help with his "guitarmanship" (43). Given this multilayered world and the stories about Johnson's sudden improvement, Johnson's alleged deal with the devil is inevitably a pivotal moment in the plot. But in his "quasi-alchemical" fashion, Greenberg nods to the famous crossroads myth, shifts the devil-pact scene to a new context, and creates several alternative ways of interpreting it.

In *Love in Vain,* Robert Johnson meets the devil at a Clark Gable movie. A "mangy guy" from a nearby bar follows him into the second row of the movie theater, where he shares his whiskey with Robert and where Robert, under the movie image of "a blinding sunrise," recognizes him as "a devilman" (46). The devilman instructs Robert to meet him at the crossroads at midnight with his guitar, but Robert, "swooning from drink and sleeplessness . . . nods out" as the Clark Gable movie morphs into a black-and-white film about an Old West saloon. The scenes that follow are phantasmagoric, as Blind Lemon Jefferson apparently becomes part of the Clark Gable movie, black-and-white film images alternate with colored ones, and we can no longer tell which images are from the film and which are Robert's restless dreams. We see Robert leave the theater and go to the appointed crossroads, where the devilman tunes his guitar and Robert furiously plays, after tossing the mangy devilman a coin because the latter claims to be "so broke, can't even buy my dick a doughnut" (49).

This scene and those that immediately follow sum up what Greenberg does best: he doesn't just retell the mythic stories, he uses them in new ways, incorporates them into different contexts, and enlarges them to mean new things. In this case, Greenberg has started with the historical fact, reported by Johnny Shines, that Johnson loved the movies, especially Clark Gable films and Westerns (*Love in Vain* 214). To this account he adds the myth of a pact with the devil and mixes modern technology (film) with folklore (the conjurer and the devilman) in a way that probably would have made sense to Johnson and his contemporaries, inhabitants of this world of frequent, jarring contrasts. Then he adds Johnson's sleepiness, a condition made probable by his wandering lifestyle and heavy drinking. Did Johnson meet the devil in the theater and follow him to the crossroads? Did Johnson dream the whole thing? Was the devil himself just a part of that dream, since Johnson largely ignores him while wailing on his guitar? Was the devilman simply a con artist, tricking Johnson into the midnight meeting so he could steal or beg for coins? The five scenes immediately following the crossroads meeting suggest that one can interpret it in all of these ways. Instead of showing Johnson, newly contracted to the devil, heading straight to Robinsonville to show off his newfound guitar skills, Greenberg includes a long sequence of scenes depicting Johnson traveling and developing his artistry. We see him in a juke house full of strangers, where he stares unflinchingly at the guitarists' hands. We see him studying a slide guitarist's technique in a roadside shanty, writing in his book, practicing on his guitar, sleeping on levees and in trucks, wandering the countryside, and getting dirtier and more disreputable looking as time passes. Weeks and months evidently go by before Johnson's triumphant return to Robinsonville. As a result of this time lag, his miraculously improved technique—a historical fact reported by various observers—may have been the result of the conjurer, the devil, a dream, studying diverse models, or hard work, long hours, and experience. *Love in Vain* does not present the actual construction of myth as *Trick the Devil* does, but it offers multiple alternative ways to see potential reality behind the myths.

This shift in perception may be the most valuable thing that history can offer. Recall that Greenberg's subtitle identifies the play as a *vision* of Robert Johnson. Film historian Robert Rosenstone sees all filmed history as visionary: "History on film . . . is history (literally and metaphorically) as vision. As vision (of a culture, an era, a civilization) that precedes any notion of 'fact.' As vision that calls 'facts' into being by providing a framework in which they make sense" (194). For Rosenstone, this visionary framework is important to understanding history; it offers new ways of seeing the world, past and present. Of such innovative historical films, which presumably Greenberg's screenplay will become,[5] Rosenstone says: "History as experiment does not make the same claim on us as does the realist film. Rather than opening a window directly onto the past, it opens a window onto a different way of thinking about the past. The aim is not to tell everything, but to point to past events, or to converse about history, or to show what history should be meaningful to people in the present. Experimental films . . . tend to make bits and pieces of our historical experience accessible, sometimes in all its confusion" (63–64). Greenberg's screenplay manifests the confusion of a world caught between scientific fact and mythic belief, between modern conveniences and folk legend, between the exploitation of sharecropping and the promise of recording contracts—a world where mules laugh and the devil goes to the movies. In blending all these seemingly disparate elements, Greenberg highlights the elements of Robert Johnson's history that should be meaningful to people in the present: the history of oppressions that Johnson strove to avoid, his solitary spirit, his persistence in the face of every obstacle, and the music-permeated culture that helped him shape his own astonishing songs. Alan Greenberg does not reinsert Robert Johnson into his historical context to strip away the accumulated myth, because for Greenberg, the myth is always already a part of that historical context. Greenberg "gives flesh to myth instead" (Christgau). Greenberg's technique of mingling realism, mythology, and imagination to re-create a world in which all three operate is akin to the positive side of double-consciousness: it allows us to see things from multiple perspectives and thus to recognize the potential validity of apparent opposites in our "contrapuntal civilization."

New Relationships with the Past

The thrust of this chapter has been to examine the various ways contemporary artists have restored Robert Johnson to some variant of his historical context and how that re-creation of history intersects with the construction of myth. Collectively, the five texts I have explored suggest that once a figure has become thoroughly mythologized—as Robert Johnson surely has—it may be impossible to uncover the historical person that first gave rise to the myths. The recirculation and reuses of his image through time inevitably accumulate meanings that adhere, and the man who was the original signifier is lost under a history of signs. But while the stripping away of all mythology may be impossible after a certain point, these texts reveal something significant about the intersection—the crossroads—of history and myth. Bill Harris's *Trick the Devil* enacts the formation of myth and so reveals it as a human construct that can never be ideologically neutral. Alan Greenberg's *Love in Vain* shows the ways that myth permeates culture, suggesting that myth itself is already embedded in history. This is not to suggest that these two texts are necessarily "superior" in an artistic sense to the others discussed here; each has merit in its own right and tells us something significant about Robert Johnson and American culture. But in terms of my analysis of the ways history can or cannot upend myth, Harris's and Greenberg's texts offer us the clearest ways to vanquish myth and restore some agency to the historical figure that was Robert Johnson. They illustrate two different methods of creating "artificial myths" that reveal the workings of the mythmaking process.

Robert Rosenstone has commented at length on what innovative films about historical events can tell us, and his comments are appropriate for other sorts of texts as well. For Rosenstone, depicting history in imaginative ways can "offer a new relationship with the world of the past" and can "even reinvent History." He defines a "postmodern history film" (or text) as a work that, "refusing the pretense that the screen can be an unmediated window onto the past, foregrounds itself as a construction. . . . Such works do not, like the dramatic feature or the documentary, attempt to recreate the past realistically. Instead they point to it and play with it, raising questions about the very evidence on which our knowledge of the past depends, creatively interacting with its traces" (12). All the historically based texts explored in this chapter exemplify this process to some degree. None of them attempts to "recreate the past realistically." All of them play with historical ideas, raise questions about those ideas, and "offer us a new relationship with the past." In this case, that new relationship includes seeing Robert Johnson within an imagined historical context and looking at the ways that myth and history intertwine around him. Rosenstone goes on to note that "[t]he best of these films [or texts] present the possibility of more than one interpretation of events—they render the world as multiple, complex, and indeterminate, rather than as a series of self-enclosed, neat, linear stories" (37). His comment succinctly sums up the nexus of things revealed by the texts examined in this chapter, from the bifurcations of American culture to the multiple perspective of double-consciousness to the reality of myth. For the artists discussed herein, as for Rosenstone, history is most valuable when it helps us reinvent our relationships to culture, past and present.

3

The Paradox of Authenticity

In the last chapter, I discussed how re-visionings of Robert Johnson in his original historical context can reveal the constructedness of myth. Many other contemporary writers import Johnson to the contemporary world, using him to comment more directly on turn-of-the-century culture. In this chapter and the next, I discuss one film and four novels that depict Robert Johnson in imagined circumstances. The texts have one main thing in common: in each Johnson is used as a focusing device, a minor player in someone else's story rather than the hero of his own tragic tale. Chapter 3 looks at texts in which Johnson functions as a background figure who sparks a contemporary character's personal quest. Chapter 4 discusses novels that invoke Robert Johnson's life, legend, and music to restore harmony to a broken civilization. In all these cases artists consciously use Robert Johnson to illustrate something about our own time and to predict a positive future, either individual (chapter 3) or communal (chapter 4).

At first glance, this process of transporting Robert Johnson to a new time and place seems like an interesting ploy, one that opens a world of possibilities. But as Ralph Ellison warns, any historical character brings an accumulation of meanings with it into a text (74). Theorist Jacques Derrida has also pointed out some difficulties in quickening the dead for artistic purposes. For Derrida, one always faces the possibility that the dead will not stay put as it (Derrida's pronoun) has been represented. It will appear as a repetition of itself and as a specter for the first time; it is both "repetition *and* first time" and so logically impossible to contain or represent. Derrida uses the term "hauntology" to refer to this condition in which "the specter is always a *revenant.* One cannot control its comings and goings because it *begins by coming back*" (10–11).

This "hauntology" is evident in the re-creations of Robert Johnson that I discuss in this and the following chapter. Johnson reappears as the uncanny, as something familiar and yet strange, always and ever slipping the bonds of history and art with which scholars and artists try to contain him. It seems fitting, somehow, that a musician noted for being haunted himself should so haunt us today. But if, as Derrida suggests, an artist who revivifies a dead character cannot control its meanings, what exactly is reanimated along with Johnson's life and legend? In semiotic terms, once you take Robert Johnson out of his original context, he becomes a floating signifier, detached from history, a specter revived for a variety of artistic and ideological purposes but never wholly in the control of his reanimator. He is like Frankenstein's monster, operating with a will beyond that of his creator.

Many of the associations that have accrued to Johnson's image were produced by its circulation in the mass media—printed texts, films, and Web sites. S. Paige Baty has created a useful term for discussing this recirculation of a historical figure in our late-capitalist, media-driven culture: "cultural re-membering." For Baty, a cultural icon (in her study, Marilyn Monroe) is remembered both as he or she was and as he or she has been recirculated in the media. The originating era of the icon is thus recalled through multiple layers of associations that have attached themselves to the icon through time and that may have nothing to do with historical reality. The idea of "re-membering" also suggests (although Baty is not explicit about this) a cultural reanimation of the dead, as if attaching new parts to a physical body. In this way, her reading of cultural re-membering echoes Derrida's notion of hauntology. Baty's work extends Derrida's, however, by emphasizing the influence of the mass media in creating cultural associations for historical icons. These mediating influences have been felt demonstrably in the Robert Johnson industry, where a platinum-selling CD set, worshipful rock stars, and popular films have helped construct current awareness of Johnson and shaped our contemporary understanding of his era and the blues in general.

The media has also had a strong impact on the ways contemporary artists recirculate Robert Johnson in literature and film. As a revenant, Robert Johnson's presence in these texts signifies a host of shifting cultural associations. It would no doubt have surprised the historical Robert Johnson to know that almost a hundred years after his birth, he is regarded as a touchstone of authenticity for individual musicians or an emblem of multicultural cooperation for America at large. As we shall see, these two contemporary ideals—authenticity and multiculturalism—have attached themselves to Johnson's image, reflecting turn-of-the-millennium concerns and allowing us, perhaps, to develop a discourse about what our individual amd communal future might look like.

Africanist Presence and Authenticity in *Crossroads*

In a brilliant series of lectures published as *Playing in the Dark,* novelist Toni Morrison describes her long-term interest in the necessary "Africanist presence" (6) in American literature, or "the way black people ignite critical moments of discovery or change or emphasis in literature not written by them" (viii). In the 1986 film *Crossroads,* written by John Fusco and directed by Walter Hill, and the 1998 novel *Crossroad Blues* by Ace Atkins, white artists use Robert Johnson in exactly the way Morrison describes. In both of these similarly titled texts, Johnson makes a cameo appearance in the prologue, either recording his songs (in the film) or making his last appearance at the fateful Greenwood juke joint (in the novel). In both, a young white man, inspired by Johnson's music, makes a pilgrimage to the Mississippi Delta in search of undiscovered Johnson songs. In both, an older African American man serves as a guide to the blues life for the young white protagonist, who in both cases is a musician striving to be a bluesman. In both, Robert Johnson's music is the holy grail that will lead the protagonist to enhanced self-expression, career fulfillment, and musical success. And in both, the blues is portrayed as a touchstone of musical authenticity in this overly commercialized, mean ol' world in which Robert Johnson (or his revenant surrogate) provokes "critical moments of discovery or change."

Crossroads is the story of teenaged Eugene Martone, a Julliard-trained classical guitar prodigy who is obsessed with the blues. Eugene's Julliard instructor discourages him from playing the blues, claiming, "Excellence in primitive music is cultural. You have to be born to it." However, once Eugene discovers Willie Brown, Robert Johnson's onetime musical partner, living in a New York nursing home, the influence of the music teacher pales and that of the African American spiritual guide takes over. Willie and Eugene strike a bargain: Eugene agrees to help Willie escape from the nursing home and return to the Delta, and in exchange Willie promises to teach Robert Johnson's apocryphal thirtieth song to Eugene. Willie then takes Eugene on the hobo's road and teaches him a series of the blues life's lessons.

As the pair travel south the film employs many conventional formulas, including elements of a grail quest, a buddy movie, a road movie, and a coming-of-age story, ending with a showdown—a headcutting contest between Eugene and the devil's prize guitarist. The twist is that Eugene identifies himself from the start as "a bluesman," much to the amusement of the well-traveled Willie Brown. Recognizing both the boy's impressive guitar technique and his lack of experience, Willie admits that Eugene has "lightning" in his hands but that "he's missing everything else. . . . No mileage." He see Eugene as "just one more white boy rippin' off our music." A central thematic issue of the film is thus introduced: who has the right to call himself "a bluesman"?

The historical Willie Brown, whose name Johnson invokes in "Cross Road Blues," was a guitarist, but *Crossroads* turns him into a harmonica player. This is only one of many liberties the film takes with blues history. A bigger problem is the film's muddled vision of the wellsprings of blues music. Many commentators see the blues as an incontrovertible product of its time. Created by men and women who lived under the constant physical and mental stresses of grinding poverty, hard labor, and ever-present racism, the blues worldview involved facing one's problems head-on, of naming them—as in the Dogon concept of "Nommo"—as a way to control their impact and survive them. Other commentators disagree and define the blues primarily by its emotional content. These critics see the music as an evolving entity with applications to today's world, regardless of its origins. Acknowledging that specific cultural conditions produced the blues, music scholar Steven G. Smith nonetheless claims that the blues mean different things to differently situated people and appeal widely because we all have felt pain at times: "A teenaged middle-class white boy's pain in being unable, for the moment, to get together with his girlfriend is a far cry from the pain Robert Johnson means when he sings, 'The sun going down, boy, dark gonna catch me here' ("Crossroad Blues"). Yet both experiences are poignantly symbolized in blues, for pain is pain, whatever its causes and implications. By absolutizing the predicament of felt oppression, blues has cut loose from its original historical situation and become amazingly democratic" (51).

Crossroads presents a vision of the blues similar to what Smith describes as its modern incarnation—a teenaged boy's cry of pain—and posits the blues as a way to express emotion and overcome despair. However, the film also suggests that Eugene must have some contact with the place and sociocultural conditions that first produced the blues in order to be an official "bluesman." Logical inconsistencies thus abound, as Eugene's adolescent attempts to live the life of an early twentieth-century bluesman fall ludicrously short of what those blues musicians endured. In place of the lifelong hardships of Depression-era Mississippi that shaped Robert Johnson and the historical Willie Brown, Eugene learns all he needs to know on a short journey over the course of a few days. Once he and Willie disembark from the air-conditioned bus that carries them comfortably from New York to Memphis, they face the difficulties of bad weather, knife threats, gun threats, and police harassment on their way to Willie's home town of Fulton's Point, Mississippi. Eugene suffers lost love in the form of a two-night stand with a runaway teen named Frances and faces the indignities of racism, albeit vicariously, since Willie is the target. He briefly experiences the rambling life of a hitchhiker, sleeps in abandoned buildings, plays his first "barrelhouse" as Willie's accompanist, and learns from Willie that the blues must come from experience and from within. Despite Willie's initial reaction to the "white boy," the movie suggests that earning the title of "bluesman" can be facilitated by a few days' change of scenery.

Throughout the journey, Willie serves as an ancestor figure, a guide who makes sure that Eugene understands the import of his experiences. When confronted by a racist bar owner who insults Willie and drives the pair off his premises, Eugene notes in astonishment that he "didn't know that kind of stuff still went on." (Evidently his Julliard instructor's comment about "primitive" music failed to register.) Willie tells him, "Now you're starting to learn some deep blues." When Frances leaves and Eugene confesses miserably to Willie that he's "really going to miss her," Willie reminds him, "The blues ain't nothing but a good man feeling bad, thinking about the woman he once was with," and nods approvingly as Eugene absorbs this message and begins improvising on his guitar. And when Willie finally confesses that there is no thirtieth Robert Johnson song, he counsels Eugene that the song wouldn't help him anyway. "You got to do it for yourself," he tells Eugene. "That's what Robert would have told you." By the end of the trip Eugene has evidently completed his crash course in becoming a bluesman, thanks to the efforts of Willie Brown. One is reminded of Spike Lee's complaint that American films are replete with "mystical, magical Negroes," black characters who happily use their extraordinary powers for the betterment of white characters. About *The Legend of Bagger Vance,* for example, Lee says, "They were hanging 'em high in Georgia then. If Bagger Vance really did have magical powers . . . do you really think his number-one concern would be helping Matt Damon with his golf swing?" (Gentry). While Willie does at one point offer Eugene "the last mojo hand in the world" to supplement his guitar-playing prowess, he probably falls a bit short of "magical Negro" status. Nonetheless, he certainly functions as Morrison's "Africanist presence" who "ignites critical moments of discovery" for Eugene.

In *Crossroads,* however, Eugene is able to repay Willie for the lessons and the insights. Near the end of the film, Willie's real reason for returning to

Mississippi is revealed. It seems that as a youth, Willie had followed Robert Johnson's lead in selling his soul to the devil—here depicted amusingly as an African American trickster figure in Wild West gambler's garb—for musical success. Feeling cheated by his lack of fame, Willie goes back to the crossroads to renege on the deal. The devil offers a new deal: pit Eugene in a headcutting contest against the devil's house guitarist, Jack Butler (played with hilarious, over-the-top energy by rock guitarist Steve Vai). If Eugene wins, Willie gets back his soul; if Eugene loses, the devil gets Eugene's soul as well as Willie's. In the ensuing guitar duel, with Eugene playing blues against his opponent's heavy metal, Eugene eventually beats Butler with, inexplicably, a classical guitar riff. The movie thus ends happily as Willie is freed from confinement and damnation, and Eugene has earned fast-track credentials as a bluesman. One might think of this as a story of immigration, with Eugene quickly gaining a green card (a blue card?) by marrying a citizen.

And what does Robert Johnson signify in this movie, the cinematic equivalent of a recent CD dubbed "RJ-lite" by one reviewer (Red Rooster 9)? His physical presence is relegated to the four opening minutes of the film, and all we see of him is a few shots in a recording studio and at a crossroads. His influence on the action, however, is powerful and operates on several levels. On one level, Johnson functions as a grail, as the ultimate musical genius whom Eugene emulates and whose untapped legacy he hopes to find. The structure of the film supports this view, taking the form of a personal odyssey, a journey toward self-fulfillment through creative self-expression, with Willie Brown standing in for Johnson as a guardian elder on a young man's quest for self-knowledge. The writer, John Fusco, admits that such a story inspired the screenplay. As a college student at New York University, Fusco learned of an old African American harmonica player living in a nearby nursing home. Hoping that the man had personal experience of the blues, Fusco went to see him, only to find him confused with age and unskilled on the blues harp. Nonetheless, he recalled his thoughts as he drove out to the nursing home for the first time: "What if he [the harmonica player] knew the legendary lost song of Robert Johnson's and, having fostered an unlikely father/son relationship with me, he passed it on. Taught it to me. Took me on the road, down to the Delta, down to . . . the Crossroads" (Fusco, "*Crossroads*"). The screenplay that emerged from this adolescent fantasy became *Crossroads,* which was Fusco's undergraduate thesis at NYU before becoming the Walter Hill film.

This reading of the film as a quest for personal growth is also emphasized by the casting of Ralph Macchio as Eugene. Known prior to *Cross-*

roads primarily as the Karate Kid, another young man who "finds himself" through the mediation of an elderly guide from a culture different than his own, the film can be seen as "a musical-drama-fantasy-coming-of-age-story with Macchio again playing Daniel-san and Joe Seneca [who plays Willie Brown] playing the role of a grizzled, black Mr. Miyogi" (Tharp). The coming-of-age formula obviously recapitulates that of *The Karate Kid,* and both films partake of the romantic impulse that inflects so many tributes to Robert Johnson. Interestingly, in her remarks about Africanist presences in American literature, Morrison explicitly links such figures to romanticism and notes that a black character often serves as the "surrogate and enabler" for a white one in romantic texts (*Playing* 51). Willie Brown (who represents Johnson) and Robert Johnson himself function in this way for Eugene.

But the quest motif that drives *Crossroads* has other, less idealistic components. Not only does Eugene want to have a bluesman's experiences, he wants to capitalize on his friendship with Willie and his knowledge of Johnson's music. He wants to gain fame and fortune with Johnson's lost song and thus power in our late-capitalist, media-driven culture. When he first tries to convince Willie to teach him the song, Eugene argues, "I could record it, you know, like Clapton did with 'Crossroads.' The Rolling Stones did it with 'Love in Vain.' I mean, it could be my whole introduction to the blues scene." Recognizing the boy's commercial motive as well as his arrogance, Willie accuses Eugene of "ripping off" African American music, and at this point Eugene responds that he wants Johnson's thirtieth song out of altruism: "We could record it together. We'd be giving it to the world." Later, however, when he explains his interest in the song to Frances (something of a hustler herself), she recognizes his baser motives right away. When she asks if Eugene thinks the lost song will make him famous, he replies, "Right. . . . It's my ticket to the blues scene." The resurrection of Robert Johnson in this film is thus linked to the related specters of cultural appropriation and the commercialization of the blues. Blues for profit as opposed to blues as personal expression compete thematically in *Crossroads,* and collision is avoided only by a plot device: the thirtieth song does not exist, so Eugene has no chance to cash in.

Despite Eugene's commercial intentions and despite the movie's puzzling abandonment of blues music in the climactic guitar contest, the thrust of the movie—and Johnson's presence in it—suggests one other important theme. By the end of the film, Eugene has completed his initiation into "the blues scene": he has gone to the crossroads and, with Willie's help and the inspiration of Robert Johnson, beaten the devil at his own game. The blues itself, represented by traditional bluesmen like Brown and Johnson, thus becomes a touchstone of authenticity, signifying supernatural powers and a depth of emotional experience presumably unavailable to most residents of the industrialized world. This point is clearest, perhaps, in the contrast between Willie's loving (if occasionally cantankerous) concern for Eugene's artistic development and the advice offered by his effete Julliard teacher, for whom technical virtuosity is of supreme importance. The teacher complains that "primitive music" is a distraction from his classical studies. He cautions Eugene, "The discipline of the classical is very exacting, and if you persist in the other [the blues], you'll squander your talent." Willie, in contrast, stresses the importance of "mileage"; rather than emphasizing technical skill (which Eugene, fortunately, already has), Willie promotes experience, feelings, innovation, and improvisation as the bases for musical genius. The blues, symbolized by the haunting shadow of Robert Johnson, is thus presented as the utterance of individual experience, honestly and creatively expressed. It and he represent the development of an inner self through contact with primal feelings and personal experiences rather than through technology or technique, a genuineness—an authenticity—available primarily through the practice of an African American cultural form.

The philosophical concept of authenticity is a vestige of romantic thought, so it is not surprising that it has become attached to Robert Johnson, a romantic icon of the 1960s and beyond. For early romantic thinkers like Jean Jacques Rousseau, who were critical of "disengaged rationality" and the eighteenth century's new emphasis on scientific thought and methods, the notion of authenticity included the beliefs that human beings have an innate moral sense and should thus be ruled by their intuition and that they each possess an individuality deserving of expression (Taylor 25–26). Within this framework that exalted the emotional over the rational, artistic creation became a paradigm for human self-definition (62).

In America in the 1960s, the concept of authenticity was resurrected, not only as an element of the era's romantic idealism but also as a counterpoint to the sense of alienation that impelled the decade's many political movements. "Alienation" could mean the lack of access to material goods and social justice that many African Americans confronted or simply the feeling of being disaffected from dominant social norms that many middle-class white liberals experienced (Rossinow 4–5). In either case, the opposite of alienation was wholeness, or authenticity, which became associated with "alternative" cultural practices like blues and jazz. During this era when alienation and marginality implied radical political agency, the cultural products of marginalized groups like African Americans automatically indicated authenticity to the young people of the liberal left (15). Robert Johnson thus became the universal signifier for the genuine, the uncorrupted. Noting that Bob Dylan included a verse from Johnson's "Stones in My Passway" in his 1963 recording of the venerable country blues "Corrine Corrina," Christopher A. Waterman remarks, "If a folk singer wanted to signal his knowledge of and sympathy for the blues—the baseline of black authenticity—there was simply no one better to cite that Robert Johnson" (189). This belief in the authenticity of alternative cultures has persisted since the 1960s, with African American music often seen to offer "a powerful critique of mainstream middle-class Anglo-America as well as an elaborate vocabulary for airing feelings of marginality and contestation" (Lipsitz, *Dangerous* 54–55).

There are several problematic assumptions underlying this equation of Robert Johnson (or the blues more generally) with authenticity. Most obvious is the assumption that blues music is the direct expression of emotion rather than the product of talent and craft. We are not too far here from the early twentieth-century glorification of "the primitive," which posited African American art forms as the natural outpouring of a simple people, their works charming and heartfelt but devoid of complexity, history, and artistry. One-time *Living Blues* editor Paul Garon defends this position this way: "Our elucidation of the blues as 'primitive' is neither gratuitous nor demeaning; for we see in the blues a suggestion of humanity's original vitality and pride. Our conception of primitive merges with our conception of non-alienation. What we seek in the blues is a glimmer of freedom; and it is there, in every song" (*Blues* 83). Others counter that African American music has too often been seen as "a primordial cure for the ills of a civilized and increasingly mechanized modern society" (Radano 460).

A second problem emerges in the supposition that the blues were part of an unchanging culture, focused on preservation and repetition and untainted by contact with the dominant society. Anthropologist James Clifford calls this approach to the study of past cultures "the pastoral/salvage" paradigm, in which western researchers attempt to preserve dying nonwestern cultures, believing that western societies are "dynamic and oriented toward change, whereas nonwestern societies seek equilibrium and the reproduction of inherited forms" (125). Authenticity is thus centered on a salvageable, static past in which the actual Robert Johnson has no place. On the contrary, as we saw in chapter 1, Johnson was an innovative interpreter of the blues forms he inherited, and during the last months of his life he apparently played an electric guitar as part of a three-man combo, with "The Robert Johnson Band" painted on the bass drum.[1] In addition, he was undoubtedly influenced by recording industry practices of his time, tailoring his songs to fit standard recorded length. Despite these romanticized re-memberings, then, the music scene that Robert Johnson knew was powerfully dynamic, and he played a leading role in its evolution.

Crossroads mostly manages to avoid the first of these pitfalls by acknowledging the skill involved in playing the blues. Thanks to his recognized talent (he has been called "a prodigy") and his Julliard training, Eugene already has "lightning" in his hands when he sets out on his blues expedition. In his showdown with Jack Butler, he wins both because of his short course in blues living and because of his mastery of the instrument. The film does, however, perpetuate the myth that Delta culture offers a wellspring of untainted culture: the devil still haunts the crossroads, and blues music is still an activity associated wholly with African American musicians and audiences, whose positive energy contrasts sharply with that seen in the white saloon that the film depicts. Most importantly, *Crossroads* expressly suggests that authenticity runs counter to commercialization, that true art must be motiveless. Eugene cannot face down the devil until he knows that there is no thirtieth song for him to cash in on; he does not go to the crossroads before learning that he has no prepaid "ticket to the blues scene." George Lipsitz notes that in the climactic headcutting contest, "heavy metal represents the contaminated culture of the music industry, while the blues appears as a precommercial form with magical powers owing to its purportedly pure and uncontaminated history" (*Possessive* 120). Thus, like many readings of blues history in general and Robert Johnson's life in particular, the film ignores the business concerns of early blues practitioners. Much of their time was spent in securing gigs and seeking recording contracts; their rambling lifestyle derived less from being footloose and fancy free than from the necessities of obtaining work as musicians wherever they could get it. Seen in this light, "The blues music that emerges in the film *Crossroads* . . . has less to do with the blues itself than with the traditions of romanticism in Western culture" (121).

Could Eugene have become "a bluesman" without the mediating presence of Willie Brown and the inspiration of Robert Johnson? And to cast this question in a larger context, can American cultural authenticity exist without an Africanist catalyst like Robert Johnson? While there is no simple answer to this question, within the world of Fusco and Hill's *Cross-*

roads, the haunting presence of Robert Johnson is required. In recirculating the legend of Robert Johnson, as he lived and in his revenant form as Willie Brown, Fusco and Hill had a prepackaged, inherently dramatic story at their disposal, an iconic tale with legendary proportions. By grafting it onto the coming-of-age story of Eugene Martone, however, they invited new meanings to accrue. When the young bluesman who seeks the crossroads is white, northern, educated, and privileged, the specter of Robert Johnson can no longer be contained. Intended or not, *Crossroads* suggests that social class doesn't matter and that authentic blues artistry is available to anyone willing to pay a few days' dues (whether that involves selling one's soul or not). *Crossroads* thus displays what I see as an underlying paradox in the contemporary search for authenticity in blues music. On the one hand, authentic music is seen to have arisen from honest emotional responses to specific, pretechnological historical and material conditions; on the other hand, residents of the technological age (like Eugene) think they can reproduce the music, despite their not having experienced the originating conditions and despite the irony of having knowledge of them primarily through media technology. Those who seek to replicate this musical authenticity are thus doomed from the start by their mass-mediated understanding of what it is and whence it springs.

Commodification versus Bohemian Authenticity in *Crossroad Blues*

Crossroad Blues begins where *Crossroads* leaves off; it features a version of Eugene Martone after he has completed his initiation experiences. The protagonist of the novel is Nick Travers, a sometime blues historian (he's sporadically writing a biography of Guitar Slim), occasional blues professor (he holds an adjunct position in the Tulane music department), and weekend blues harmonica player. Before we meet Nick, however, a five-page prologue recounts the last night of Robert Johnson's life. In Atkins's version, Johnson does take a free drink from a suspicious juke joint owner, but his real killer is a fat, white record producer who tracks him down outside the juke. Speaking to Johnson from inside his black Buick, eerily identifiable by his bulk, by the glowing tip of his cigarette, and by the sulfurous smoke that emanates from the car, the record producer accuses Johnson of stealing nine unreleased tracks of his own recorded music. The producer's words link him explicitly with the devil figure of Johnson mythology: "'Thought you'd left me behind huh, Bob? Thought you could leave our deal? But you and me keep together. . . . When you sign a contract with me, I own your soul. . . . I own your ass. . . . I captured that sound you made and I own it'" (4). He proffers a glass of whiskey, ordering Johnson to drink and "'[f]inish the deal, Bob. . . . Finish the deal'" (5), which Johnson, feeling world-weary and hell-hounded, does.

On page six, the scene changes to a blues bar, the time and place defined as "last night, New Orleans, Louisiana." After this shift occurs and Nick is introduced, the plot of the novel is similar to that of *Crossroads.* One of Nick's Tulane colleagues, a music professor with little knowledge of the blues, has gone to Mississippi in search of the missing nine recordings from the prologue, and disappeared. The chair of the music department sends Nick, who has conducted interviews in the Delta and knows the territory and the people, to find him. Once again we have a young white man's quest to the Mississippi Delta in search of missing Johnson music, this time complicated by Nick's parallel search for his colleague, Michael Baker. Even from these opening chapters, however, we can already see evidence of a cultural dynamic similar to the one informing *Crossroads.* Nick, the "authentic" blues man, hates the missing Baker, who offered "pompous lectures or erroneous facts based on his political ideology. Guys like Baker took the stick and muddied the waters of a diminishing river of information" (19). Nick speculates that a trip to the Delta must be difficult for someone like Baker, who would be "afraid his Gucci loafers would get a speck of cowshit on them" (19). Nick, in contrast, plays blues harmonica regularly at local blues clubs, dresses casually in jeans and chambray shirts, has done both fieldwork and academic research on blues figures, and despises pretension of any kind. In Nick's differences from his erstwhile colleague, we see the beginning of this text's configuration and approval of "authentic" blues culture.

Since Nick is a more mature—or at least older—character than Eugene Martone, his understanding of and relationship to Robert Johnson is more complicated than Eugene's simple desire to cash in on the music. Nick does romanticize Johnson, however. He considers him "the holy grail of blues" (31) and claims that "Johnson didn't play blues. He was blues" (32). Uneasy about searching for the truth about Johnson's death, Nick notes, "To most researchers, Johnson's life was a beautiful woman better men [than Nick] had tried to court unsuccessfully" (116). But Nick's interest in Johnson extends beyond research projects. He strongly identifies with Johnson himself, claiming, "The crossroads are wherever you want them to be" (48). Indeed, the novel offers many parallels that promote Nick as a contemporary version of Johnson. We meet Nick just after his former girlfriend decides to marry another man. His heartsickness, like that attributed to

Johnson in the prologue, "sits in his stomach like a jagged stone" (40). A former NFL football player, Nick lost his job by dumping a Gatorade bucket over the head of his "racist" black coach (43), who refused him playing time in favor of a high-priced yet less competent rookie. This action renders Nick the champion of the underdog, his action cheered on by "a bunch of dockworkers who liked what he'd done to the bossman" (44). He is thus, like Johnson, the victim of racial injustice, restricted opportunity, and class bias. Nick also spends one night in jail and finds the experience to be "about humiliation, loss of freedom," ordeals Johnson repeatedly encountered. Finally, throughout the novel, lyrics from Robert Johnson songs are used to comment on current predicaments in Nick's life. In one instance, when a friend refuses to tell him the truth, the chapter closes with the verse from "Stones in My Passway" that begins, "My enemies have betrayed me" (159). In another, after Nick has suffered an early morning beating by some hired thugs, these lines from "Me and the Devil Blues" punctuate the action:

> Early this mornin'
> when you knocked upon my door.
> And I said, "Hello, Satan,
> I believe it's time to go." (150)

A man with "[n]o immediate goals" (11), Nick represents working-class values, real blues music, self-made men, and heartbreak survivors everywhere. Like Johnson and unlike the missing Baker, he is presented as an "authentic" bluesman.

This image of Nick Travers—whose surname, we are told, means "dweller at a crossroad" (ix)—reflects Nick's view of himself as well as the view Atkins encourages us to take of him. But just as Eugene Martone's attempt to be an authentic bluesman conflicts with his privileged upbringing, so is Nick's self-image undermined in part by his background and even by some of his thoughts. The holder of a Ph.D. in music from the University of Mississippi at Oxford, Nick conducted many of his Delta travels with the graceful Ole Miss campus as his base of operations. He is happy to share a beer with a homeless man in the laundromat, whom he nonetheless thinks of as "a classic wino" and a "derelict" (10–11). Eventually, he uses his knowledge of blues history as currency in his Delta travels. He makes friends with an African American Delta resident named James by telling him stories about Robert Johnson, including the story of Johnson's disrupting producer Don Law's dinner to borrow money for a prostitute. In the company of James and his friends, Nick feels "glad to pass on a small tale they'd surely repeat on other nights" (61). In this way he earns James's trust, and this contact leads to Nick's eventually solving both the mystery of the missing Baker and the mystery of Johnson's death. Nick does not literally profit from Johnson's music, as Eugene hopes to. He does, however, use his knowledge as capital in seeking the true story of Robert Johnson's murder, thereby gaining information that will surely solidify his academic position and further his career. Nick himself is uncomfortable with his own motives, noting that this discovery could "make a career" for him, even though "[i]t was selfish, he knew, to think in those terms" (181). Nonetheless, in this age of information management, Nick puts his knowledge to a potentially commercial purpose. In Fiske's terms, Nick presents himself as one of the people despite his power-bloc credentials and advantages.

Nick's capitalizing on his blues knowledge, however, is not damning in the world of *Crossroads Blues;* it is, after all, earned currency, and Nick's (and Atkins's) information is well researched. The villain role is saved for the postmodern version of the devil who complicates Nick's search and, since Nick is living partly in parallel to Robert Johnson, threatens his life. No longer a crossroads trickster, a western gambler, or a fat man in a Buick, the devil who tries to buy Nick's soul is Pascal Cruz, a former Los Angeles record producer. Cruz looks a lot like Mephistopheles, the original purveyor of Faustian bargains, as we learn from one of Cruz's hitmen: "Dressed all in black. Sport coat over one of those collarless shirts. Long black hair and pointed beard. Black eyes with arched upside-down V's for eyebrows. A face long and thin like he was on a hunger strike. Tall and bony. Loose limbed. Cruz reminded him of Satan from all those Baptist comic books he had to read as a kid" (70). Later in the story we learn about Cruz's lurid history of lucrative scams, drug excesses, seductions, and violence; we see his "satanic smile spreading wide" (75).

Cruz's most important credential as a blues villain, however, comes from his ownership of a nightclub called the Blues Shack, a thinly disguised version of the House of Blues chain. A powerful example of the mass-mediated re-membering of blues culture, the real House of Blues opened its New Orleans venue in 1994, and the slick, highly commercial chain continues to incite dismay among blues purists everywhere. One commentator has called the House of Blues "a blues theme-park" in which elements of African American culture are rendered exotic by their removal from their original social context (Lieberfeld 219–20). Cruz's club fits this pattern. Focused on marketing rather than on music or the preservation of history, Cruz believes that it "[d]idn't matter if it was blues or mayonnaise, he knew how to package and sell anything" (108). Like the House of Blues clubs, his Blues Shack offers premium sound in a folksy setting. "Cruz knew if someone could present blues performance in the right way it would sell. He needed to build a high-tech juke joint. Old wood and rusted signs with video and state-of-the-art sound. Make it feel like you were in Mississippi with a little *Star Trek* mixed in" (108). In the worldview of *Crossroad Blues,* Cruz's callous commodification of authentic blues music is the most obvious outward sign of his inner corruption.

The counterpoint to Cruz is Nick's African American mentor JoJo Jackson, the owner of the "last of the old New Orleans juke joints" (6), where Nick plays a regular Friday night gig. Like Willie Brown to Eugene Martone, JoJo functions as a tribal elder to Nick, guiding him into blues manhood. In a series of flashbacks, we learn that Nick was a college freshman when he first began hanging out at JoJo's club. Their friendship solidified when JoJo saved the teenaged Nick from a violently jealous husband (like the one who may or may not have poisoned Robert Johnson) and taught him to play harmonica. Just like Willie Brown's vision in the film *Crossroads,* JoJo's definition of the blues is based on the emotional expression of personal experience. We learn: "For some reason, JoJo had decided to take Nick on as his harmonica prodigy. . . . He said he could show Nick how to use it. But the rest would have to be what was inside. The harp was just a tool for bringing the soul out. . . . It wasn't about being fancy, JoJo told him. It was about bringing the right emotion out at the right time" (112–13). JoJo teaches Nick in the spirit of mentorship, of transmitting a cultural legacy: "The way he'd learned from his mentor back in Clarksdale, JoJo said he was just passing it back around the loop" (113). JoJo has no mystical powers to provide him with "magical Negro" credentials, but like *Crossroads'* Willie Brown, he is an Africanist presence who helps Nick develop into adulthood and become a practicing blues musician. But it is not kindness and mentoring alone that provide JoJo's power in Nick's life or that define him as the antithesis of the devil, Pascal Cruz. Unlike Cruz, JoJo has real blues credentials: he is African American, from the Delta, a musician, and one step removed (in his musical acquaintances) from Robert Johnson. After JoJo warns Nick to "[w]atch your white ass" in Mississippi, Nick thinks, "That was the reason he liked blues and blues people. They all hated bullshit, not a phony bastard among them" (30).

Unlike the Hill and Fusco film, Atkins's novel takes few liberties with what is known of blues history. Rather, the book depends on the solid scholarship of both Nick Travers and Ace Atkins to make its case for blues authenticity. One reviewer, Marilyn Stasio, justly applauds Atkins's re-creation of the voices of the old bluesmen whom Nick interviews, remarking that their "scratchy voices catch the ragged cadences and downbeat mood of the delta. . . . [W]hen his old guys open up you can really hear the music everybody talks about so reverentially" (32). And when Nick does finally track down the juke owner who may have poisoned Johnson, their encounter follows closely the details related by the blues researcher Mack McCormick, who described his meeting with Johnson's alleged, unnamed murderer in the 1992 documentary film *The Search for Robert Johnson.* Like McCormick's source, Atkins's murderer greets Nick with a shotgun and, before he even knows the purpose of Nick's visit, offers an alibi for his whereabouts on the 1938 night of Johnson's death. In Atkins's version, however, Johnson's actual killer turns out not to be that long-sought juke owner but, as we have seen, the white record producer in the black Buick. As was the case in Alan Greenberg's screenplay *Love in Vain,* the power-bloc recording industry that exploited Johnson and his peers, personified here by the smoking fat man of 1938 and the fiendish Pascal Cruz of the present, turns out to be the devil in *Crossroad Blues.*

Given the thorough research of *Crossroad Blues* and the respect both it and *Crossroads* pay to the blues itself, both texts can be seen as offering models of intercultural understanding. The white protagonists of both works gain wisdom and maturity through the intercession of their black mentors, and just as Eugene helps Willie escape from his contract with the devil, so Nick helps JoJo save his bar from the nefarious Cruz. The benefits are reciprocal. And since both texts also offer accessible introductions to blues history and culture, they may introduce blues heritage to uninitiated consumers of popular films and detective novels. However, both texts overlook the importance of race and class in creating blues music and culture and thus engage in the paradox of authenticity that I described above. The protagonists use Robert Johnson's music in an attempt to capture a presumed pretechnological, anticommercial purity despite the fact that they both know of Johnson because they live in a mass-mediated world, and both have acknowledged profit motives somewhere on their agendas.

This use of Robert Johnson's music brings us back to Morrison's Africanist presences. Echoing Derrida's language of hauntology, Morrison notes, "Even, and especially, when American texts are not 'about' Africanist presences or characters or narrative or idiom, the shadow hovers in implication, in sign" (*Playing* 46–47). In both *Crossroads* and *Crossroad Blues,* Robert Johnson is the shadowy sign who inspires the protagonist and defines his quest, and in each text he is triply represented. First, he himself appears briefly in the prologue to each story, a specter enacting a moment of his own life story. Second, he is embodied in the present by his contemporary avatars, Willie Brown and JoJo Jackson, African American bluesmen from the Delta who experienced much that Johnson did and who pass on the music and the blues culture to their acolytes. These mentor characters perform the functions Morrison sees as typical of the Africanist persona, as each helps his student eschew capitalist goals, confirms the student's emergence as a "bluesman," and reinforces the student's vision of himself as culturally authentic.

Finally, the white protagonists themselves stand in for Johnson, and, as in the case of Chris Hunt's film *The Search for Robert Johnson,* the cross-racial surrogation process contains some inevitable slippage. Both protagonists find inspiration in Johnson and seek to follow in his footsteps: Eugene goes to the crossroads, deals with the devil, and hopes to record Johnson's music; and Nick believes that crossroads are with him wherever he goes. However, neither one routinely faces the prejudice, poverty, or exploitation suffered by Johnson or by their mentors. By removing the blues from its social and historical context, the two texts express, as Daniel Lieberfeld says of House of Blues clubs, "a desire for limited contact with selected decontextualized aspects of African American culture" (219). Morrison connects such white "manipulation of the Africanist narrative" (*Playing* 53) with the shameful tradition of blackface minstrelsy: "Just as [blackface] entertainers . . . could render permissible topics that otherwise would have been taboo, so American writers were able to employ an imagined Africanist persona to articulate and act out the forbidden in American culture" (66). Eugene and Nick can sample the bluesman's life: they can travel, tangle with the law, engage in temporary sexual relationships, and play heartfelt music. But they also have safety nets to fall back on—a secure Long Island home and parental guardianship in Eugene's case, a converted loft and a teaching job in Nick's.

Yet imitation is a form of flattery. Eric Lott has argued convincingly that blackface minstrelsy, as practiced in the nineteenth century, was not about mockery and degradation of African Americans so much as about imitation and desire. He writes: "Minstrel performers often attempted to repress through ridicule the real interest in black cultural practices they nonetheless betrayed. . . . The very form of blackface acts—an investiture in black bodies—seems a manifestation of the particular desire to try on the accents of 'blackness' and demonstrate the permeability of the color line" (6). Eugene and Nick likewise seek to inhabit Robert Johnson's life and music. Products of the romantic reinvention of Johnson, however, neither Eugene nor Nick engage in ridicule at all, and this may be what saves them from charges of minstrelsy even as they engage in related practices. Lott talks further about minstrelsy's initiating an important strain of American bohemianism, and it may be here that the connection of *Crossroads* and *Crossroad Blues* to blackface is clearest. Noting that in early blackface minstrelsy, a set of "racial attitudes and cultural styles that in America go by the name of bohemianism first emerged" (50–51), Lott claims that blackface stars "inaugurated an American tradition of class abdication through gendered cross-racial immersion which persists . . . to our own day" (51). W. T. Lhamon Jr. extends this analysis, noting that early blackface performers were often "[d]isempowered youths" who applied blackface in defiance of dominant cultural norms, using it as a working-class reaction, a protest against "merchant-defined external impostures" as well as to "express a distinctive style" (43–44). While neither Eugene nor Nick is really culturally disenfranchised, they both feel deeply disaffected from societal norms. Eugene rebels against the passionless classroom guitar in which he is being schooled; Nick, in his continual ranting against "goddamn phonies" everywhere, seeks to define himself through his music and by his distance from conventional expectations. Both also affect the style of the bluesmen they emulate, Nick in his working-class wardrobe and Eugene in the anachronistic fedora hat he buys to match the guitar Willie picks out for him. Both thus continue the tradition of engaging African American cultural practices as alternatives to the perceived sterility of mainstream life, using a re-membered Robert Johnson—an Africanist presence, a revenant—to signify what has been lost.

Given this history of minstrel traditions, can Eugene and Nick ever earn the right to call themselves "bluesmen"? Both texts convey an investment in constructing a superficial blues authenticity for their protagonists. In both cases, the superficiality may simply be the unavoidable by-product of genre: neither Hollywood films nor popular detective novels are conceived to offer in-depth cultural analysis. But could characters (or people) like Eugene and Nick ever claim to be bluesmen, given their whiteness and relative privilege? This question has long been hotly debated in blues scholarship, and the varied answers reveal both fissures and odd coalitions in postmodern American culture.

At one extreme end would be those essentialists who believe that only African Americans can play real blues music. The editors of *Living Blues* magazine, whose stated mission is to "preserve the African American blues tradition," are regularly held up as exemplars of this position, especially after publishing Paul Garon's 1993 editorial claiming that "blues is defined culturally and not acoustically" (Garon, "Speak"). And indeed, the magazine's Letters to the Editor column revisits this vexed question periodically.[2] Near this end of the spectrum would also be Julio Finn, whose reading of Robert Johnson's crossroads encounter richly informed chapter 1. Finn makes a clear distinction between white and black blues artists, claiming that white artists with dedication and expertise can be proud of being blues musicians, but "they can never be *bluespeople.* Why not? Because the blues is not something they *live* but something they do—which makes all the difference in the world. What distinguishes the bluesperson from the blues performer is cultural-racial make-up, which can only be inherited by a descendant of an ex-American slave" (*Bluesman* 229). Finn echoes Garon's tenet that "very specific sociological, cultural, economic, psychological, and political forces faced by working-class African Americans—forces permeated with racism—produced the blues. *Nothing else did!*" ("Speak"). Recognizing the contributions of committed and talented white artists and acknowledging that the blues is part of all Americans' heritage, Finn nevertheless argues that "[t]he blues is the cultural memorial of slavery, a musical memoir commemorating the history of blacks in the United States. Unlike other arts, its intrinsic spirit can only be transmitted by blood or, if you like, physically. No amount of enthusiasm, no amount of time spent living with black people, will ever endow a non-Afro-American with it" (*Bluesman* 230). Finn is evidently trying to salvage the blues from years of profit-driven cultural appropriation. Despite his intentions, however, his comment is startlingly similar to the claim made by the fictional Julliard teacher: "Excellence in primitive music is cultural. You have to be born to it." Mouthed by Eugene's effete white teacher, this statement clearly reveals the character's racist assumptions and his ignorance of the blues' complex artistry. When a similar statement is made by an African American bluesman and researcher on a mission to preserve his cultural heritage, we see a perfect example of Fiske's point that issue-centered coalitions can form despite differences in social categories and long-term goals (*Power Plays* 10–11). This odd overlap of interests in preserving the blues's racial purity thus illustrates two of Fiske's points: that strange bedfellows often unite against perceived threats from the culture at large, and that membership in a specific interest group does not depend on an unchanging identity position.

At the other end of the spectrum is white blues harmonica player Adam Gussow, who for ten years performed with multi-instrumentalist Sterling

Magee, a.k.a. Mr. Satan, as part of Satan and Adam, an interracial, intergenerational blues duo. After enjoying the tutelage of an African American harmonica player named Nat Riddles and then performing widely as Mr. Satan's partner, Gussow sees in such interracial apprenticeships a potential reversal of the master/slave relationship upon which American racism was built. Writing that what binds the older black mentor and his young white apprentice is "earned mutual respect and the transmission of needed knowledge," Gussow explains:

> I've always felt that the critique of American music as one long, white rip-off of black genius, true as it could be at points, was distorting and misrepresenting a far more interesting parallel dynamic. Why not allow for the possibility of sweated-for spiritual progress? . . . Interracial apprenticeship—the extraordinarily generous gift of black musical wisdom to those who would reciprocate with gifts of reverence and responsive attention—is not merely widespread in the contemporary blues scene: It may well be the deeper purpose of the whole enterprise. What is being undone gig by gig, it might be argued, is a long and traumatic past (slavery, sharecropping, segregation) in which American race relations took the form of soul-murdering mastery, white over black. The blues world has been engaged for the last 30 years, perhaps without knowing it, in an unprecedented experiment. Hard-working black masters and their younger white apprentices, shoulder to shoulder, have been confronting and unmaking the remnants of the master-slave dialectic.[3] ("My Master" 106)

I have quoted Gussow at some length because I think his vision of the present and the future is important. He acknowledges the African American cultural roots of the blues and the history of white exploitation of blues artists but sees the contemporary blues scene as moving in a different and positive direction. Moreover, his experience has been repeated by other white blues musicians of his generation, such as Iowa native Hawkeye Herman. Herman learned much about the blues world from playing with Cool Papa Sadler, whom he describes as "a father, friend, and mentor to all who approached the music and life with sincerity and humility" ("Jokin'"). Perhaps the blues, like Robert Johnson, will not stay put as it has been represented. It exists in the twenty-first century as both repetition and first time, an evolving entity beyond the control of any one person or any one school of thought.

Gussow's model of apprenticeship, however, does not really apply to either *Crossroads* or *Crossroad Blues.* Instead of envisioning a future of cross-cultural understanding born from evolving blues traditions, both texts take their heroes back to the past, back to the Delta, back to an irrecoverable historical context that had no determining influence on the lives of the two protagonists or on their music. Their journeys remain individual quests for personal fulfillment and self-expression; they form no part of any larger, forward-looking social project. The three novels discussed in chapter 4, however, all reflect, to some degree, Gussow's vision of the blues as a potential bridge to present and future multicultural harmony. All three texts share Paul Gilroy's understanding that the blues encodes "a politics of transformation" within its lyrics and structures (37), and all three personify these transformative blues with the haunting presence of Robert Johnson.

4
The New Cultural Politics of Difference

In chapter 1, I observed that no one has yet reported seeing Robert Johnson hanging around House of Blues clubs. If you read enough contemporary fiction, though, you will find him roaming a Spokane Indian reservation, winking at you in a New York City park, and playing music with other dead bluesmen in the Ozark mountains. In texts that import him to such far-flung locales, Robert Johnson is used as a signifier of something larger than himself, larger even than the artistic inspiration that he provided for others in *Crossroads* and *Crossroad Blues.* In the novels discussed in this chapter, Robert Johnson personifies a different ideal: the value of crossing cultural boundaries.

In the introduction, I spent some time discussing the multicultural initiatives that many scholars see as crucial to turn-of-the-millennium culture. Significant among such thinkers is philosopher Cornel West, who in 1990 noted a shift in aesthetic and political values away from notions of the universal and the homogeneous and toward a new appreciation of diversity, hybridity, and cultural variety. For West and many others, this "new cultural politics of difference" offers an important step forward in dismantling hierarchical paradigms of race and race relations. It also offers "ordinary people" a way to see that they have the power to shape society. Emphasizing the grassroots partnerships for cultural change that evolved in the late twentieth century (including such varied groups as Jesse Jackson's Rainbow Coalition and the revolutionary factions in Eastern Europe), West notes:

> The most significant theme of the new cultural politics of difference is the agency, capability and ability of human beings who have been culturally degraded, politically oppressed and economically exploited by bourgeois liberal and communist illiberal status quo. This theme neither romanticizes nor idealizes marginalized peoples. Rather it accentuates their humanity. . . . The new cultural politics of difference affirms the perennial quest for the precious ideals of individuality and democracy by digging deep in the depths of hu-

> man particularities and social specifics in order to construct new kinds of connections, affinities and communities across empire, nation, region, race, gender, age and sexual orientation. ("New Cultural" 34–35)

In other words, at the turn of the century scholars like West see political and social value in recognizing and celebrating diversity. In contrast to those who decry "Balkanization" as a debilitating symptom of cultural fragmentation, West sees positive benefit in affirming differences and forming new coalitions based not on identity politics but on common goals. His work seeks to promote new and complex iterations of racial identity and practice, such as that articulated by Adam Gussow at the end of chapter 3, and it echoes John Fiske's conviction that coalitions of "the people" can and do effect social change.

The three novels discussed in this chapter—Alan Rodgers's *Bone Music,* Sherman Alexie's *Reservation Blues,* and Walter Mosley's *RL's Dream,* all published in 1995—share this interest in the possibilities of a pluralistic society. It is not surprising that contemporary novelists should participate in this multicultural initiative. The social movement toward cultural pluralism identified by West and others has been paralleled by changes in studies of American literature, as critics and scholars begin to celebrate texts that recognize America's characteristic mixing of cultures and perspectives. Paul Lauter's groundbreaking *Heath Anthology of American Literature,* which debuted in 1989, is only the most comprehensive example of a widespread academic movement to expand the canon of American writers and to celebrate diversity in literary subjects and styles. And since Rodgers, Alexie, and Mosley all depict Johnson's blues and their own art of storytelling as powerful agents of multicultural transmission, they all participate in this contemporary trend in literature and literary study.

What makes these three novels stand out from other recent fiction with multicultural themes, however, is the authors' choice of Robert Johnson as a representative figure, a haunting reminder of human possibilities. Each writer places Robert Johnson in a late twentieth-century world where cultures intermingle. The advantages of these fusions vary and include such diverse gifts as inspiration for the dispossessed, the sharing of cultural heritage through stories and music, and an ethics of community care. In each case, a re-membered Robert Johnson becomes a signifier for a positive future society with multicultural possibilities. And in the case of *Bone Music,* a cross-cultural coalition led by a reanimated Robert Johnson actually saves the world.

The Nation That the Crossroads Built

Bone Music begins much like *Crossroads* and *Crossroad Blues:* by depicting imagined scenes based on the historical Robert Johnson's life. In *Bone Music,* however, the scene of Robert Johnson's death is extended to almost thirty pages. In addition, although Robert Johnson the Delta musician dies in this early section of the novel, he returns as the literal undead, and we follow him throughout the novel as he negotiates life after death in varying circumstances. A horror novel, *Bone Music* ignores the bonds of realism that *Crossroads* and *Crossroad Blues* at least superficially embrace. The Johnson of this novel is literally a revenant, and his post-death acknowledgement of his earthly sins eventually enables him, along with a cohort of dead blues musicians and living members of America's ethnically diverse culture, to sing an eruption of hellhounds back into hell.

The Robert Johnson of the first thirty pages, however, is as callow and foolish as Eugene Martone or Nick Travers ever was. Courting his own death by flirting outrageously with a juke joint owner's wife in front of the provoked husband, then drinking from a whiskey bottle that he knows is poisoned, Johnson arrogantly expects his musical genius to protect him from death. And indeed, he does survive the poisoning but quickly succumbs to a resultant bacterial infection, deadly in this pre-antibiotic era. But Johnson's musical gifts afford him certain advantages, bringing forces from several spiritual traditions to his deathbed assistance. In the deathbed scene, we discover that in *Bone Music,* when great blues musicians die they do not go directly to heaven or hell. Instead, they end up in a community somewhere near the Ozark mountains, where they rule as Wizard Kings or their attendant Hoodoo Doctors, with powers to help the living. Robert Johnson is thus attended by both Blind Willie Johnson, a living Christian preacher and gospel singer, and bluesman Blind Lemon Jefferson, here some nine years dead and a "Hoodoo Doctor." This odd pairing of historically based spiritual guides, one Christian and one hoodoo, offers the novel's first indication that the action takes place in a world of multiple, overlapping cultural traditions.

In this case, however, Johnson goes too far for even this alliance of forces to save him. Recognizing that he is about to die and furious about it, he sings the song "Judgment Day" (apparently not Johnson's recorded "If I Had Possession over Judgment Day"). While all great bluesmen know this song in their hearts, we learn, none have the temerity to sing it, for the song will crack the "Eye of the World," the structure that protects earth from the demons of hell. "Brash and vainglorious," the young Robert Johnson of *Bone Music* sings "Judgment Day" "because he knew that he was dying and he thought that was the end of the world" (1).

> He mistook his own death for the end of the world. Such a hubris had that Robert Johnson!
>
> Oh, he wasn't the first to think such a thing, and God knows he won't be the last. But few before Robert Johnson ever had the *gift* he had, and no other living soul could ever sing the song he sang; and when he mistook his own doom for the Battle at the End he did a thing no other man has ever done:
>
> He sang a song to make it true. (26)

Rodgers's Robert Johnson is thus a very different reanimation than the model of musical authenticity we saw in *Crossroads* and *Crossroad Blues*. In *Bone Music* Johnson becomes an emblem of intemperate youth and the incarnation of a modern society created from multiple spiritual, literary, musical, and historical traditions. In this deathbed scene, the novelist invokes western Christianity, hoodoo (with its traces of African Vodun), modern scientific knowledge, and epic tragedy (Johnson's "hubris") in explaining the cause of Johnson's death. And while Johnson's selfish actions are apocalyptic—the potential source of the world's destruction—through his second earthly life (beginning in 1948) and his underworld experiences, he learns to become its eventual savior. In the first thirty pages, Rodgers's overarching project becomes clear: he is defining contemporary America as a hybrid culture, whose beauty and strength comes from the intermingling of diverse traditions. According to Rodgers, *Bone Music* is "about the way things interact to make the world the way it is—there are connections down inside all the seemingly discrete bits. . . . What the book is trying to do, ultimately, is define us as a people" ("Re: Robert Johnson" [17 July 2001]).

The hybridity of culture that Rodgers sees as "defining" contemporary America is apparent not only in the Robert Johnson sections of the novel but in its overall structure as well. For while Johnson appears frequently throughout the novel, his story is only one of a handful of disparate plots that remain largely separate until the climactic ending scene, when all the characters must band together to repair the damaged Eye of the World. The first part of the book alternates between the story of Robert Johnson and the parallel story of Lisa Henderson, an eight-year-old African American girl living in Spanish Harlem who dies of a cancerous tumor in the first few pages of the novel. Her death is thus juxtaposed to Johnson's, and it is not until late in the novel that we discover she is his granddaughter.

Unrecognized links between cultures past and present are thus personified in Lisa.

Like Johnson, Lisa doesn't exactly die, either. In a nightmarish section of the book, Lisa's distraught mother Emma, a Baptist, calls upon Mama Estrella Perez, a Santeria priestess, who helps Emma bring Lisa back to life as a zombie child. The religious and ethnic fusions apparent in Johnson's death scene are invoked even more directly in the story of Lisa's death and horrific rebirth. As she dies, Lisa is guided by a mysterious, calming female presence, who is variously identified as Santa Barbara, the Santeria "virgin with the sword" (3); Our Lady of Sorrows, suggesting connection with the Catholic Virgin Mary (7); Shungó, the loa of Yoruba tradition (2); and "*the goddess who repented*" (2). Later in the book we find this same female figure also called Polly, apparent consort to John Henry, the steel-driving hero of African American folklore and song. This palimpsestic character thus embodies multiple races, ethnicities, folklores, and spiritual traditions and sets them in action during multiple time periods, from Johnson's death in 1938 to Lisa's in "the present."

A central event of the novel occurs in 1952, well before the millennial "present" of the climax. On a ridge overlooking Memphis, two hundred dead blues artists who once ruled the Delta (including such luminaries as Peetie Wheatstraw, Charley Patton, Blind Lemon Jefferson, and Ma Rainey) gather under John Henry's leadership. Their purpose is to heal the cracked Eye of the World with communal song. Employing a blues-based version of Beethoven's "Ode to Joy" as their weapon, the musicians sing together, but the song fails and they all perish. Apparently the Wizard Kings of the Delta did not have enough power to reverse the damage done by Johnson's singing "Judgment Day," even when they allied their forces to Beethoven's; unlike Eugene Martone, they can't beat the devil with a classical riff. The collective power necessary to heal the ruptured Eye would not come until years later, at the turn of the millennium, but the preparation for it begins with this scene. A vision of the Wizard Kings' demise enters the dreams of a boy named Dan Alvarez, who will grow up to be a West Coast studio musician. In his dream Dan hears "Ode to Joy" "rebroken, syncopated, twisted, and remade into blues, but it was still Beethoven's melody, beautiful as it was the morning that the master wrote it" (160). He also experiences a vision of the young Elvis Presley stealing John Henry's smoking guitar from the rubble of the Wizard Kings' destruction. Years later, when an adult Dan revivifies a newly dead and now revenant Elvis Presley, the ingredients necessary to put down the demon insurrection are finally assembled.

The second half of the novel traces three separate groups as they travel through the underworld: Lisa, Robert Johnson, and Santa Barbara/Shungó; Emma Henderson (seeking her lost zombie daughter Lisa) and Leadbelly (the evil genius and only survivor of the Hoodoo Kings); and Dan Alvarez, Elvis, and Polly. Each group is thus composed of various kinds of characters (historical, legendary, spiritual, and musical, dead or alive) and each group discovers on its separate journey that music—from folk song to classical melody—has the power to protect them from the demons. At the end of their journeys, the three groups of underworld travelers are joined by a new generation of blues kings, including the historical bluesmen Furry Lewis, Tampa Red, Washboard Sam, and Stevie Ray Vaughan, all of whom died after the 1952 debacle. Together they discover that while the blues, even in combination with Beethoven, was not powerful enough in itself to repair the cracked Eye of the World, when further combined with a multitude of other musical traditions, music can rid the world of demons. In the chaotic climax, order is finally restored to the world at a revival meeting/carnival/jubilee in the center of New Orleans, where the combined efforts of the new blues kings, Santa Barbara/Shungó, Robert Johnson, Elvis Presley, Dan Alvarez, and Polly in singing "Jesu Joy of Man's Desiring," accompanied by Lisa on kazoo, strike the demons back to hell.

This frenzied scene, the culmination of the many cultures, musical heritages, locations, eras, and peoples that Rodgers intermixes in *Bone Music,* suggests what I take to be the overall point of this sometimes frazzling novel. The scene works to do what Cornel West describes in his call for a new world order that recognizes the power of culturally dispossessed peoples ("New Cultural" 34). No one group, even the powerful coalition of dead blues artists, can preserve the harmony of the world in *Bone Music.* It takes the joint effort of people of multiple ethnicities and races, of varying degrees of talent, of all ages, of varied religious backgrounds, from different parts of the country and different socioeconomic classes to form "new kinds of connections, affinities and communities across empire, nation, region, race, gender, age and sexual orientation" (West, "New Cultural" 35). Each of them plays a unique and necessary part. As Santa Barbara tells Lisa early in the novel, when the dead child pleads to stay dead: "The world still needs you, child" (6). And when I asked Alan Rodgers why Dan Alvarez, a mere studio musician, gets to play such a large part in saving the world, Rodgers replied, "Don't we all?" ("Re: Robert Johnson" [17 July 2001]).

But it is not only coalition or West's "politics of difference" that Rodgers is extolling in *Bone Music.* He goes further by suggesting that identity positions like race and religion are not fixed or even necessarily different from each other. This point is evident in the Santa Barbara/Shungó character, who embodies multiple religions in one being and so suggests that the spiritual traditions they represent not only coexist but are one and the same, or at least spring from the same source. In an intriguing turn of phrase, Rodgers asserts that this overlap of cultural images is "actual folklore" ("Re: Robert Johnson" [17 July 2001]). Most interesting in this context, however, are the Three Blind Lords of the Piedmont, who preside over the novel's climactic celebration scene. These characters, early East Coast blues artists (and so not present at the 1952 disaster of Delta musicians), are crucial participants in the final overthrow of demons. They are also racial shape-shifters. The narrator tells us:

> Two of them were white and one was black, or maybe one of them was white and two were black, or maybe they were all black, the paintbrush touches us all in its way, doesn't it? We are a nation made at the crossroads where two things meet, and the consequences of that meeting make us all the people who we are. . . .
>
> Two of them were white, now, and one was black. These things change from time to time, depending on the circumstances and the context. They aren't nearly so important as they seem.
>
> Because we are the nation that the crossroads built, and after that what else matters? (282)

In "the nation that the crossroads built," differences are inevitable, coalition brings strength, and racial differences are cultural constructs, liable to change with time. Even the music, which Rodgers posits as the product of a hybrid culture, gains power from its fusion of western and African forms.

Given Rodgers's interest in the supernatural, in cultural collaborations, and in musical and spiritual traditions that abide, his reasons for choosing Robert Johnson as a literally haunting presence seem obvious. Johnson's alleged deal with the devil implies a set of spiritual concerns similar to those Rodgers explores in *Bone Music,* where he reanimates Johnson first to destroy the world and then to save it. Curiously, however, the pact at the crossroads is never mentioned in *Bone Music.* When questioned about this omission, Rodgers replied, "The deal with the devil story wouldn't have worked in this. At all. Doesn't even work in my understanding of theology. Why should the devil pay for what he owns anyhow? Or can't take title to, no matter what? And the devil sure isn't responsible for music like that. It's something divine, in fact" ("Re: Robert Johnson" [18

July 2001]). Rodgers's reference to divinity resonates in this context. Taken as a whole, the novel offers a metaphor for sin and redemption, with the pattern of repentance repeated in the various stories of Johnson, Lisa, Elvis, and others. As one reviewer describes it, Rodgers "turns history into myth," blending American Christian beliefs with other U.S. legends to create "an intelligent morality play" in which the forces of good and evil are equally interesting and powerful (Padol 20–21).

But maybe Robert Johnson signifies something more in *Bone Music.* Given a world where cultures intermingle and generations must work together to preserve cosmic harmony, some sort of cultural transmission is crucial. Robert Johnson's function as a gifted musician comes into play here, since he can learn old songs, write new songs, and pass them on to his musical successors like Stevie Ray Vaughan and to his own descendants, especially Lisa, whom he guides through hell and instructs on the kazoo. While Robert Johnson may be, as one reviewer claims, simply a plot device in *Bone Music* (Eldridge), he does facilitate the intercultural, intergenerational passing down of knowledge necessary to encourage redemption in others and preserve order in a messily pluralistic culture.

And it is not only music that Johnson passes on. *Bone Music* is replete with orally transmitted stories, from the legend of Johnson himself to the tales about John Henry. The narrator tells us: "There are a thousand stories about John Henry, and a thousand thousand variations on those tales. Some of the stories are literally true; some of them are figuratively true; some of them are wrong. That's the nature of stories, isn't it? They show us all the highlights of the world, but they never leave us certain that we can trust the things we know" (118). This statement, from a storyteller about storytelling, suggests the power of stories to shape reality and the instability of the truths they purport to tell. The religious traditions, music, and tales that are passed down from one generation to the next and traded between cultures inevitably mutate, usually contain some element of truth, and are necessary for cultural continuation in any case.

As my description probably suggests, *Bone Music* is a somewhat frenetic novel, its multiple plot lines animated by dozens of characters, dead and alive, who ceaselessly traverse the nation and the underworld, representatives of various religious traditions, regions, eras, and ethnicities. Demons roil around every corner. Possibly because of its exuberant hybridity, the novel sometimes seems to suggest contradictory things about "the nation that the crossroads built." On the one hand, it is only through the joining and mingling of various cultural forces that the world is preserved from demon usurpation, so the novel presents cultural hybridity as a source of strength. On the other hand, when race is immaterial and madonna figures from diverse religions are really all the same being, the differences that provide strength are not really differences at all. One might argue that I am asking a horror novel to do too much philosophical work, that like the Hollywood film and detective novel discussed in chapter 3, its very genre precludes serious cultural critique. But Rodgers himself and some critics would take issue with this notion of genre restrictions. Rodgers claims, "I write about ideas. Fiction is where I do it" ("Re: Robert Johnson" [17 July 2001]). And reviewers have hailed *Bone Music* as "a work of mythological proportions" (Mosiman) and "a book that define[s] us as a people—a Nibelungenlied for America; an Odyssey for Main Street" ("*Bone Music* Book Description"). Rodgers's work is philosophically informed, but because of the complicated plot, he ends up *presenting* thoughtful ideas without really *exploring* them. Despite Rodgers's intentions, *Bone Music* may be a prisoner of its genre, as surreal scenes of ghouls and zombies intersect with "actual folklore" to snarl the basic philosophy of the morality tale. Since neither Alexie's *Reservation Blues* nor Mosley's *RL's Dream* is bound by conventional literary formulas or driven by a complicated plot, they can more fully and more subtly examine the implications of cultural hybridity, empowerment through music and stories, and a re-membered Robert Johnson.

On the Edge of the Twenty-first Century

Sherman Alexie's *Reservation Blues* and Walter Mosley's *RL's Dream* take place in contemporary fictional worlds where dreams are part of reality, where stories can create the truth, and, in the case of *Reservation Blues,* where magic is a part of daily life. Both novels, however, also depict the material here and now, specifically the poverty and limited opportunities that define late twentieth-century life on an Indian reservation (Alexie) and in New York City's tenements (Mosley). This similarity of vision is perhaps not accidental. In a 1994 interview, conducted while Alexie was working on *Reservation Blues,* he praised Walter Mosley for breaking down genre barriers with his Easy Rawlins detective series. Alexie said: "'[Mosley's] hero is a black detective in Los Angeles during the 1940s. While it's still formula writing, there's some sly social commentary, real insidious stuff'" (qtd. in Bellante 26). In *Reservation Blues,* similar "sly social commentary" intermingles with the magical realism that characterizes much recent Native American fiction. The result is a novel that conducts a form of Barthes's third-order semiotic analysis, unpacking the mythic Robert

Johnson created in the 1960s and reinvesting him with historical significance. In this case, however, Johnson is no revenant but still wholly alive, re-membered as both a Depression-era African American and a resident of a contemporary American Indian reservation.

Reservation Blues takes place on a Spokane Indian reservation in 1992, where Robert Johnson unexpectedly shows up carrying his guitar, having faked his death in 1938 in an attempt to escape the "sickness" of his musical genius (6). He arrives seeking the help of "a woman who lives on a hill," known as Big Mom to the Indians. Big Mom is a supernaturally long-lived member of the Spokane tribe who remembers the nineteenth-century slaughter of hundreds of Indian horses at the hands of Generals Sheridan and Wright. A musical genius and "a part of every tribe" (199), Big Mom is "the teacher of all those great musicians of the twentieth century" (201), from Les Paul to Paul McCartney, including the tragic figures Janis Joplin, Jimi Hendrix, and Marvin Gaye, whom she sees as reincarnations of the slaughtered horses. Like Alan Rodgers's Santa Barbara/ Shungó character, Big Mom is an equal opportunity spiritual guide, willing to help musicians from any culture who seek her aid. Robert Johnson is one such supplicant, and by the end of the novel he has traded in his cursed/enchanted guitar for the harmonica she carves for him. Healed of his "sickness" by the end of the novel, Johnson plans to stay on the reservation. "'I think I jus' might belong here,'" he says. "'I think this Tribe's been waitin' for me for a long time. . . . I think the Indians might need me. Maybe need my music'" (303).

Alexie suggests that Johnson is able to make a home on the reservation because conditions there so resemble those of slavery and sharecropping, elements of Johnson's own heritage. This connection is expressed when Thomas Builds-the-Fire, a compulsive storyteller and one of the novel's main characters, hears multiple racial histories in Robert Johnson's blues. First he hears "Robert Johnson's grandmother singing backup" in "some tattered cabin. No windows, blanket for a door, acrid smoke. Johnson's grandmother was not alone in that cabin. Other black men, women, and children sang with her. The smell of sweat, blood, and cotton filled that room" (174–75). Thomas also hears the history of his Spokane Indian people in Johnson's blues, blues that "were ancient, aboriginal, indigenous . . . [but the Spokanes] would not speak about any of it" (174–75). The resemblance between Robert Johnson's history and contemporary Native American life is invoked even more specifically in an earlier Alexie short story in which the young Victor Joseph, who would grow up to appear as one of the main characters in *Reservation Blues,* says: "The first time I heard Robert Johnson sing I knew he understood what it meant to be an Indian on the edge of the twenty-first century, even if he was black at the beginning of the twentieth" (Alexie, "Because" 35). In *Reservation Blues,* Alexie shows the similarities of cultural conditions for these two disadvantaged groups. And as Rodgers did in *Bone Music,* Alexie uses Robert Johnson to portend a future where diverse racial and ethnic cultures might mingle harmoniously, for mutual benefit and support.

In *Reservation Blues,* Johnson begins to be healed of his "sickness" when he gives away his guitar. The guitar is enchanted: it can speak, play by itself, transport itself, and turn whoever plays it into a virtuoso performer. When Johnson gives it to Thomas Builds-the-Fire, Thomas passes it on to Victor Joseph, here an adult, unemployed alcoholic with no future. Together with Victor's friend Junior Polatkin and with Thomas's female friends Chess and Checkers Warmwater, the two form a band called Coyote Springs and achieve quick, startling success. Much of their fame comes from Victor's impassioned playing on Robert Johnson's guitar, which burns and scars Victor's hands and occasionally even sets a room on fire. And just as Robert Johnson suffered from the gift and curse of his talent, so too does Victor. When the group is flown to New York for a recording session at the behest of the ominously named producers Sheridan and Wright of Cavalry Records, Victor finds he can no longer control the guitar: it slices open his palm, flies out of his hands, and ruins the session, spoiling the group's only chance to record. In this scene, the recording industry represents the continued exploitation of native peoples by white power-bloc forces and also, as we have seen in works as various as *Love in Vain* and *Crossroad Blues,* the devil to whom the group may have sold its collective soul.

The chapter following the recording session further develops the theme of selling oneself for art. In a flashback to Johnson's early life, the devil, here "a handsome white man" in a "perfectly pressed wool suit in the hot Mississippi heat," appears to Robert Johnson, offering him musical talent if he will give up whatever he loves the most (264). For Johnson, the son of sharecroppers and grandson of slaves, the thing he loves the most is freedom, and it is freedom (from his own ambition, perhaps) that he hopes to regain in the present by getting rid of his guitar. This flashback scene resonates with a dream of Victor's in the same chapter. In the dream, the guitar—which Victor had smashed and left in the New York studio—returns to the reservation. "*You can have me back,*" the guitar tells him, "*and you can be anybody you want to be. You can have anything you want to have. But you have to trade me for it. . . . You have to give up what you love the most. . . . What do you love the most? Who do you love the most?"* (255). Outside, while Victor dreams, his lifelong friend Junior hears Victor whisper his name, and shortly thereafter Junior commits suicide. Alexie uses Johnson as a warning: genius, or perhaps fame, will cost one dearly and may finally come at too high a price.

But Alexie's Johnson does survive and finds a new place for himself on the reservation, where he feels he might be of use. Johnson's newfound purpose in life suggests that music can have an important function in preserving culture and transforming sorrow. Literary critic Jerry Wasserman calls this "blues telescoping," noting that "*Reservation Blues* explores how blues music spans time, space and race to express and transcend the pain of oppressed peoples." But part of what makes this positive outcome possible is the focus of the artist—in this case, a reborn Robert Johnson—on helping the community rather than on simply expressing himself, seeking recognition, or making a living. While achieving fame can involve devastating personal sacrifice, the actual making of art can and perhaps must serve an important communal function.

We see this communal function of music illustrated early in the novel, when Thomas has a conversation with Johnson's magic guitar. "'Y'all need to play songs for your people,'" the charmed guitar tells him. "'They need you. . . . Y'all need the music'" (23). And indeed, as the guitar plays blues music through the night, it invades the people's dreams. "Music rose above the reservation, made its way into the clouds, and rained down. The reservation arched its back, opened its mouth, and drank deep because the music tasted so familiar. . . . The music kept falling down, falling down" (24). Alexie echoes the common blues refrain "blues falling down like rain" and, in repeating the line, invokes Johnson's own "blues falling down like hail, falling down like hail" from "Hellhounds on My Trail." He is also once again commenting on the similarly hard lives of early blues pioneers and contemporary Native Americans on the reservation, where "the music tasted so familiar." But most importantly, the image of rain and of the people drinking deeply suggests that the music can also sustain and nurture growth. In a place where dreams are "murdered" (7), blues music offers new dreams, new possibilities; in speaking for the troubles of the weary everywhere, it helps transcend them. This is perhaps why Alexie is so careful to document the specific living conditions of the reservation—the hunger, loneliness, alcoholism, and suicidal despair. The blues ethos suggests that one must face, recognize, and name one's demons to move beyond them. As music writer and musician Mark Buechler has noted: "blues music is not about surrendering to sorrow, as so many uninformed listeners believe. It's about grappling with that sorrow down in the rag-and-bone shop of the heart and transforming it—through impassioned vocals, through a groove or through a bent note—into a kind of affirmation of the human spirit. But it's an affirmation without sentiment and without delusion, one that never fails to acknowledge the tragedy at the heart of being" (59). Alexie creates a world of poverty and diminishment in which blues music can speak for the dispossessed, giving them voice and giving meaning to their lives (Sublett). He acknowledges the "tragedy" at the heart of their being yet offers art, personified by the rehabilitated Robert Johnson, as a source of inspiration for the future.

I use the word "art" rather than the more specific "music" because *Reservation Blues,* like *Bone Music,* suggests that storytelling also is important for cultural transmission and for survival. "'Indians tell a lot of stories,'" Alexie commented in an interview. "'It ties people together'" (qtd. in Bellante 14). Within the novel, Thomas Builds-the-Fire is as compulsive a storyteller as Robert Johnson ever was a guitar player. When he first meets Johnson seeking a cure for "a sickness" he can't get rid of, Thomas sympathizes. "Thomas knew about sickness. He'd caught some disease in the womb that forced him to tell stories. The weight of those stories bowed his legs and bent his spine a bit" (6). Throughout the novel this "misfit storyteller of the Spokane tribe" (5) attempts to document tribal history (real or metaphoric), preserve tradition, and heal wounds with his stories, to which nobody listens. Yet Thomas's stories, however unwelcome, contain a powerful magic of their own: "Thomas Builds-the-Fire's stories climbed into your clothes like sand, gave you itches that could not be scratched. If you repeated even a sentence from one of those stories, your throat was never the same again. Those stories hung in your clothes and hair like smoke, and no amount of laundry soap or shampoo washed them out" (15). And even though the Spokanes reject Thomas's stories, the novel proposes that the stories offer one way to survive individually and communally. Janine Richardson observes that Thomas as storyteller "works against the willful forgetting and denial that is in operation on the reservation among the population at large" (41). In this way, his stories share the cultural work of the blues, which, as the magic guitar reminds Thomas, "always makes us remember" (22). The blues also share some stylistic similarities with Native American storytelling, notably in their use of repetition. According to P. Jane Hafen, the purpose of this device in Indian stories is to allow the storyteller to speak in a collective voice that illustrates tradition, much as blues lyrics often directly connect the speaker's experience with that of his or her community (73). The blues and storytelling thus fulfill similar cultural functions in *Reservation Blues:* they preserve communal truths, link artist to community, and pass down tools necessary for survival.

Another possible reason for Alexie's drawing such clear-cut comparisons between storytelling and the blues, and between contemporary Native American and early twentieth-century African American culture, is to avoid charges of cultural appropriation. Such theft of indigenous art forms is one of the major themes of the novel, and Alexie goes to great lengths to suggest that Native Americans like the members of Coyote Springs have earned the culturally determined right to sing the blues. Not so for many of the white characters in the book. Elvis Presley appears in Thomas's dreams as "*a cavalry scout in a previous life*" (73), symbolizing the "white pillaging of all marginalized cultures" (Cox 65). Even more glaring examples of rip-off artists are two white folk singers whose names, Betty and Veronica, amusingly connect them to the sanitized 1950s pop culture depicted in the Archie comics. Both have long blonde hair, wear "too much Indian jewelry" (41), and believe that Indians possess special spiritual knowledge. "'You have all the things we don't have,'" Betty tells Thomas and Chess. "'You live at peace with the earth. You are so wise'" (168). Betty and Veronica run a New Age bookshop in Seattle called Dopplegangers, and Alexie obviously uses them as foils to the Native American characters.

Multiple levels of irony occur through Alexie's use of these recurring doppelgangers, culminating when Sheridan and Wright offer Betty and Veronica a recording contract and re-create them as Indians. Sheridan tells his boss: "'These two women here had grandmothers or something that were Indian. We can sell that Indian idea. We don't need any goddamn just-off-the-reservation Indians. We can use these women. They've been on the reservations. . . . These women have got the reservation experience down. . . . We dress them up a little. Get them into a tanning booth. Darken them up a little. Maybe a little plastic surgery on those cheekbones. . . . Dye their hair black. Then we'd have Indians. People want to hear Indians'" (269). After agreeing to this "fine tuning" of their image (271), Betty and Veronica end up with a lucrative recording contract, an obvious comment on the commodification and marketing of Native American culture. The deal that Betty and Veronica make, however, cuts both ways. For while Cavalry Records, with a stipulated "economic need for a viable Indian band" (272), does record and promote them in preference to Coyote Springs, the women have to sell part of themselves in the process. Arguing that he is in the business of making dreams come true, Wright convinces them to give up playing their own music, to perform in redface, and to offer "'a little something in exchange for our hard work'" (272). As they acquiesce, Betty and Veronica "could hear the drums" (273). This image implies that in handing over their appearances, their music, and their futures to the exploiters from Cavalry Records, they are about to become culturally more Indian (or more African American) than they ever imagined. Like Robert Johnson and like Victor, they may give up too much and pay too high a price for the promise of stardom.

Despite this critique of the imitation Indians in this book, Alexie ends the novel, as Rodgers does in *Bone Music,* on a note of hope for intercultural understanding, personified by the newly healed Robert Johnson. After the debacle in New York, the members of Coyote Springs return, humiliated, to the reservation, where they languish in depression, waiting for shipments of commodity food, until Thomas, Chess, and Checkers decide to move off the reservation and seek work in nearby Spokane. On the night of their departure the community is having a feast, which Alexie marks from the start as culturally inclusive. When Big Mom encourages Father Arnold, the reservation Catholic priest, to attend with her, she tells him, "'You cover all the Christian stuff; I'll do the traditional Indian stuff. We'll make a great team'" (280). At the feast, Big Mom takes up a collection to give Thomas and the Warmwaters some start-up money, reminding the people of their "tribal responsibilities" (304). Thomas, Chess, and Checkers are thus, in a sense, reinstated in the tribe even as they prepare to depart from it, an inverse parallel to the spiritually restored Robert Johnson, who at the feast announces his intention to stay on, to play his music and so possibly help the tribe. As Johnson tells Thomas, "'We both have places we need to be'" (303), and those places are defined by potential social function rather than by static notions of racial identity. In this way, Alexie uses Johnson and the remaining members of Coyote Springs to create a fictional representation of the cross-cultural coalition building, based on communities of interest, that Cornel West has called for.

To Face the Truth and Still Be a Man

Walter Mosley's *RL's Dream,* another 1995 novel that imagines cross-cultural understanding, offers perhaps the truest example of Robert Johnson as a haunting presence. In this novel, a departure for Mosley from his Easy Rawlins detective series, Robert Johnson is neither a guiding ancestor, nor the undead, nor the still alive. He exists only in the mind and memory of a dying black septuagenarian named Atwater "Soupspoon" Wise, a homeless New Yorker whose life was changed forever during the brief period of his Mississippi youth that he spent performing with Robert Johnson. Soupspoon's memories and occasional visions of Johnson strengthen him during his last few months of life. Johnson thus functions as what Genevieve Fabre and Robert O'Meally would call a "lieu de mémoire" or "site of memory." For Fabre and O'Meally, people create such lieux de mémoire to help structure identity in a rapidly changing world: "Threatened by a sense of discontinuity and forgetfulness, we seek new moorings and props, new means of reactivating the processes of remembrance as we reach toward a better sense of who we are and whence we have come" (7). Lieux de mémoire such as Soupspoon's recollections of Robert Johnson are the products of "interaction between history and memory, of the interplay between the personal and the collective" (7). "Collective" experience is especially relevant to *RL's Dream,* which uses the haunting presence of Robert Johnson to epitomize the sustaining powers of the blues and its importance in creating community.

Like *Reservation Blues, RL's Dream* sets its characters in a world of dispossessed people. In this case, the setting is the tenements of contemporary New York City, where life is not much better than it was in Depression-era Mississippi. As the novel begins, Soupspoon, suffering severe pain from hip cancer, is being evicted from the apartment he has inhabited for twenty-seven years. As he sees his few possessions being dragged into the street, Soupspoon feels sorry for the young black man working on the eviction team, "who didn't even know how to act with his elders," and thinks, "*Them two men could go from 'partment to 'partment an' th'ow out ev'ryone. An' ain't not nobody gonna lift a hand t'stop'em. We was poor in the Delta, but we wasn't never that poor*" (28). Soupspoon specifically connects Delta hardships with New York conditions and laments the loss of community support in the unfeeling city. His feelings of alienation turn out to be unfounded, however. Swooping unexpectedly to his rescue is Kiki Waters, a thirty-something white woman who lives in an upstairs apartment and to whom Soupspoon has spoken only once. With an Arkansas background and southern cultural values similar to Soupspoon's, Kiki takes him into her own one-room home, engineers a scam on the insurance firm for which she works to get medical coverage (and so chemotherapy) for Soupspoon, and nurses him back to temporary health. This unlikely pair form an alternative sort of household, a "cooperative life style built upon exchange and reciprocity" typical of networks for survival often created by the urban poor (Stack, *All* 125).

Kiki herself is another of the culturally disenfranchised when we meet her. As a child, she was sexually abused by her father, a memory she daily attempts to drown by drinking to excess. On the day she rescues Soupspoon she is recovering from a painful stab wound inflicted when she intervened in a mugging. Soupspoon and Kiki are thus both victims of the violence and lack of compassion that mark life in the modern city, and as Paula W. Woods notes, they share "differently colored yet fundamentally common Southern roots" (12). Mosley has commented on the widespread experience of dispossession that affects people of all races in late-capitalist culture. In the extended essay *Workin' on the Chain Gang,* he explicitly states what he implies with his fictional Soupspoon and Kiki:

> What black people have experienced as a group for centuries many whites now experience as solitary and alienated individuals. In their various groups white Americans might feel that they belong, that there is a group spirit that looks out for them. But individually they suffer the barbs of bureaucratic indifference and the vicissitudes of corporate whims like everyone else. . . .
>
> Every American is a unit of labor. That labor is possessed by an employer. . . . The employer owes the laborer nothing. He may depend on our labor, but the advantage of supply and demand is in his favor, not ours. In a very real way this unites the historical experience of African Americans and the new day dawning on the rest of the nation. (14–15)

Given this fictional world ruled by heartless bureaucracies, riddled with violence, and shadowed by poverty, what hope avails? *RL's Dream* offers two answers to this question: the development of a cultural ethics of care and the transmission of positive social values, illustrated primarily through Robert Johnson and the blues.[1]

In her book *In a Different Voice,* Carol Gilligan posits the existence of two different moral orientations: "justice reasoning," which requires that we treat others fairly, and "care reasoning," which demands that we assist those in need. Soupspoon's lament about the eviction men suggests that he is the product of the latter, and Kiki's extraordinary action of installing Soupspoon in her own home—an action some critics find implausible (Ulin 3)—reflects a similar ethical orientation. Building on Gilligan's work, Carol B. Stack has found that care reasoning is prevalent among African American residents of small southern towns—exactly the environment that produced Soupspoon and influenced Kiki ("Different Voices" 293). Many scholars argue that this community ethics of care stems from an "Afrocentric morality" that emphasizes interdependence, reciprocity, and communal responsibility for those in need. For many black thinkers, past and present, "Identity is not some Cartesian abstraction grounded in a solipsistic self-consciousness. . . . In place of Descartes' 'I think, therefore I am,' we find in this black tradition, 'I am because we are; and since we are, therefore I am.' If individual identity is grounded in social interaction, in the life of the community, then that individual's good life is inseparable from the successful functioning of his or her society" (Hord and Lee 7–8). Seen within this context, Kiki's actions are consistent with her upbringing in a small Arkansas town and the care she received there from an African American woman named Hattie, who ultimately rescued Kiki from her abusive father. Unlike the eviction man who does not know how to respect his elders, Kiki does, and her actions in protecting Soupspoon help her reframe her own identity in a way that eventually saves her life as well as prolonging his.

It is not only through Kiki's ministrations, however, that Soupspoon gets a last chance to live. As Andrea Stuart remarks, he is "brought back to life by [Kiki's] care and his fervent desire to get back to the blues." Soupspoon idolizes the Robert Johnson of his memory. He remembers Johnson as one of the few products of the Delta who could not only transcend the experiences of poverty and violence but, through his music, help others to do the same. Soupspoon recalls that in his Mississippi youth, "'Livin' was bein' a slave. An' all you could really do was lose yo'self in whiskey, women, and the blues. An' when you got tired'a that it was time to die. An' the onliest man I ever met who could face that truth and still be a man was Robert Johnson'" (225). While he does link Johnson's musical power with the demonic—he calls Johnson "Satan's favorite son"—this supernatural energy seems positive to Soupspoon, a way to express a freedom that African Americans in the 1930s South could experience in no other way. And after Johnson's death, Soupspoon's own music was "'just a weak shadow, just like some echo of somethin' that happened a long time ago. They [his listeners] was feelin' somethin', but not what Robert Johnson made us feel in Arcola. They cain't get that naked. . . . Robert Johnson's blues get down to a nerve most people don't even have no more'" (143). Once Kiki helps him back to health and mobility, Soupspoon's primary goal is to play the blues again, to have one more chance to touch people's lives in the way that Robert Johnson did.

Given this portrait of Johnson as Satan's child, a man with musical power to sing himself out of jail (as he does in one of Soupspoon's remembered tales), whose music "'would rip the skin right off yo' back'" (143), Mosley has sometimes been criticized for romanticizing Johnson and the blues in this novel. George Lipsitz complains about Mosley's "nostalgic" portrait of Johnson: "Once again, the blues are deployed as an antidote to the shallowness of contemporary commercial culture, as an art form precious because it is unapproachable and unknowable, locked into the past but superior to anything we can imagine in the present" (*Possessive* 121). David L. Ulin concurs that the novel is flawed by a "romanticism . . . that belies the intention an artist as sophisticated as Robert Johnson must have brought to his music" (8). This tendency to indulge in myths about Satan and about supernatural blues agency is probably what led the Delta Haze Corporation, dedicated to "the preservation and promotion of traditional American blues," to officially castigate *RL's Dream* for its "abundance of factual inaccuracies."

These scholars and reviewers may be overlooking two things. First, the book is a work of fiction, and thus "factual accuracy" is irrelevant. Second, it is Soupspoon and not necessarily Mosley who mythologizes Robert Johnson. Given the detailed descriptions of the socioeconomic and cultural conditions in which the characters live, one might reasonably assume that Mosley is presenting a culturally specific portrait of a man, Soupspoon Wise, who has lived too long in the past and in memory. Indeed, in several scenes of the book it is not simply memories of Robert Johnson that haunt Soupspoon but actual appearances: Soupspoon sees Johnson kissing a girl, drinking, smiling devilishly in the park (an apparition the other characters do not share), and also sitting on his bed smoking a cigarette while Soupspoon dies. Soupspoon has lived his life haunted by his memories of Robert Johnson and paralyzed by his sense of his own inferior skills. It is not until he can bring these memories to light—share them with Mavis, his estranged wife and once Johnson's girlfriend, as well as with Kiki and her friend Randy, who have never heard of Robert Johnson—that Soupspoon can reemerge as a blues artist and have an impact on the community himself. Unburdened of his romantic recollections, Soupspoon is free to create and to enspirit, suggesting that Mosley's Robert Johnson is more a device of characterization that an attempt at a factual representation of the man. He is not a signifier of any "truth" but Soupspoon's.

Preserving what he knows about Johnson and then playing the blues with the passion of a man who knows he's dying (as Johnson did, in Soupspoon's mind) are the two forces that impel Soupspoon's actions after his chemotherapy sessions allow him a few last months of life. Soupspoon feels compelled to tell his stories of Robert Johnson. At first he tries to make contact with others who knew Johnson, but the only other old Delta bluesman he can find in the city is too senile to help him. He then buys a tape recorder so that he can talk his stories into it, but he is frustrated by the solitary experience. Finally he corrals Kiki into listening while he talks and the recorder turns. "'Just listen to me,'" he begs her, in an appeal that Thomas Builds-the-Fire would surely understand. "'I'm a storyteller. Storytellers need somebody wanna hear what they got to tell'" (130). With Kiki's presence, Soupspoon's memories come tumbling out, his call eliciting her response, and at the end of the session Soupspoon is pleased by the personal release he feels and by his sense of transmitting important cultural information. He claims proudly, "'They ain't nuthin' Robert Johnson did worth rememberin' except the way he played guitar and how he made livin' just that much more easy t'bear. You got botha them things now, here today. They got his records t'listen to an' me t'bear witness'" (145). Soupspoon is proud to be a transmitter of cultural history, capturing his memories of Johnson and so potentially creating new lieux de mémoire for Kiki and others.

Mosley also uses Johnson as "a touchstone for the oppressive historical experience of two races, embodying the transformative impulse of the blues" to express pain in an affirmation of hope (Wasserman). Once relieved of his memories, Soupspoon feels driven to play the blues again, to make people feel at least a bit of what Johnson's audiences felt. His first opportunity comes with Kiki and Randy, as the three sit drinking and laughing around Kiki's table one evening. Kiki sings and Randy beats a tin spoon on a jar in accompaniment to Soupspoon's guitar, and, in acknowledgement of the hardships that birthed the blues and that all three had endured, "Soupspoon realized somewhere near midnight that they were playing music. These children weren't even born when he came around but they were playing his music. They were living it, too" (182).

Soupspoon's first public foray back into life as a bluesman comes when he plays at a street fair, and it is here that the blues most dramatically takes on its healing, intergenerational, interracial function. At first, Soupspoon himself is transported to the past, reliving his history mentally as he plays, suggesting that music unites past and present, functioning as a lieu de mémoire in itself. Soupspoon becomes "a spectacle and a witness all in one. . . . He saw the way people walked with music in their step even when they didn't stop to listen. . . . When the music got good, and he closed his eyes to feel it right, he saw the backside of his life—the people who he'd walked with and left behind" (209). He also sees its influence on his listeners, from the cultural memory it encapsulates for African Americans to the reflexive appreciation of white passersby: "Thousands of people passed by, hundreds stopped to listen to the blues. Almost every black man and woman stopped and cocked their ears. They heard something in Soupspoon's notes. Something that people call Africa" (210–11). Yet as old friends stop by and new ones are created, we are told that "Soupspoon's music was for everybody and everything" (211). For critic Christine Levecq, Soupspoon's performance at this street fair offers a clear and optimistic vision of future possibilities, albeit a temporary one. The scene reunites most of the characters of the book, black and white, and "creates a sense of a possible, interracial community brought together by the music. In this movement toward a sense of community not based on race, the novel leaves behind the melancholic depiction of former racial certainties. The community may dissolve when the music stops, but we get a glimpse of a possible future."

Shortly after this street fair, Soupspoon dies, alone and unrecognized by all but Robert Johnson, who sits on the edge of his bed, smoking a cigarette. While this ending is poignant, it is not entirely sad. Soupspoon has fulfilled his dreams: he has recorded his recollections of Robert Johnson, and he has moved people by playing the blues as only a man who knows he's dying can. Despite the novel's critique of systemic cultural apathy toward the disempowered, and despite its depiction of the modern city as unfeeling, violent, and dangerous, *RL's Dream* offers a thin thread of hope. It suggests that with the development of a societal ethics of care, and with individual action based on supporting others through music or through more direct action, our culture may yet recover the "agency, capability and ability of human beings who have been culturally degraded, politically oppressed and economically exploited," just as Cornel West has prophesied ("New Cultural" 34). In this novel Robert Johnson is re-membered—by Soupspoon and perhaps by Mosley—as the piston that can propel us into this brave new world.

The Skin of the Goat

In an essay on African American popular culture, performance artist Coco Fusco relates an Afro-Cuban proverb from the Abakua religion: "Chivo que rompe tambor, con su pellor paga": "the goat who breaks the drum will have to pay with his skin." For Fusco, this proverb has two meanings: not only does a troublemaker pay for his or her actions, but he or she "turns him or herself into the instrument, in order to continue the music" (279). I see this maxim as relevant on several levels to Robert Johnson at the turn of the century. Many of the stories about Johnson suggest that he may have paid for his ambition, or perhaps for his unfettered lifestyle, with his life, a theme that we have seen recapitulated in the Robert Johnson character of *Bone Music* and in Sherman Alexie's Victor Joseph. But Fusco's second interpretation of the saying—that the goat himself becomes the instrument for future music—seems most relevant in the context of this chapter. Each of these writers uses Robert Johnson to continue some tradition related to the blues, whether it be the importance of basing community on common experiences and goals or the concern for preserving culture through memory and oral tradition. They all employ their imagined versions of Robert Johnson to predict a future where the music continues its social functions. He becomes the goat who pays with his skin to perpetuate the musical tradition.

Joseph Roach has described a cultural process that he calls "surrogation," by which "culture reproduces and re-creates itself" using the "three-sided relationship of memory, performance, and substitution" (2). Each of the texts examined in this chapter uses Robert Johnson as the fulcrum on which these three elements pivot and which in turn re-creates our culture. As we have seen repeatedly in chapters 3 and 4, the historical Robert Johnson cannot be contained in these contemporary uses of his image and legend. Roach explains: "Because collective memory works selectively, imaginatively, and often perversely, surrogation rarely if ever succeeds. The process requires many trials and at least as many errors. The fit cannot be exact. The intended substitute either cannot fulfill expectations, creating a deficit, or actually exceeds them, creating a surplus" (2). In this hauntology of Robert Johnson, I have tried to show how the meanings that have accumulated around his image through time have created a host of such surpluses. The thrust of my discussion in this chapter and the preceding one has been to explore these surpluses, to see what value is added when Robert Johnson is imported to new contexts and for new purposes. When he loses his historical self and the historical world that produced him, he reveals some essential concerns of the era that is recirculating his image, reanimating him from the dead, re-membering him.

Specifically, in the texts explored in chapters 3 and 4 Robert Johnson is used to represent two often competing values: individual growth and personal fulfillment, on the one hand, and community survival, on the other hand. This decisive split in what the surrogate is made to signify should not, by this time, surprise us. As we saw in chapter 2, American culture is built on such paradoxes, and contemporary uses of Robert Johnson frequently reveal the fundamental contradictions in our culture. As in *Crossroads* and *Crossroad Blues,* we strive for the American Dream of financial security and personal happiness, but the dream recedes before us. I write at a time when the fulfillment of this dream is available to fewer and fewer Americans. The gap between rich and poor has become enormous, and the recent economic downturn has caused the collapse of hundreds of dot-com dreams. In contrast, the events of 11 September 2001 have reinvigorated (at least temporarily) the American ideal of community service. The confluence of these events suggests, as do *Bone Music, Reservation Blues,* and *RL's Dream,* that our individual prosperity depends in great measure on building coalitions around issues of social justice and social change. Yet the individual dream of *Crossroads* and *Crossroad Blues* lingers. In the five works discussed in this Robert Johnson hauntology, Johnson serves as a lieu de mémoire for our entire culture, made to stand for the individual goals we desperately cling to and also for the community presence demanded of us if the cultural politics of difference is to become a permanent condition.

5
Virtual Robert Johnson

Earlier in this book, I remarked that no one had yet seen Robert Johnson impersonators hanging around blues clubs. As it turns out, I was wrong. There *is* a Robert Johnson impersonator, a musician named Rocky Lawrence who allegedly worked fifteen hours a day for three years while he "learned and relearned every note, every tuning, every vocal inflection of [Robert Johnson's] fabled 29 songs." After this period of study, Lawrence "emerged with the songs and soul of Robert Johnson." I know this now because I found his home page on the Internet.

It should come as no surprise, given the preceding chapters, that Robert Johnson, in various guises, is a notable Internet presence. At the end of chapter 1, I proposed Robert Johnson as an exemplary representative of postmodern culture, given his chameleon-like personality, the bricolage techniques of his music, and the myriad uses of his image that reflect contemporary cultural segmentations. The Internet shares many of those same qualities. In the words of media theorist David Tetzlaff, "The Web is a mass medium for a fragmented postmodern culture—a mass medium without an actual mass, at least in the sense that millions watch the same TV show at the same time. . . . There's a mass of people online at any time, but they're all off in their own special little corner, the total audience scattered across the multiple nodes of the Web" (102). Since the Internet is thus a powerful mirror for contemporary culture in general—a culture that S. Paige Baty has called a network of "competing discourses" (10)—it is an ideal place for the inevitably manifold representations of Robert Johnson to appear. Visible in places that offer everything from encyclopedic facts to interpretive essays, merchandise sales to promotional materials, and the services of at least one impersonator, Robert Johnson is alive and well in cyberspace.

In this chapter I explore several different virtual Robert Johnsons. First I will examine uses of his image, legend, and music on the Internet. Then I will turn to a different mass medium, film, to analyze another virtual Robert Johnson, one created by an excited group of scholars and fans who mistakenly thought that an anonymous musician captured on silent film was Robert Johnson. In both cases, we will see how "readers" of Robert Johnson project themselves onto the image at hand. These explorations will yield a number of related results: we will see how online community is formed, how identity is constructed in a world permeated by the Internet and other mass media, and how Robert Johnson the icon has ultimately become completely severed from Robert Johnson the musician.

R.J. in the Information Age

Serious study of Internet dynamics—what is sometimes called "cyberculture"—began around 1990 and still tends to revolve around a few recurring topics.[1] Some cyberculture scholars focus on the primary uses of the Internet, such as information sharing and commerce. Others study Internet "community" formation, debating whether or not cyberculture offers real community as we know it offline. Some examine identity construction on the Internet, where users can log on as anyone or anything they wish, while others explore how the presence of links and hypertext may be changing the way we read and know.

The most obvious and probably the most widespread use of the Internet is as a source of information. Whether we seek directions to a blues festival or a new approach to teaching *The Sound and the Fury,* those of us with online access usually turn first to the Internet. Not surprisingly, the Internet offers information on almost any aspect of Robert Johnson's life and music that a fan could want.[2] Those looking for basic biographical and historical information about Johnson, such as that found offline in an encyclopedia, have a host of sites to choose from, including About.com's entry on the Blues; Music Central—"music from/for the road"; BluesNet, the self-proclaimed "longest-running blues site on the Web"; the All Music Guide to the Blues; the FolkLib Index; the Rock and Roll Hall of Fame site; and HitsQuick—"a fast, comprehensive music site for the rest of us." One can find information on how to play Johnson's music at "Playing Robert Johnson's Songs," at Blues Lyrics On Line, and (sometimes) at OLGA, an online archive of guitar tablature that occasionally breaks down over copyright challenges. Those seeking the chance to participate in discussions of Johnson's life and music can drop into the Blue Flame Cafe, an "interactive biographical encyclopedia of the blues," or join the discussion forums on the Blue Highway (such as "Muddy's Cabin," a chat room). One can read online blues fanzines, such as Mudcat Cafe, "a magazine dedicated to blues and folk music," or the Blues

Enquirer, where I discovered an astrologer's explanation of the celestial forces at work in Robert Johnson's death. And in addition to bulletin boards like the Blues Board and Blueschat, the venerable Blues-L discussion list, hosted at Brown University, often features conversations about Robert Johnson in its recent postings and in its extensive, searchable archives. For late-breaking R.J. news—such as stories about his latest "true" grave site or about the Claud Johnson legacy law suit—these online discussion lists and chat rooms provide the quickest access to information and debate, provided by sources in the know and opinionated fans alike.

Other sites focus more narrowly on Robert Johnson himself rather than broadly on the blues. The Delta Haze Corporation's Web site, "devoted to providing information about Robert Johnson," bills itself as the "official" Robert Johnson Web site. Not only does it offer extensive biographical and historical information (including an often updated version of Stephen C. LaVere's liner notes for the 1990 CD boxed set), it provides application forms for those hoping to reprint one of the two known photographs of Johnson or to copy his lyrics and music. Sometimes individual fans also sponsor Robert Johnson sites, although these hosts tend to come and go and often have specific agendas. One site, for example, identifies itself as the "Crossroads Curse" site. In addition to recounting the legend of Johnson's deal with the devil, the site offers links to other musicians (Eric Clapton, the Allman Brothers, Lynyrd Skynyrd) who recorded versions of Johnson's "Cross Road Blues" and, according to the Web site, suffered some variant of the crossroads curse themselves.

As we saw in chapter 1, Robert Johnson is the subject of much learned discourse as well as myth, so various academic studies of Robert Johnson are, naturally, available on the Internet. Some of these provide scholarly analyses of Johnson's music, such as Joseph L. Monzo's microtonal analysis of Johnson's "Drunken Hearted Man" or Mike Daley's discussion of timbre and style in Johnson's singing. Those interested in gender issues can read Potent.com's "Constructions of Masculinity in the Music of Robert Johnson." Other sites take a pedagogical cast and provide information on using Robert Johnson in the college classroom. The most celebrated and long-lived of these is *The Robert Johnson Notebooks,* the record of a 1997 University of Virginia English course that focused on analyzing Johnson's lyrics as poetry. According to the students who designed the Web site, the teacher, Victor Cabas, created his Mississippi in Story and Songs class "as an excuse to teach Robert Johnson" and discovered that the class's papers on Johnson, written after a period of immersion in the songs and some training in lyric analysis, "[were] often the best that he [got] for the entire session." In addition to the student papers posted there, the site offers information on Johnson's life and legend, a teaching plan, a chart to facilitate verse analysis, a glossary of poetic terms, and information on citation formats. While other teaching sources tend to be less ambitious single pages rather than comprehensive sites, several, such as the Hypermedia Projects for Musicological Research and Education (at Berkeley) do feature Johnson prominently, and at least one other, posted by Catherine Lavender for an honors history class at the City University of New York–Staten Island, offers intriguing research and discussion questions about Robert Johnson's lyrics and his place in blues history.

In addition to sites offering information or discussion, many others are designed to promote Johnson-related projects or to sell Johnson-related merchandise. Some hawk basic fan items, like T-shirts, posters, sheet music, books, and CDs. Others advertise films about Johnson, including *Can't You Hear the Wind Howl?* and *Crossroads.* There are even government-sponsored sites promoting Robert Johnson–related tourist information, such as the Trail of the Hellhound Web site, maintained by the National Park Service, which provides information on blues-related locations throughout Mississippi.

By now you are probably asking, "But what does all this tell me about Robert Johnson?" The answer is, not much, at least not much that we can't learn just as well from print sources and interviews. A better question to ask, and one similar to the one I have asked throughout this book, is, "What does this glut of information about Robert Johnson reveal about turn-of-the-century culture?" Just as the texts discussed in the preceding chapters reflect our current values and assumptions, so Robert Johnson's appearances on the Internet can tell us a host of things about today's burgeoning cyberculture as well as about the broader culture that engendered it.

Cyberpower

In his provocative book on power relations on the Internet, British sociologist Tim Jordan describes "cyberpower" as "flow[ing] around the three connected principles of identity fluidity, renovated hierarchies and informational spaces" (87). I will discuss identity fluidity in a later section of this chapter; first I will take up the ideas of power hierarchies and information exchange as illustrated by Robert Johnson's appearances on the Internet.

The first and most obvious conclusion one could draw from my catalog of Robert Johnson–related sites is that the Internet is an excellent source of data. A student assigned to give an oral presentation on Robert Johnson could find everything he or she needed there: biography, pictures, music, lyrics, historical background, and connections to other musicians. Because the knowledge of so many is shared so widely on the Internet, many scholars see it as promoting positive change in our culture. Psychologists Gary Shank and Donald Cunningham, for instance, observe that the Internet allows people to have instantaneous access to each other's expertise, permitting nontraditional syntheses of information and ideas (37–38). Furthermore, since decision making is no longer restricted by time and space, the Internet may begin to undermine conventional social hierarchies (Jordan 81). Anyone with a health care question, for example, knows of the wealth of expert information and advice available on the Internet. Such information, easily accessed at one's leisure, can greatly assist a patient in choosing a course of treatment that differs from a doctor's perhaps more traditional advice. In short, optimistic cybercritics see the Internet as leveling the playing field so that nonexperts can compete.

This vision has merit, of course, provided that one has access to the Internet in the first place. It may seem obvious to note that not everyone has Internet access, but the extent of the limitations and the ramifications of those limitations are profound. Taking a global perspective, Ziauddin Sardar sees Internet access as a luxury, available to very few people in the world. After estimating the costs of hardware, software, repeated necessary upgrades, connection to an Internet provider, and telephone bills, Sardar notes, "One can feed a family of four in Bangladesh for a whole year for that sort of money" (739). In the United States, households with incomes over seventy-five thousand dollars are most likely to be hooked up, and in the Third World only the very wealthy can afford an Internet connection. For Sardar, "that leaves most of humanity at the mercy of real reality" (739). Even in the United States, "cyberspace is expensive space. True believers who tout the Internet as democracy actualized, as an electronic town hall meeting, live with class blinders in a muddle of self-delusion. One might as well call suburban country clubs models of classless integration" (Lockard 220). These analyses give one pause in praising the ready availability of Robert Johnson information on the Internet. Surely someone living today in conditions of poverty similar to those Robert Johnson endured would never see that information. He or she would get to touch a computer only in a library or a school—if he or she had a library card or a school affiliation, and only if his or her library or school were equipped with computers and offered Internet services. Rather than undermining social hierarchies, as Jordan suggests, the Internet may simply magnify them.

The issue of Internet access is further complicated in that the flow of information runs both ways. This means that those who can *read* the Internet are also the ones who can *write* the Internet—who can send email, post messages on bulletin boards, create home pages, participate in chat rooms, design Web sites, and disseminate information. As we saw earlier in this book, creating discourse is a way of exercising power; it always reflects the social conditions of its production (Fiske, *Power Plays* 15). In the case of Robert Johnson on the Internet, we see many examples of this principle at work. Who constructs Robert Johnson Web sites? By and large they are the same class of people who write books and articles about him: researchers with media access, usually white, usually male, and usually well educated. True, the Internet does allow more participation by more kinds of people: there are Robert Johnson Web pages designed by high school and college students as well as by simple fans—people who would not have access to media distribution without the Internet. But one wonders what Robert Johnson on the Internet would look like if the Internet really were universally accessible, the movement of information as uninhibited as some idealists like to imagine. What other kinds of information would be available? Would we have more anecdotes from his family members and other people who knew him? More photographs? More documents? As S. Paige Baty reminds us, such "mass mediated rememberings" reflect who in a culture knows things, how they know them, and how they wield power through that knowledge (19).

One way to wield power is to have money, so it is not surprising that numerous Johnson Web sites are designed for the sole purpose of selling paraphernalia related to him and his music. As a random exercise, on 10 July 2002 I used the Vivisimo search engine to look for "Robert+Johnson+blues." Vivisimo is useful because it clusters hits by category, in this case under such topics as lyrics, reviews and albums, profile, and merchandise. The search engine found 140 references to Robert Johnson. Of the first hundred, thirty-one were not related to the Delta Johnson and another thirteen were duplicate listings, leaving sixty-six discrete sites. Thirty-eight of those sites—over half—had something to sell, either directly (such as artists marketing their prints) or through links to book and CD distribution centers like Amazon.com. This marketing function of the Internet, like access to information, is simply a reflection of our society, not a reordering of it (Slevin 67). What it shows is that over half of those with Internet capability and interest in Robert Johnson see selling his image as a fundamental part of spreading his fame. Culture is a commodity, and those with the power of the Internet at hand have the best opportunities for sales and consumption. In Sardar's trenchant analysis, cyberspace offers an amoral arena for colonization, capitalism, and the commodification of minority cultures—what he calls "the 'American Dream' writ large" (735).

Robert Johnson on the Cybercommons

Another facet of the American Dream is the ideal of community. Starting with John Winthrop's famous 1630 sermon encouraging Puritan settlers to work together to form "a city upon a hill," Americans continually reiterate, in words if not in deeds, the national goal of "entertain[ing] each other in brotherly affection." Yet as we saw in chapter 2, this goal of human interdependence exists in perpetual tension with our other national characteristic of unfettered individuality. Many commentators see the goal of true community growing ever more impossible in postmodern culture, with its fragmented audiences, shifting coalitions, increasingly transient and diverse population, and myriad time pressures. Some, notably Howard Rheingold, lament this loss of "a sense of a social commons" in contemporary life and suggest that the Internet can replace it, providing "access to a tool that could bring conviviality and understanding into our lives and might help revitalise the public sphere" (5). The example of Philcat, a member of an early cyberspace community called WELL, illustrates this point. When his young son was diagnosed with leukemia, Philcat received an outpouring of medical information and emotional support from his fellow list members that lasted throughout his son's treatment. For cybercritic Tim Jordan, this is exactly how an offline neighborhood or professional community would respond. He observes: "The moral of Philcat is that people do not communicate with computers but use computers to communicate with each other. And, in doing so, genuine, heartfelt communities may be built" (57).

Many cybercritics disagree with this positive view of online community, sometimes labeling it "utopian." For some, even the desire to experience such community is mere nostalgia, a desire to return to an orderly, 1950s-style world that never truly existed (Willson 644).[3] Others question whether online community is really equivalent to the personal interaction we experience offline, in "real life." Joseph Lockard thinks that Internet communities are limited to one function: communication. He argues that Internet space addresses "a desire for community rather than the difficult-to-achieve, sweated-over reality of community" and that "[t]o accept only communication in place of a community's manifold functions is to sell our common faith in community vastly short" (225). Some critics go so far as to claim that membership in cybercommunities can have deleterious effects on other relationships, claiming that individuals who spend a great deal of time in virtual reality tend to isolate themselves from offline social reality (Willson 644–45).

Yet Robert Johnson's appearances in cyberspace suggest that online groups of individuals with a shared interest do fulfill some of the traditional functions of a community. My experience with T. Coraghessan Boyle's Web site provides an excellent case in point. As part of my research for my discussion of Boyle's story "Stones in My Passway, Hellhounds on My Trail," I went to the site. There I found not only biographical information and descriptions of Boyle's works but also a message board where readers can ask questions and discuss issues pertaining to his books and where Boyle himself frequently posts answers to readers' queries. On 3 May 2001, I posted a question for Boyle, asking if his choice to depict Robert Johnson in historical context was an attempt to overturn myth. Boyle graciously answered me on 6 May. Shortly thereafter the thread took on a life of its own, as Robert Johnson fans who also happen to be T. C. Boyle fans began offering information and engaging in debate, none of it having much to do with my original question to Boyle. Several blues fans assumed I wanted to know more about Johnson and jumped in with sources of information. Another took the opportunity to ask if anyone had seen the recent film *Chocolat* and wondered if it were true that a new Robert Johnson song was included in the score. This led to a conversation about the Tommy Johnson character in the also recently released *O Brother, Where Art Thou?* including discussion of whether or not the character was really based on Robert Johnson as well as reviews of the film's musical score. Finally, one participant directed me to an earlier discussion of Boyle's "Stones in My Passway." That thread offered one reader's summary of Johnson's life and death, followed by a series of posts on Johnson's music and blues history in general.

My brief foray into the world of Internet bulletin boards illustrates several things about both Robert Johnson and online community. First, it shows that even on the bulletin board of a contemporary writer, whose fourteen hefty tomes of fiction contain one ten-page story about Robert Johnson, Robert Johnson fans abound. He shows up in all sorts of unlikely places, a testament to his fame and to the way the Internet enlarges the culture of celebrity—even on a Web site devoted to somebody else.[4]

Second, we learn that Robert Johnson fans are quite helpful, eager to provide information to a perceived novice and to share each other's interests. My experience there supports Rheingold's assertion that the Internet is "a tool that could bring conviviality and understanding into our lives" (5) and suggests that Winthrop's ideals are being enacted in some Internet locations. Third, it reveals the diversity of interests of people who are also fans of Robert Johnson, as popular films, blues history, other kinds of music, and interest in Boyle's fiction all provided avenues into the discussion. The T. C. Boyle message board thus presents one unlikely node where the network of competing discourses about Robert Johnson folds over on itself, forming a temporary coalition of fans in a space reserved for discussion of an entirely different topic. Finally, and perhaps most importantly, my experience indicates that for many participants in such online forums, any difference between online and offline community is wholly in the mind of the perceiver. As Nessim Watson has argued, "The distinction between 'virtual' community and 'real' community is unwarranted. . . . My experience has been that people in the offline world tend to see online communities as virtual, but that participants in the online communities see them as quite real" (129).

This last point—that online community may be quite similar to offline community—is recapitulated daily on interactive Web sites. This likeness is not surprising, since online interactions are never wholly separable from the offline contexts within which participants sit down at their computers to use the Internet (Kendall 58). The time people spend at the computer does not erase the time they spend negotiating daily stresses and power inequities, all of which they inevitably carry with them into cyberspace. Furthermore, Internet sites are created and used by people who seek interaction with individuals who share their interests—who seek at least temporary "community." These points can be well illustrated by a brief look at the Blues-L discussion list. Blues-L is a mail list "devoted to the discussion of the Blues in all of its forms—from predecessors of blues music to contemporary performers" (Blues-L FAQ). Hosted at Brown University, where its founder, Jack Haller, started it in April 1993, the list boasts over 750 subscribers from all over the world. I confess to being a member for many years now. However, since list members typically receive eighty to one hundred messages a day, I prefer to read the threads only in weekly digest form, and I rarely post a message. This information will matter to some scholars of cyberculture, who object to critique from "lurkers" who do not participate in the discussions. I see their reaction to lurkers as further evidence that online communities do indeed function in ways similar to communities throughout human history, as members try to protect their group from the perceived threat of a potentially critical outsider.

In May 2002 I spent several days searching through Blues-L's archives from 1999 through May 2002 and reading all messages that mention Robert Johnson. What I found there reinforced my suspicion that members of online communities behave in many of the same ways as their offline counterparts. First I noted the subject matter of the various Johnson-related threads: his music, his recordings, his influence, his contested biography, reviews of books and films about him, the perennial debate over Stephen LaVere's right to the published songs and photos, and discussion of recent events, such as the lawsuit brought by Claud Johnson. As we saw in chapter 1, these are the same issues that Robert Johnson fans have been discussing for decades in print sources. Next I looked at the nature of the interactions within any given discussion thread. Some participants, like my fellow participants on the T. C. Boyle message board, were eager to share information and to learn new facts about Johnson. One of them, a college student (I surmise from his email address), introduced himself excitedly to the group in January 1999 and directed them to his Robert Johnson Web page, of which he was quite proud. When I searched for the page in 2002 it had disappeared into cyberspace, a fate not uncommon to individual Web pages but also not uncommon among college students, who graduate and form new communities not based on campus affiliation.

Most interesting to me, however, were the occasional disputes between list members and the way they were resolved. Blues-L is an unmoderated list, but it is managed by a group of volunteer subscribers (all male, as far as I could tell) known as "list moms." It also has specific rules of etiquette, including one that all postings be blues-related, and others prohibiting merchandise sales and personal attacks. Their FAQ page states: "As with any good, high-volume list or newsgroup, Blues-L has its share of unsolvable and continually recurring controversies. Unfortunately, the discussion of these topics typically leads to flame wars, name calling, personal attacks, and, in general, messages sent to Blues-L that stray far from the topic of the Blues. The most controversial topics have something to do with white/black issues." My days spent browsing posts about Robert Johnson verified this analysis and also confirmed my opinion that online communities and hierarchies recapitulate those offline.

Let me describe a case in point, a discussion thread that continued over a three-week period in May 2000 about an article published in the April/May 2000 issue of *Living Blues*.[5] The article, written by Tom Freeland (a regular contributor to and manager of the Blues-L list as well as a *Living Blues* writer), focuses on the hearings about Claud Johnson's paternity and his possible entitlement to the Robert Johnson estate. In addition to summarizing court testimony, Freeland provides a synopsis of what was known about Robert Johnson and offers information newly available from the trial transcripts. One regular contributor to the list, who used the nickname "Ocky Milkman" (a character in a Dylan Thomas play) and an email address of "Boris Batanov" (another obvious pseudonym, as Rocky and Bullwinkle fans will recognize), wrote a detailed critique of Freeland's article. While "Ocky," as the other list members called him, made some unkind reflections on Freeland's writing style and organizational framework, he also offered thoughtful commentary on what the article tells us about contemporary culture. Ocky pointed out that Johnson's life history illustrated the loose formation of family structure among African Americans in early twentieth-century Mississippi, which he identified as the lingering legacy of slavery. He also complained that while the story mentions in passing the young Robert Johnson's making a one-stringed diddley bow, elsewhere in the magazine one was offered for sale for $285, an example of "the exploitation and marketing of anything pertinent to . . . rj" (Milkman). Finally, he lamented the cult of celebrity that has attached to Johnson. When another list member, defending Freeland's writing style, noted that Freeland's story had been based on trial witnesses who were "remote and impersonal," Ocky replied (on 11 May) with another incisive cultural analysis. He noted the "culture clash" between the criminal justice system and the black Mississippi residents being interviewed; while he didn't mention the power-bloc and the people, he could have. He also complained about *Living Blues*'s lack of "journalistic integrity" in not disclosing Freeland's status as a lawyer (and thus presumably an insider to the events he describes). His post ended by lamenting that "the white media establishment's" excessive attention to Robert Johnson has overshadowed the contributions of other early blues musicians.

Thus far, I found the discussion fascinating, even though I had read the Freeland piece in question and found it clear and informative. While the analysis of Freeland's article in a space frequented by Freeland himself embarrassed some list members, the issues that Ocky brought up were important ones to any race-conscious individual. Given his double pseudonyms, I do not know anything about Ocky's racial background, and I refer to the persona as "he" simply because his fellow list members did. But Ocky patently intended to project an African American persona by means of his repeated, trenchant analyses of the function of race in everyday interactions, which often goes unrecognized by white people; through his signature file, which included this quotation: "'God made a mistake when he gave the white man a guitar'—Martin Mull, picking up his guitar"; and through his informational postings, such as a link to "Black Radio Stations" around the country (20 April 1999).

The Blues-L FAQ sheet was right in claiming that racial issues cause the most problems in the discussion list—as they often do offline—and the story of Ocky's critique took several sharp turns away from the blues, just as the list hosts feared and predicted. Tom Freeland himself replied to the list on 11 May to challenge Ocky's contention that *Living Blues* should have identified him as a lawyer. Freeland explained that he had been working as a journalist when he covered the story and had no inside information. He ended his post with this pointed comment about the doubly pseudonymous Ocky: "Ocky, of course, has a unique perspective on what one must ethically reveal about oneself in order for one's comment to be viewed as legitimate" (Freeland, "Re: *Living Blues*").

While Ocky Milkman and Tom Freeland had so far remained relatively civil, the discussion took an ugly turn when someone named Steve posted an insulting, off-color slur about Ocky's sexuality and appearance, about which he presumably had no knowledge. Ocky, now apparently enraged, responded in kind, ending his equally offensive response to Steve with a plea: "list mom, you there?" Enter the peacemakers. First a list member named Cookie chimed in to agree with some of Ocky's points, noting that he had a history of being abused on the list. On 13 May Cookie wrote, "He was only stating 'his' opinion. You may not like it or agree with it, and that is fine, but he, like the rest of us, has that right. And he does take a lot of flack for his personal opinions." Apparently (and my subsequent archival search confirmed this), Ocky's attempts to keep race at the center of blues-related discussions had caused dissension on Blues-L before. Another list member named John attempted to calm the debate in a different way, by reviewing the good points Ocky had made and turning discussion away from the personal and back to the merits of Freeland's article. Both failed, however, as abuse flew to and from Ocky, accompanied by more pleas for mom's intervention. I don't know whether mom ever contacted any of the parties individually, but if he did, he left no tracks on the discussion board. Instead, the sensible voices of Cookie and John were heard more often, and finally a discussion of independent thinking as well as a metadiscourse—a discussion of discussion tactics—ended the thread, which disappeared by the fifth week of May.

Does any part of this scenario sound familiar? The discussion begins with a thoughtful, if challenging, critique, with race at the center. Counterarguments are heard, the day wanes late, tempers flare, and insults (veiled and otherwise) are exchanged. Cooler heads intervene and attempt to reconcile both the parties and the ideas, until eventually the group veers completely off the track of the initial project, bogged down in procedural debate. I have sat through many committee meetings within my campus community that followed this pattern exactly, especially when a racially charged issue—such as whether to require a "diversity" course in the core curriculum—was under discussion.

The point with which I began this discussion—Kendall's claim that online relationships and group dynamics are not separable from their offline social and political contexts—is demonstrated in this discussion thread about Robert Johnson's legacy. As Kendall further notes, "Participants come to on-line forums from different positions of power within society, which affects both their own actions on-line and their interpretations of others' actions" (71). It really doesn't matter if Ocky Milkman is male and African American, two roles he consciously performed on the Blues-L discussion list in May 2000. Ocky chose to make race a central issue in discussing Robert Johnson, as it certainly is if one examines, as Ocky did, the power inequities between the black court witnesses and the U.S. justice system, between black musicians and white reviewers, or the persistent impact of slavery on contemporary African American culture. Whether these observations provoke overt hostility or a desire to squelch controversy to preserve community peace, they are always difficult to deal with, as we saw in the contested biography of Robert Johnson and in the controversies over the postage stamp. In fact, this online discussion corresponds precisely to the decades-long debate (in *Living Blues* and elsewhere) over the role of race in determining who has the right to be called a "bluesman" or "blueswoman."

My analysis thus far has shown that the Internet is a space where real community can form and prosper; it also shows that online communities are not much different from offline ones. The same tensions exist in both realms, with hierarchies of race and gender (however these attributes may be constituted online) providing a significant context for interaction. Instead of embodying the impossible dream of "a color-blind space with equality for all" (Herman and Sloop 85), the Internet may simply be masking the problems in a world where, as various scholars have shown, participants are assumed to be white and male unless specifically identified otherwise (Kendall 66–67; Silver 29–30). That real-world problems invade online communities does not make them any less communities, but they are not utopian communities. They are products of the offline institutions that promote and develop them as well as the offline concerns of the participants. It is in this context of social and political realities that we must assess their value (Robins 79).

But Ocky Milkman's carefully guarded real identity brings us back to Tim Jordan's point about the three circulating principles of cyberpower being "identity fluidity, renovated hierarchies and informational spaces" (87). I have already discussed information and hierarchies, but the issue of identity fluidity—the idea that on the Internet people can present themselves as anyone they choose—needs further examination in conjunction with a virtual Robert Johnson.

The Flexible Self

Who is Ocky Milkman, really? I don't know anything about his offline life, but the identity he performed on Blues-L in 2000 was very specific. His wide-ranging knowledge of many types of music marked him as a extremely avid fan, if not a musician or musicologist; his impressive vocabulary and well-written postings bespoke a high level of education; his unflagging attention to racial inequities and subtexts suggested African American ancestry; and his vitriolic outbursts, which twice led to his suspension from the list before he finally quit on 22 August 2000, reveal either barely suppressed rage or devout libertarianism, or both. His final posting offered a descriptive menu of the list's regular contributors with a pithy, usually unflattering phrase attached to each name. The last item on his list: "Ocky Milkman. doesn't even exist (poof)." Self-constructed personae online (unlike the offline variety) can be abandoned or re-created at will; cybersuicide may simply provide the clearest path to a fresh start.

Many commentators see this flexibility of identity as one of the glories of the Internet. The most obvious example this ability appears in the icons chosen by players in interactive fantasy worlds like MUDs and MOOs; in many of them I could present myself as, say, Lara Croft or a dragon. But even on serious discussion lists like Blues-L, where concealing one's offline identity is not a goal for most participants, individuals nonetheless construct personae for themselves—as expert, as peacemaker, as gadfly, for example—all guises that may be unrelated to the roles they perform offline. Sherry Turkle, a prominent scholar in the discussion of online identity creation, enthuses about the possibilities this fluidity presents. For Turkle, Internet identity play can help prepare participants to negotiate an increasingly multivalent offline world. She writes that online experiences "admit multiplicity and flexibility. They acknowledge the constructed nature of reality, self, and other. . . . [They suggest] the value of approaching one's 'story' in several ways and with fluid access to one's different aspects." In her view, the Internet allows us to transform ourselves, to test possibilities, "to develop models of psychological well-being that are in a meaningful sense postmodern" (263).

The construction of Web pages is another way that the Internet allows us to create a flexible identity. The home page differs from a text resume in that it fully reveals its constructedness—and therefore its mutability—in multiple ways. Rob Shields notes that a Web page is not a discrete entity but accumulates meaning from other elements accessed through links and from the reader's actions in choosing which links (if any) to follow (150–51). For Shields, a Web page identity is thus relational and dialogic, its meaning dependent in large part on the external doors it offers and on the readers' selection of thresholds to cross. The idea that a reader supplies part of the meaning of a text will not come as news to any student of contemporary literary theory. But in the case of home pages, it seems that a new concept of identity itself is being conceived. Mark Poster has argued convincingly that the Internet, as a fundamental component of postmodern society, collaborates with culture at large to "constitute subjects as unstable, multiple and diffuse" (612). Poster predicts that this process will accelerate as traffic on the information highway increases. He concludes that identity construction in the computer age "occurs through the mechanism of interactivity" (618–19).

These twin themes—that the Internet emphasizes the constructedness of identity and that readers participate in this construction—correlate to Robert Johnson himself as well as to contemporary uses of his image. First, one can look at some elements of his biography (at least as we know it) and see further evidence of the point I made in chapter 1: Robert Johnson prefigured postmodernism. If it is true, as scholars like Obrecht, McCormick, and Wardlow allege, that Johnson tried on various surnames throughout his life, then we can see Robert Johnson himself in the very act of identity construction that I have described throughout this section, developing avatars as the need arose. His vaunted ability to play whatever kind of music the audience wanted to hear, from "My Blue Heaven" to his own harrowing blues songs, attests to his ability to "link" himself to various musical contexts, as his "readers" required. His musical creations, those masterpieces of bricolage assembled from bits and pieces of what he heard and what he imagined, offer an analog to personal home pages which, as Daniel Chandler has observed, include preexisting elements, allusions, adaptations, and borrowings. Perhaps our current fascination with Johnson stems in part from his ability to maneuver so nimbly through challenging times. His transient lifestyle and changeable character—"'Close to a split personality,'" according to his running mate Johnny Shines (qtd. in Welding 103)—may seem an emblem for Internet users today. He thus exemplifies the lives (online and off) that many people now lead, with multiple roles, changing locations, and impermanent relationships, all forged in a world of unstable connections and disappearing links.

Second and more important is the concept that *readers* of a home page partially create the identity of the page owner. In addition to following links, a reader can filter, peck, impose, transgress, and fragment. These activities, all made possible by the computer, do not lead to archivable "hard facts" or to "consistent results" but to variable constructions by diverse readers (Sosnoski 136). The identity presented on a Web page is thus partly the projection of each individual reader. This process is exactly what I have described throughout this book regarding readers of Robert Johnson. As different individuals and different constituencies interpret what they read about Robert Johnson and fill in the gaps in his story, they project their own experiences and expectations onto him. For romantic 1960s musicians and fans, Johnson was the wandering troubadour of myth, the touchstone of musical authenticity; for researchers and folklorists, he was an elusive source of material, hard to track down; for the promoter, he was a potential source of revenue. His identity as a cultural icon at the turn of the twenty-first century has, in short, been largely created by everyone who has ever looked at it. He has become a creature composed by a multitude, each reader/creator pursuing different links and attending to different facets of what the man left behind. Robert Johnson is thus the perfect embodiment of Internet culture, where people can shift identities, participate in communities not bounded by space, and construct others as they imagine them to be.

And so, with this discussion of Robert Johnson on the Internet, my analysis of contemporary uses of Robert Johnson has come full circle, back to the vision presented in chapter 1 of Robert Johnson as the unlikely representative of postmodernity. In the next section I will introduce a new virtual Robert Johnson, one who will take this examination one final step further. We will see Robert Johnson the man, who became a sign, and whose sign became a myth, now displaced completely by Robert Johnson the symbol.

Projected Robert Johnson

In April 1998, at the Delta Studies Symposium held annually in Jonesboro, Arkansas, a startling announcement was made: a short (maybe five-second) film clip of Robert Johnson had been found. As a participant at that symposium, I could feel the electricity in the room as the assembled scholars imagined seeing the living, playing Robert Johnson, whose image had heretofore been circulated only in two published photographs.[6] According to Leo Schumaker, a California disc jockey who had seen the film clip, an anonymous Greenville movie theater owner had found some old reels of film in the theater's attic, 1930s footage of musicians who had been hired to perform outside the theater to attract customers. One young man looked remarkably like Robert Johnson: hat slanted over one eye, exceptionally long and agile fingers, and to the astonished delight of the audience (who sensed the emergence of a new fact about Robert Johnson), he wore a harmonica rack around his neck. We were disappointed that the clip was not available for viewing—evidently the as-yet-unidentified theater owner was guarding it jealously—but according to Schumaker, the owner claimed that Robert Lockwood Jr. and Honeyboy Edwards had recognized the musician as Robert Johnson. Furthermore, although Schumaker had turned down an offer to buy the clip, it had so excited the interest of several British rock stars that they had flown to Mississippi to see it. Adding to the buzz, respected blues historian David Evans was in the room, and he had seen stills from the film. Noting that he had at first been skeptical about the musician's identity, Evans explained that he was now almost convinced by this cinematic ghost because of the white rim on his guitar (similar to that in Johnson's photo-booth picture), because of his clothing, and most of all because of his remarkably long fingers. Evans had observed in detail the musician's left-hand technique and saw therein a possible explanation for some of the complexities of Johnson's music. In the following issue of *Living Blues,* Evans was quoted as saying, "'Nothing is inconsistent with what we know of Johnson'" (qtd. in Cheseborough, "Robert Johnson").

In the months following the symposium, controversy swirled around the film clip, around who really owned it, where it was shot, who believed it was Robert Johnson and why, what it might tell us about Johnson's musical techniques, who wanted to purchase the film, and for how much. We now know that the musician on the film clip is definitely not Robert Johnson (see figure 3). But the energy expended on defending, explicating, and finally defusing this false alarm tells us much about the Robert

Figure 3. Still figure from *Black Hometown Movie:* This is not Robert Johnson!

Johnson industry at the turn of the century, in which Robert Johnson himself is a completely absent presence, apparently no longer needed to fuel the R.J. machinery.

Throughout the middle months of 1998, however, before the truth was known, many well-regarded scholars continued the debate, and *Living Blues* magazine, along with *Blues Access* and *Guitar One,* continued to publish articles and letters about it. David Evans wrote a long letter for *Living Blues* no. 141 (Sept./Oct. 1998) in response to Steve Cheseborough's first report in *Living Blues* no. 140 (July/Aug. 1998). Since Cheseborough had quoted him in the first piece, Evans wanted to clarify his position. First, with his trademark caution, Evans urged readers to withhold their speculation about the identity of the filmed musician until they could see the clip for themselves. He also explained that he had seen only a very small still photograph and not the whole clip. He summed up his position this way: "On the basis of what I've seen, and I reserve the right to change my opinion later, I think there is a strong likelihood that the musician in the footage is indeed Robert Johnson."

It wasn't long after that letter appeared, however, that the film was discredited as a Robert Johnson artifact. Musician Hawkeye Herman recalls hearing "via the grapevine" that "the person in the film clip was definitely not RJ" as early as May 1998, while he was in Memphis for the Handy Awards ("Re: Question"). Scholarly notice took a bit longer, and it was not until September 1998, during the week-long ceremonies to celebrate Robert Johnson's induction into the Rock and Roll Hall of Fame in Cleveland, Ohio, that the truth was finally made public. At a showing of the film on a large screen, it was noticed that the musician was performing in front of a poster for a movie released in 1941, three years after Robert Johnson's death. Whoever he was, he was clearly not Robert Johnson. One might suppose that this definite proof would end the conversation, but not so. Evidently even things that *might have been* Robert Johnson now leave an afterglow.

First there was some scholarly backtracking. Evans, who from the start had been no more than cautiously optimistic about the film, explained why he had fallen for the hoax. Focusing intently on the internal evidence of the film clip itself, Evans had neglected to assess the conflicting stories told by the previously anonymous owner of the film clip, a Memphis entrepreneur named Leo "Tater Red" Allred. Allred had claimed that the original film footage disintegrated shortly after he had transferred it to video. As it turns out, copies of the film, which was shot by the theater owner, B. F. Jackson, in Ruleville (not Greenville), Mississippi, survive in several repositories in the South, including the Mississippi Department of Archives and History in Jackson. The can in which the Allred film clip was found was labeled "1942"; Honeyboy Edwards and Robert Lockwood Jr. never identified the musician as Johnson; and one of the British rockers whom Allred alleged offered him millions for the clip called the story "hogwash" (Evans, "Letter" [1999] 8–9). After describing Tater Red's Beale Street souvenir shop, which sells T-shirts proclaiming "only the devil knows for sure," Evans summarizes his feelings this way: "It is now clear that a trail of misinformation about the film's source and background led to a kind of 'pyramid scheme' of speculation, expert opinion, and authentication, all supported by the notion that this was footage of the legendary Robert Johnson. Instead, it appears that the whole thing was nothing more than an opportunity to hobnob with rock stars, market t-shirts, and achieve somewhat more than fifteen minutes of fame" (9). Evans was not alone in recanting. David Rubin of *Guitar One* magazine hastened to note that the positive opinions on the film attributed to him and Edward Komara in a *Living Blues* article were accurate but misleading, since the film was discussed only in a one-page sidebar to an eight-page essay on Johnson's musical techniques (Rubin, "Somebody" 7). An irony of this situation is that so many well-respected experts on blues music were duped by an irresponsible hustler seeking fame and fortune. The power-bloc of academia did not prevent one of the people from exploiting the Robert Johnson industry for his own gain, at the expense of those with expertise and media access. While Allred's scheme ultimately failed to win him riches, it did illustrate John Fiske's point that power does not always flow from the top down.

Fiske also argues that the meaning of an artifact or icon is determined by the circulation of responses to it, both among individuals and through the media. The story of the film clip certainly corroborates this point, since even its definitive debunking as an image of Robert Johnson does not end the story. Present at the Rock and Roll Hall of Fame's induction ceremonies for Johnson (where the public discrediting of the film took place) was filmmaker Robert Mugge, who covered many of the week's events for his documentary film *Hellhounds on My Trail: The Afterlife of Robert Johnson*. In addition to wonderful concert footage of the numerous blues luminaries who performed Robert Johnson songs, Mugge shot interviews with panelists, selections from keynote speeches, and conversations with participants about the film clip. We see Allred describing the clip and still hedging the details. We see conference attendees viewing the film clip, hear some of their commentary as they repeatedly watch it, and commiserate with Robert Lockwood Jr., who reportedly announced in frustration, "I don't care how many times you look at this film—it ain't never gonna be Robert Johnson."

I began this book by discussing Robert Johnson in semiotic terms, as a man who became a sign and whose sign then came to signify much more about current cultural mythologies than it did about the man and his music. Throughout the subsequent chapters, I have shown that Robert Johnson's image has been used to signify all sorts of things, from cultural authenticity to the paradoxes of American history to millennial multiculturalism. With this film about a film that is not Robert Johnson, however, the original Robert Johnson loses even his iconic status and becomes, in semiotic terms, a symbol—a very different kind of sign than an icon. An icon resembles the thing it represents, so a photograph of Robert Johnson, or a story based on what we know about him, is iconic—it retains real traces of the original. A symbol, in contrast, bears only an arbitrary relationship to the thing it purports to represent. Words, for example, are symbols, because a word like "guitar" has no literal relationship to the shape or sound of a guitar; its use is purely customary. In the Allred film clip, Robert Johnson is conspicuously absent. The anonymous musician is thus a symbol, despite Allred's attempt to fix a marketable iconic significance to him; the film clip's relationship to Johnson is arbitrary, based on Allred's usage rather than on likeness. I return here to semiotics to make a simple but important point: Robert Johnson is no longer needed to stir interest in Robert Johnson. Once the Robert Johnson apparatus touches something, to such an extent that a film *once thought to be* Johnson is screened at the Hall of Fame ceremonies in honor of Johnson, the reality of Robert Johnson no longer matters.

Despite the definitive absence of Robert Johnson, the film clip has continued to generate commentary from blues scholars. Some have raised the issue of who the young musician might be, since, as Lockwood reminds us, he's not ever going to be Robert Johnson; others extol the importance of the film as a historical document.[7] Still others offer emotional responses to the haunting film clip, with its ghostly retention of the Robert Johnson mystique simply through symbolic association. In a review of Mugge's film, Gil Asakawa explains, "Watching it a couple of times, you can see how many music fans would *want* it to be Robert Johnson, because it would be such a priceless record of the man" (25). Finally, there are the comments of Robert Mugge himself, who believes that Johnson's vociferous fans, as well as the musicians who play his music and the scholars who endlessly debate it, are the "hellhounds" on the bluesman's trail. Mugge told an interviewer, "'It greatly amused me that all these people won't leave Robert Johnson in death'" (qtd. in Asakawa 25). The irony of this remark from the filmmaker, who evidently excludes himself from this group of hellhounds even as he makes a movie about Robert Johnson, must not be overlooked. It suggests the degree to which even an artist using Robert Johnson as a unifying device in his work no longer sees Robert Johnson as an iconic sign. And within this critique of a film about a film that is not Robert Johnson, Robert Johnson himself has disappeared entirely, subsumed into a symbol onto which we project our own desires and dreams.

x x x

I began this chapter by introducing you to Rocky Lawrence, a Robert Johnson impersonator, who at least dresses like Johnson and plays Johnson's actual music, attempting to reproduce faithfully the sounds we hear on the recordings. Lawrence's Web page assertion that he has successfully re-created "the songs and soul of Robert Johnson" testifies to the fact that once there was an artist named Robert Johnson and perhaps might explain (to the impishly inclined) where that bartered soul went. In Robert Johnson's other Internet appearances, he still exists in iconic mode, with his photographs, his music, and his life story all widely available for entertainment and debate. And even if Internet readers of Johnson project their own fantasies onto that icon, at least there is a historical/imagined/constructed Robert Johnson, however illusory, at the core of the discussion.

Not so in this metacommentary about the commentary about a film clip that is not Robert Johnson. Just as the Internet allows users to construct identities at will, Robert Johnson has now become a wholly imagined creature, composed of bits, bytes, and cinematic and personal projections, represented less by his image and music than by arbitrary symbols that scholars, fans, marketers, and hucksters have associated with him. While the central purpose of my own inquiry has been to expose these workings of the R.J. machinery, the irony of my role in perpetuating the discourse is not lost on me. One can't escape the culture one inhabits. We live in a hall of mirrors, seeing reflections of ourselves as we try to construct a virtual Robert Johnson. And from it all only one hard fact emerges: the person who once lived as Robert Johnson, like Ocky Milkman, now "doesn't even exist. (poof)."

Conclusion: Robert Johnson, a Strange Attractor

> Man is an animal suspended in webs of significance he himself has spun.
> —Clifford Geertz

Chaos theory, like the Internet, is a powerful embodiment of postmodern culture. Its development over the past thirty years has enabled scientists to find patterns in systems that once were thought to be random. Chaos, it seems, contains "deeply encoded structures called 'strange attractors'" (Hayles 9) that, like Robert Johnson, are surrounded by unpredictable forces. A strange attractor is an undetectable point of attraction around which other things revolve, its presence indicated only by the activity around it; it is the stable focal point of a pattern, or the "general trend of a system around which the details oscillate" (Grace).[1] Because this surrounding motion is the only way we can identify strange attractors—we can never touch or see them—they are often visually represented as an empty center, the hole in the donut.

Although strange attractors create different sorts of patterns than those accounted for by the traditional, linear sciences, once those patterns are recognized, chaos appears to be everywhere. Chaos theory has been used to describe outbreaks of disease, the movements of the Nile River, unsteady eye movements in schizophrenics, changes in weather patterns, the way cars group together on the highway, the way oil flows through pipes, and why two identical pots of water boil at different times.[2] It appears that much human behavior and many natural phenomena follow this recently recognized pattern. But as some of those well-known examples suggest, the utility of chaos theory to explain phenomena has expanded beyond science and into the culture at large. James Gleick notes that it has changed the way "business executives make decisions about insurance . . . [and] the way political theorists talk about the stresses leading to armed conflict" (5). It has been used in literary studies, as recent works by N. Katherine Hayles, Harriett Hawkins, Gordon E. Slethaug, and Adalaide Morris attest.

It has even influenced artistic productions. In addition to its explicit impact on the novels of writers like John Barth, Thomas Pynchon, and Don DeLillo, chaos has literally been embodied in the Petronio Dance Company's production "Strange Attractors," with choreographer Stephen Petronio defining a strange attractor as "a moving and magnetic focal point in a seemingly chaotic field of particles."

The widespread applicability of this concept suggests that it is closely connected to prevailing ideas of our culture, or what Hayles calls "the cultural dominant." For her, "At issue is not only what chaos implies as a new paradigm but what it can tell us about the culture in which it is embedded" (146). In fact, one of the scientists who named "strange attractors"—one of the key paradigms of chaos theory—selected the name specifically for its cultural resonance. In his groundbreaking 1980 paper "Strange Attractors," David Ruelle wrote: "I have not spoken of the esthetic appeal of strange attractors. These systems of curves, these clouds of points suggest sometimes fireworks or galaxies, sometimes strange and disquieting vegetal proliferations. A realm lies there to explore, and harmonies to discover" (137). This is extraordinarily poetic language for a scientific journal and suggests that chaos theory in general, and strange attractors in particular, form a compelling paradigm for contemporary cultural productions of all kinds.

No doubt you see where I'm going with this metaphor and its application to Robert Johnson.[3] Throughout this book I have looked at the way cultural productions eddy around him in complex and varied ways. Like a strange attractor, he is the focus of a pattern, a presence detectable only through the whirlpool of activity surrounding him. We have seen Robert Johnson used to honor the blues, to propagate supernatural myths, to create a usable past, to illustrate African American double-consciousness, to expose racial inequities, to suggest the interweaving of myth and reality, to inspire personal quests and artistic ambitions, to portend a utopian future of interracial harmony, to structure psychological experience as a lieu de mémoire, to promote an ethics of care, to construct Internet community, to model identity formation in the postmodern world, to attract celebrity, and to sell T-shirts. What exists at the center of this maelstrom is an image of a man who once was real but who now exists only as symbol or myth. His assumed but unverifiable presence is a strange attractor to various activities that have little in common except for an ever-shifting focal point, the apparently empty center that was once Robert Johnson. But that seemingly empty center is what unifies the system. As Briggs and Peat note on the shape of strange attractors, "There will always be missing information, a hole (or should we say a *whole*) at the center of these logics. . . . The attractor is the shape created in phase space by 'missing information,' the shape of uncertainty" (175). Robert Johnson, who cannot be unambiguously identified except by the current of information around him, is likewise "the shape of uncertainty."

I have discovered one artist, however, whose work acknowledges the profound absence of Robert Johnson within the cultural industry that has been created around him. In a 1996 collection of poems entitled *Whirling round the Sun,* Suzanne Noguere includes a captivating portrait of Robert Johnson, which I quote here in its entirety:

Robert Johnson
When Mr. Johnson has the blues you'd think
that glass would crack, floors jolt, and the needle coax
from the spinning disk his yet unsettled ghost

as genies have been rubbed from lamps—if not
his ghost, at least that genius of a muse
who made the blues apocalyptic news.

Is it she, heard falsetto through his voice,
who is the ultimate ventriloquist,
or is it he whose prodding makes the gist

come from the dummy sitting on his knees?
It talks, tells, urges, cries, chimes, and rings
and yet it is nothing but wood and strings.

Bent over his aggrieved guitar and bent
on being, all the same he doesn't shrink
to come so early to the brink

of death; for every Southern song has taught
the heart that always goes for broke can't last
longer than to write its fast epitaph.

And it is useless, sitting here, to wish
for once to see the smile or hear the laugh
of the dead man pleading from the phonograph.

This poem provides a fitting ending to my study. Listening to Robert Johnson's powerful music, Noguere's speaker constructs a hauntology of Robert Johnson. At first, she hears destruction in the music—floors cracking, glass breaking—and surmises that she is hearing Johnson's still "unsettled" ghost through the medium of inanimate objects—the needle, the record. But then another possibility occurs to her: perhaps what she hears is not his ghost but the eternal muse who inspired him in the first place. "Is it she," the speaker asks (referring to the female muse), whose presence is indicated by Johnson's falsetto singing voice and by the human cries emanating from the inanimate wooden box—"the dummy"—that was his guitar? With these images, Noguere links Johnson to the dark forces of his Faustian legend as well as to the history of western civilization, in which the Muses—daughters of Zeus and Memory—are thought to be the origins of all artistic inspiration. From contemplating the sources of his powers, the speaker goes on to envision the mind and heart of Johnson himself. She imagines him facing the truth embedded in the music he has inherited, both from the muse and from his southern blues heritage: that death is inevitable, especially for those whose hearts "go for broke"—that is, who are uncompromising about their goals. He wants to live—he is "bent / on being"—but still does not "shrink" from the abyss to which his "going for broke" leads him.

In this lyrically compressed form, Noguere evokes many issues that have been central to my analysis of Robert Johnson at the turn of the century: she recognizes something powerful and unknowable in the music, suspects supernatural forces at work in his songs, imagines different possible scenarios to account for his musical prowess, and assumes that his music is self-consciously apocalyptic, portending the musician's early, tragic death. The poem even riffs on the formal structure of many of Johnson's blues compositions, with the abb rhyme scheme of her three-line stanzas echoing his characteristic aab. For me, however, the poem's real power lies in the last stanza. There, the speaker recognizes the futility of hoping to see or know Robert Johnson the man. He is dead, and wishing to see him smile or hear him laugh is a poignant exercise in futility. With this realization, Suzanne Noguere achieves a fuller understanding of the Robert Johnson mystique than most of the fans, researchers, critics, musicians, and scholars whose speculations have filled the pages of this book. She recognizes Johnson as a strange attractor, the invisible force holding together a system that spins chaotically around him. Her speaker, like the Robert Johnson she imagines, faces a hard truth: he may seem to be alive and pleading, but Robert Johnson is "the dead man"—an empty center, gone for good.

The ending of Noguere's "Robert Johnson" leaves us with a paradox: the speaker of the poem avows that Johnson is dead, gone, and unrecoverable, yet she still *wishes* to recover him, and in fact, the poet does create the poem, itself an attempt at revivification. Her poetic re-creation, like the fictional revisionings, cinematic imaginings, virtual allusions, and biographical resuscitations that I have explored throughout this book, thus underscores an important theme of my study: contemporary responses to Robert Johnson are fraught with paradox and inconsistency. He has disappeared from view but remains defined by a surrounding current of seemingly chaotic activity. Like the strange attractor, Robert Johnson has become a paradigm that resonates with the culture in which it is embedded.

Coda

The epigraph with which I began this conclusion comes from anthropology, a field of study that, like science, literary criticism, and others, is drawn to problems that reflect the prevailing cultural context. N. Katherine Hayles calls our current context "cultural postmodernism," which she defines as "the realization that what [have] always been thought of as the essential, unvarying components of human experience are not natural facts of life but social constructions" (265). Geertz's contention that humans create their own "webs of significance" is one manifestation of this insight about the constructed nature of reality. And if culture is a human invention, then it can best be understood not through "an experimental science in search of law but an interpretive one in search of meaning" (5). Commenting on Geertz's work, media theorist James W. Carey takes this emphasis on interpretation of culture a step further. He understands Geertz's statement about "webs of significance" as a comment on the importance of making fictions, a word he uses "in its original sense—fictio—a 'making,' a construction" (62). For Carey, this fiction making is the highest achievement of the human mind, and understanding it is one of the most important goals of contemporary social sciences. He further insists that assessing, interpreting, and theorizing the "wide variety of cultural forms through which reality can be created" (62) is best achieved through the methods of cultural studies.

Throughout this book, I have attempted to show that Robert Johnson is the strange attractor to which conflicting and often unlikely social constructions have attached themselves. In unpacking these various fictions, examining them, and assessing the cultural assumptions that underlie them, I have been creating my own webs of significance—my own fictions about the fictions. One's implication in one's culture is inevitable, and the self-reflexivity represented in my study is fundamental to postmodern thought. Nonetheless, this work is intended to do more than illustrate my own fiction making. I hope to have offered a better understanding of how Robert Johnson's image has been used and what those uses tell us about American society in general and postmodern culture in particular. In creating my own fictions, I hope also to have exemplified what cultural criticism can do and how it can help us understand the extent to which we create ourselves, our culture, and our own significance.

And now, having spun my webs of significance, I believe I'll dust my broom.

Appendix: Web Sites

This appendix is not intended to offer a comprehensive listing of all web sites that include information about Robert Johnson. It is simply a reference list of sites I mention in chapter 5, collected here rather than scattered throughout the bibliography, for the reader's convenience. I list them by site rather than by page, since that's how I describe them in the text of this chapter. All sites listed herein were last accessed in July 2002.

About.com ("Robert Johnson Profile")
<http://blues.about.com/library/weekly/aa062700a.htm>

All Music Guide to the Blues ("Robert Johnson")
<http://www.allmusic.com/cg/amg.dll?p=amg&sql=Bwt9gs31ba3vg>

"Appreciating Robert Johnson"
<http://www.ingworld.com/appreciating/robertjohnson>

Blue Flame Cafe ("Robert Johnson")
<http://www.blueflamecafe.com/index.html>

Blue Highway
<http://www.thebluehighway.com/tbh1.html>

Blues Board
<http://www.thebluesboard.com/bluesboard/index.shtml>

Blueschat
<http://www.4-lane.com/musicchat/pages/blueschat.html>

Blues Enquirer, Astrologer to the Stars ("Robert Johnson Makes the Charts")
<http://www.astrologertothestars.com/reports001/robert.shtml>

Blues-L
<http://listserv.brown.edu/archives/blues-l.html>

Blues Lyrics on Line: Robert Johnson
<www.geocities.com/BourbonStreet/Delta/2541/blrjohns.htm>

Bluesnet ("Robert Johnson")
<http://bluesnet.hub.org/artists/robert.johnson.html>

Blues on the Big Road
<http://www.bigroadblues.com/>

The Crossroads Curse
<http://stormloader.com/users/crossroads>

Daley, Mike ("'You Hear Me When I Moan': Timbre and Style in the Singing of Robert Johnson")
<http://www.finearts.yorku.ca/mdaley/robertjohnson.html>
Delta Haze Foundation (Official Robert Johnson Web Site)
<www.deltahaze.com/30/rj.html>
FolkLib Index ("Robert Johnson")
<http://www.folklib.net/index/j/johnson_robert.shtml>
HitsQuick ("Robert Johnson")
<http://www.hitsquick.com/music/Artist/Johnson,Robert>
HyperMedia Projects for Musicological Research and Education
<http://www.cnmat.berkeley.edu/~adrian/blues.overview.html>
Lavender, Catherine ("Robert Johnson's Blues")
<http://www.library.csi.cuny.edu/dept/history/lavender/bluesques.html>
Lawrence, Rocky
<http://www.rockylawrence.com/>
Monzo, Joseph L. ("Use of Microtones in the Vocals of Robert Johnson")
<http://www.ixpres.com/interval/monzo/rjohnson/drunken.htm>
Mudcat Cafe ("Did Robert Johnson Sell His Soul at the Crossroads?")
<http://www.mudcat.org/rj-dave.cfm>
Mudcat's Robert Johnson Room
<http://www.mudcat.org/rj.cfm>
Music Central ("Johnson, Robert")
<http://www.univie.ac.at/Anglistik/easyrider/data/Robert%20Johnson.htm>
OLGA: The On-line Guitar Archive
<http://www.olga.net/dynamic/browse.php?printer=1&local=main/j/johnson_robert/>
"Playing Robert Johnson Songs"
<http://www.ingworld.com/playing/robertjohnson>
Potent.com ("Constructions of Masculinity in the Music of Robert Johnson")
<http://www.potent.com.au.monthly_jul99.html>
Rock and Roll Hall of Fame ("Robert Johnson")
<http://www.rockhall.com/hof/inductee.asp?ID=134>
Robert Johnson Notebooks
<http://www.xroads.virginia.edu/~MUSIC/blues/rjhome3.html>
Trail of the Hellhound
<http://www.cr.nps.gov/delta/blues/>

Notes

Introduction

1. Throughout this text I follow Baty's lead in using "America" to refer to the United States. Like Baty, I use the word "for its resonances as marker of a generic nation and mass-mediated political cultural condition/terrain" (Baty 8). In addition, since much of my text deals with African American culture, "America," despite its imperializing associations, seems a better parallel term than the more accurate "United States."

2. See, for some good examples, Baty; Marcus, *Dead Elvis;* Engle; and Brooker.

3. Some of the notable influences on Fiske's thinking are Michel Foucault, for his revision of Marx's theories of power, Antonio Gramsci, for his recognition that categories like "the power-bloc" and "the people" are fluid rather than permanently fixed, and Mikhail Bakhtin, for his emphasis on the creativity of the people. See Fiske's excellent short summary in *Power Plays* (7–10).

Chapter 1: Robert Johnson as Contested Space

1. See Calt and Wardlow, as well as comments by Wardlow and Mack McCormick in Hunt.

2. This early mentor's name has usually been given as "Zinnerman." Stephen C. LaVere, however, has recently uncovered a document with his signature from the cemetery where he buried his wife and where he was himself buried a short time later. The signature on the document is spelled "Zinermon."

3. For a fascinating look at details of Johnson's recording sessions, see Wald 131–86.

4. The historical pattern of migration is obvious. For a good study of the literary pattern, see Griffin.

5. Finn dramatizes the story of such an encounter in his 1986 short story "The Blue Bayou," using a nameless blues musician as the Johnson-like protagonist.

6. See chapters 10 and 11 of Pearson and McCulloch for an excellent analysis of the sources of these song lyrics and how the songs themselves have come to connote (to some listeners) Johnson's alleged pact with the devil.

Chapter 2: The Invention of the Past

1. For other discussions of the distinction between documentary and docudrama, see Corner and Woodhead.

2. This vision of Johnson as tragically naive is shared by Stanley Booth. In his short play *Standing at the Crossroads,* Johnson meets a hoodoo con man at a bayou crossroads who convinces Johnson that he has sold his soul to the devil, when all the barefoot man really wants (and gets) is Johnson's shoes.

3. For further discussion of the duality of American literary traditions, see Fiedler, *Love and Death;* Chase; and Lewis.

4. See Davis (78–80) for a good summary of this legend about Bessie Smith's death. Davis reports that the story has been reported by researchers from John Hammond to Alan Lomax, but that Chris Albertson's biography of Smith explains what actually happened. The tragic events do involve an automobile accident and ambulances but suggest that her death was more a matter of the poor judgment of those who found her than of racist ambulance policies.

5. Greenberg's screenplay has a long and troubled preproduction history. It has been optioned variously by Mick Jagger, Prince, the Sundance Institute, and Warner Brothers and has attracted the interest of Martin Scorsese (McGonigal). At this writing, the film is currently in production at HBO Films, under the direction of Tim Blake Nelson.

Chapter 3: The Paradox of Authenticity

1. This rumor about Johnson's three-piece band has been variously reported. See Palmer (131); Obrecht (14); and Delta Haze.

2. For two examples that came easily to my hand, see *Living Blues* no. 111 (Oct. 1993) and no. 131 (Jan./Feb. 1997). Other examples abound.

3. This passage comes from Gussow's regular column in *Blues Access* magazine, entitled "Journeyman's Road." For a longer, fuller look at his views on interracial apprenticeship, see his memoir, *Mister Satan's Apprentice.*

Chapter 4: The New Cultural Politics of Difference

1. My discussion of the ethics of care is informed throughout by the unpublished work of Erin Gorman.

Chapter 5: Virtual Robert Johnson

1. For a succinct overview of the development of cyberculture studies, see Silver.

2. The online addresses of each Web site mentioned in this chapter are included in the appendix. I will not repeat them in the text so as not to disrupt your reading.

3. See also the summary of such critiques in Fernback (212).

4. For two fascinating discussions of fandom on the Internet, see Senft; and Clerc.

5. The entire discussion is available in the Blues-L archives for May 2000, running through weeks two, three, and four. The archives are available to all members, and membership is free.

6. A third photograph of Robert Johnson does apparently exist, but it has never been published or widely circulated. According to Tom Freeland, a writer for *Living Blues* magazine and one of the managers of the well-established Blues-L discussion list, Mack McCormick showed Peter Guralnick the photograph while Guralnick was doing research for his 1982 monograph on Johnson, and Guralnick believed the subject to be Johnson. Evidently Stephen C. LaVere has sued McCormick over ownership of the photograph, claiming it to be the property of the Johnson estate, and because of the lawsuit the photograph has been kept under wraps. See Freeland, "Robert Johnson Books/photo."

7. See, for example, Evans "Letter" (1999; 9); Freeland "NOT on Film"; and Cheseborough, *Blues Traveling* (110).

Conclusion

1. See also Petree and Judge for good attempts to describe this complex structure in simple terms.

2. Hayles (150); Gleick (5); Briggs and Peat (76–77).

3. I am grateful to Peter X. Feng of the University of Delaware for this insight about strange attractors and to Margot A. Kelley for helping me apply it sensibly to Robert Johnson.

Works Cited

"Absent Cigarette Sparks Debate over Stamp." *New York Times,* 18 September 1994, 27.

Ainslie, Scott. *Robert Johnson at the Crossroads—The Authoritative Guitar Transcriptions.* Milwaukee: Hal Leonard, 1992.

Albertson, Chris. *Bessie.* New York: Stein and Day, 1985.

Alexie, Sherman. "Because My Father Always Said He Was the Only Indian Who Saw Jimi Hendrix Play 'The Star-Spangled Banner' at Woodstock." In *The Lone Ranger and Tonto Fistfight in Heaven.* 24–36. New York: Harper Collins, 1993.

———. *Reservation Blues.* New York: Warner Books, 1995.

Asakawa, Gil. "Mug Shots." *Blues Access* 38 (Summer 1999): 21–27.

Ashare, Matt. "Can't You Hear the Wind Howl? The Life and Music of Robert Johnson." *Boston Phoenix.* 11–18 September 1997. 8 May 2001 <http://www.bostonphoenix.com/archive../CAN_T_YOU_HEAR_THE_WIND_HO.htm>.

Atkins, Ace. *Crossroad Blues.* New York: St. Martin's, 1998.

Bakhtin, M. M. *The Dialogic Imagination.* Ed. Michael Holquist. Trans. Caryl Emerson and Michael Holquist. Austin: University of Texas Press, 1981.

Banks, Russell. "The Devil and Robert Johnson: The Blues and the 1990s." *New Republic* 204:17 (1991): 27–31.

Barnes, Bertrum, and Glen Wheeler. "A Lonely Fork in the Road." *Living Blues* 94 (November/December 1990): 26–28.

Barthes, Roland. *Mythologies.* Trans. Annette Lavers. New York: Hill and Wang, 1972.

Baty, S. Paige. *American Monroe: The Making of a Body Politic.* Berkeley: University of California Press, 1995.

Baudrillard, Jean. *America.* Trans. Chris Turner. London: Verso, 1988.

———. "Simulacra and Simulations." In *Selected Writings.* Ed. Mark Poster. Trans. Paul Foss, Paul Patton, and Philip Beitchman. 166–84. Stanford, Calif.: Stanford University Press, 1988.

Bellante, John, and Carl Bellante. "Sherman Alexie: An Excerpt from an Interview." *Bloomsbury Review,* May/June 1994, 14–15, 26.

Bennighof, James. "Some Ramblings on Robert Johnson's Mind: Critical Analysis and Aesthetic Value in Delta Blues." *American Music,* Summer 1997, 137–58.

Blues-L FAQ. 12 March 1999. 15 July 2002 <http://www.blues.net/blues-FAQ.html>.

"*Bone Music* Book Description." *Amazon.com Editorial Reviews.* 13 July 2001 <http:/ /www.amazon.com/exec/obidos/tg/stores/detail/-/book../107-4333536-75901>.

Booth, Stanley. *Standing at the Crossroads.* In *Rythm Oil: A Journey through the Music of the American South.* 3–12. Cambridge, Mass.: Da Capo Press, 1991.

Boyle, T. Coraghessan. Frequently Asked Questions. *T. Coraghessan Boyle Website.* 3 May 2001 <http://www.tcboyle.com/faq/html>.

———. Message Board. *T. Coraghessan Boyle Website.* 3 May 2001 <http:// www.tcboyle.com/msgboard/>.

———. "Stones in My Passway, Hellhound on My Trail." In *Greasy Lake and Other Stories.* 146–52. New York: Penguin, 1979.

Briggs, John, and F. David Peat. *Turbulent Mirror: An Illustrated Guide to Chaos Theory and the Science of Wholeness.* New York: Harper and Row, 1989.

Brooker, Will. *Batman Unmasked: Analysing a Cultural Icon.* London: Continuum, 2000.

Brooks, Van Wyck. "On Creating a Usable Past." *The Dial* 64 (11 April 1918): 337–41.

Broomer, Stuart. "Licked by All: A Postage Stamp of Robert Johnson." *Coda, the Journal of Jazz and Improvised Music* 264 (November/December 1995). 22 November 2000 <http://www.jazzhouse.org/files/broomer1.php3>.

Buechler, Mark. "The First Time." *Blues Revue* 28 (April/May 1997): 58–59.

Calt, Stephen. Liner notes. *The Roots of Robert Johnson.* Yazoo Records, 1990.

Calt, Stephen, and Gayle Dean Wardlow. "Robert Johnson." *78 Quarterly* 4 (1989): 41–51.

Campbell, Joseph, with Bill Moyer. *The Power of Myth.* New York: Doubleday, 1988.

Can't You Hear the Wind Howl? Official Website. March 2001. 8 May 2001 <http:/ /freehosting1.at.webjump.com/7a1ad1fd/ro/robertjohnsononfilm/ Reviews.html>.

Carey, James W. *Communication as Culture: Essays on Media and Society.* Boston: Unwin, 1989.

Cash, Stephanie. "New Postage Stamp Features Pollock." *Art in America.* May 1999. 29 October 2000 <http://www.findarticles.com/m1248/5_87/54574803/ p1/article.jhtml>.

Chadwick, Vernon. "Introduction: Ole Massa's Dead, Long Live the King of Rock 'n' Roll." In *In Search of Elvis: Music, Race, Art, Religion.* Ed. Vernon Chadwick. ix–xxvi. Boulder, Colo.: Westview Press, 1997.

Chandler, Daniel. "Personal Home Pages and the Construction of Identities on the Web." 1998. 15 May 2002 <http://www.aber.ac.uk/media/Documents/ short/webident.html>.

Chase, Richard. *The American Novel and Its Tradition.* Garden City, N.Y.: Doubleday, 1957.

Cheseborough, Steve. *Blues Traveling: The Holy Sites of Delta Blues.* Jackson: University Press of Mississippi, 2001.

———. "Robert Johnson on Film?" *Living Blues* 140 (July/August 1998): 8.

Christgau, Robert. "Rock Bios." *Village Voice,* 20 December 1983, 72.

Clerc, Susan. "Estrogen Brigades and 'Big Tits' Threads: Media Fandom On-Line and Off." In *The Cybercultures Reader.* Ed. David Bell and Barbara M. Kennedy. 216–29. London: Routledge, 2000.

Clifford, James. "Of Other Peoples: Beyond the 'Salvage Paradigm.'" In *Discussions in Contemporary Culture.* Ed. Hal Foster. 121–30. Seattle: Bay Press, 1987.

Corner, John. "British TV Dramadocumentary: Origins and Developments." In *Why Docudrama? Fact-Fiction on Film and TV.* Ed. Alan Rosenthal. 35–46. Carbondale: Southern Illinois University Press, 1999.

Cowley, John. "Shack Bullies and Levee Contractors: Bluesmen as Ethnographers." In *Songs about Work: Essays in Occupational Culture.* Ed. Archie Green. 134–62. Bloomington: Indiana University Press, 1993.

Cox, James. "Muting White Noise: The Subversion of Popular Culture Narratives of Conquest in Sherman Alexie's Fiction." *Studies in American Indian Literatures* 9:4 (Winter 1997): 52–70.

Crouch, Stanley. "Introduction: Printing the Legend." In *Love in Vain: A Vision of Robert Johnson,* by Alan Greenberg. ix–xiv. New York: Da Capo Press, 1994.

Custen, George F. "Clio in Hollywood." In *Why Docudrama? Fact-Fiction on Film and TV.* Ed. Alan Rosenthal. 19–34. Carbondale: Southern Illinois University Press, 1999.

Davis, Francis. *The History of the Blues.* New York: Hyperion, 1995.

"The Death of Robert Johnson." Interviews. *Living Blues* 94 (November/December 1990): 8–20.

DeCurtis, Anthony. "A Punk's Past Recaptured." *Rolling Stone,* 14 June 1988, 54–57.

Delta Haze Corporation. "Robert Johnson Biography." 2000. 27 September 2000 <http://www.deltahaze.com/johnson/bio.html>.

Derrida, Jacques. *Specters of Marx: The State of the Debt, the Work of Mourning, and the New International.* Trans. Peggy Kamuf. New York: Routledge, 1994.

Doss, Erika. *Elvis Culture: Fans, Faith, and Image.* Lawrence: University Press of Kansas, 1999.

Du Bois, W. E. B. *The Souls of Black Folk.* In *The Oxford W. E. B. Du Bois Reader.* Ed. Eric Sundquist. 97–240. New York: Oxford University Press, 1996.

Edgar, David. "Theater of Fact: A Dramatist's Viewpoint." In *Why Docudrama? Fact-Fiction on Film and TV.* Ed. Alan Rosenthal. 174–87. Carbondale: Southern Illinois University Press, 1999.

Edwards, David Honeyboy, as told to Janis Martinson and Michael Robert Frank. *The World Don't Owe Me Nothing: The Life and Times of Delta Bluesman Honeyboy Edwards.* Chicago: Chicago Review Press, 1997.

Eldridge, Cat. "Robert Johnson Lives (Sort Of)." *Green Man Review.* 3 July 2001 <http://www.greenmanreview.com/crossroads.html>.

Ellison, Ralph. "The Uses of History in Fiction." *Southern Literary Journal* 1 (1969): 57–90.

Engle, Gary. "What Makes Superman So Darned American?" In *Signs of Life in the U.S.A.: Readings on Popular Culture for Writers*. Ed. Sonia Maasik and Jack Solomon. 677–85. Boston: Bedford/St. Martin's, 2000.

Evans, David. *Big Road Blues: Tradition and Creativity in the Folk Blues*. New York: DaCapo Press, 1982.

———. "Letter to the Editor." *Living Blues* 141 (September/October 1998): 9.

———. "Letter to the Editor." *Living Blues* 143 (January/February 1999): 8–9.

———. *Tommy Johnson*. London: Studio Vista, 1971.

Fabre, Genevieve, and Robert O'Meally. Introduction to *History and Memory in African-American Culture*. Ed. Genevieve Fabre and Robert O'Meally. 3–17. New York: Oxford University Press, 1994.

Fernback, Jan. "There Is a There There: Notes toward a Definition of Cybercommunity." In *Doing Internet Research: Critical Issues and Methods for Examining the Net*. Ed. Steve Jones. 203–20. Thousand Oaks, Calif.: Sage Publications, 1999.

Ferris, William. *Blues from the Delta*. Garden City, N.Y.: Anchor, 1979.

Fiedler, Leslie. *Cross the Border—Close the Gap*. New York: Stein and Day, 1972.

———. *Love and Death in the American Novel*. 1960. Reprint, New York: Anchor, 1992.

Finn, Julio. "The Blue Bayou." In *B Flat, Bebop, Scat: Jazz Short Stories and Poems*. Ed. Chris Parker. 137–45. London: Quartet Books, 1986.

———. *The Bluesman: The Musical Heritage of Black Men and Women in the Americas*. New York: Interlink Books, 1992.

Fiske, John. *Power Plays Power Works*. London: Verso, 1993.

———. *Understanding Popular Culture*. Boston: Unwin Hyman, 1989.

Flowers, Arthur. *Mojo Rising: Confessions of a 21st Century Conjureman*. New York: Wanganegresse Press, 2001.

Floyd, Samuel A., Jr. *The Power of Black Music: Interpreting Its History from Africa to the United States*. New York: Oxford University Press, 1995.

Freeland, Tom. "Robert Johnson Books/photo." Online posting. 20 February 2002. Blues Music List. 17 May 2002 <http://listserv.brown.edu/archives/blues-l.html>.

———. "Re: *Living Blues* #150: Tom Freeland on Robt. Johnson." Online posting. 11 May 2000. Blues Music List. 17 May 2002 <http://listserv.brown.edu/archives/blues-l.html>.

———. "Robert Johnson NOT on Film." *Living Blues* 142 (November/December 1998): 11.

———. "Robert Johnson: Some Witnesses to a Short Life." *Living Blues* 150 (March/April 2000): 43–49.

Fusco, Coco. "Pan-American Postnationalism: Another World Order." In *Black Popular Culture*. Ed. Gina Dent and Michele Wallace. 279–84. New York: The New Press, 1998.

Fusco, John. "*Crossroads*—Writer's Comments." Waterhorse Productions Web Site. 5 July 2001 <http://waterhorseprod.com/writerscomcross.htm>.

Garon, Paul. *Blues and the Poetic Spirit*. 1975. Reprint, San Francisco: City Lights, 1996.

———. "Speak My Mind." *Living Blues* 109 (May/June 1993): 53.

Gates, Henry Louis, Jr. *The Signifying Monkey: A Theory of African-American Literary Criticism.* New York: Oxford University Press, 1988.

Geertz, Clifford. *The Interpretation of Cultures: Selected Essays.* New York: Basic Books, 1973.

Gentry, Cynthia. "Festivals." *IndieWIRE.* 13 March 2001 <http://www.indiewire.com/film/festivals/fes_01Cinequest_010313_wrap.html>.

Gilligan, Carol. *In a Different Voice: Psychological Theory and Women's Development.* Cambridge, Mass.: Harvard University Press, 1982.

Gilroy, Paul. *The Black Atlantic: Modernity and Double Consciousness.* Cambridge, Mass.: Harvard University Press, 1993.

Gleick, James. *Chaos: Making a New Science.* New York: Viking, 1987.

Grace, Roger. "Chaos in Prehistory: The Potential of Complexity Theory for the Study of Palaeolithic Archaeology." *Prehistoric Chaos.* 1996. 27 July 2002 <http://www.hf.uio.no/iakk/roger/lithic/CHAOS/chaoscon.html>.

Greenberg, Alan. "Re: Robert Johnson again." Email to author. 15 June 2001.

———. "RJ." Email to the author. 2 June 2001.

———. *Love in Vain: A Vision of Robert Johnson.* New York: Da Capo Press, 1994.

Griffin, Farah Jasmine. *"Who Set You Flowin'?" The African-American Migration Narrative.* New York: Oxford University Press, 1995.

Guralnick, Peter. *Searching for Robert Johnson.* New York: Plume, 1989.

Gussow, Adam. Letter to the author. 29 May 2001.

———. *Mister Satan's Apprentice: A Blues Memoir.* New York: Pantheon, 1998.

———. "My Master, Nat (Part One)." *Blues Access* 30 (Summer 1997): 106–7.

Hafen, P. Jane. "Rock and Roll, Redskins, and Blues in Sherman Alexie's Work." *Studies in American Indian Literatures* 9:4 (Winter 1997): 71–78.

Hall, Stuart. "Encoding, Decoding." In *The Cultural Studies Reader.* Ed. Simon During. 90–103. London: Routledge, 1993.

Handy, W. C. *Father of the Blues.* New York: Collier Books, 1941.

Harris, Bill. *Robert Johnson: Trick the Devil.* In *The National Black Drama Anthology.* Ed. Woodie King Jr. 1–46. New York: Applause, 1995.

Hawkins, Harriet. *Strange Attractors: Literature, Culture, and Chaos Theory.* New York: Prentice Hall, 1995.

Hayles, N. Katherine. *Chaos Bound: Orderly Disorder in Contemporary Literature and Science.* Ithaca, N.Y.: Cornell University Press, 1990.

Herman, Andrew, and John H. Sloop. "'Red Alert!' Rhetorics of the World Wide Web and 'Friction Free' Capitalism." In *The World Wide Web and Contemporary Cultural Theory.* Ed. Andrew Herman and Thomas Swiss. 77–98. New York: Routledge, 2000.

Herman, Hawkeye. "Re: Question about 1998 Delta Studies Symposium." Email to the author. 12 June 2002.

———. "Re: Hawkeye—Best Original Music, Phila. Inquirer." Email to the author. 10 June 2000.

———. "Jokin' on the Harp Player." Email to the author. 12 January 2002.

Heron, Laura. "The Message on the Envelope: Canadian Stamp Design, 1949–69." *The Archivist* 115 (1997): 44–54.

Hill, Walter, dir. *Crossroads.* Video tape recording. Columbia Tristar Home Video, 1986.

Holman, Curtis. "Down to the Crossroads: Jomandi Sings the Blues." Review of *Robert Johnson: Trick the Devil,* by Bill Harris. *Creative Loafing.* 9 March 1996. 11 April 2001 <http://web.cln.com/archives/atlanta/newsstand/atl030996/A_CURT.HTM>.

Hord, Fred Lee, and Jonathan Scott Lee. "'I Am Because We Are': An Introduction to Black Philosophy." In *I Am Because We Are: Readings in Black Philosophy.* Ed. Fred Lee Hord and Jonathan Scott Lee. 1–16. Amherst: University of Massachusetts Press, 1995.

Hughes, Langston. *The Collected Poems of Langston Hughes.* Ed. Arnold Rampersad. New York: Knopf, 1994.

Hunt, Chris, dir. *The Search for Robert Johnson.* Narrated by John Hammond. Video tape recording. Sony, 1992.

Jameson, Frederic. *Postmodernism, or, the Cultural Logic of Late Capitalism.* Durham, N.C.: Duke University Press, 1991.

Johnson, Matthew. "Interview with Honeyboy Edwards." *Living Blues* 94 (November/December 1990): 18–20.

Jordan, Tim. *Cyberpower: The Culture and Politics of Cyberspace and the Internet.* London: Routledge, 1999.

Judge, Anthony. "Human Values as Strange Attractors." Union of International Associations Web Page. 1993. 27 July 2002 <http://www.uia.org/uiadocs/values93.htm>.

Kakutani, Michiko. "Books of the Times." Review of *Greasy Lake and Other Stories,* by T. Coraghessan Boyle. *New York Times,* 22 May 1985, 22.

Kammen, Michael. *People of Paradox: An Inquiry Concerning the Origins of American Civilization.* New York: Alfred A. Knopf, 1972.

———. "T. Coraghessan Boyle and *World's End.*" In *Novel History: Historians and Novelists Confront America's Past (and Each Other).* Ed. Mark C. Carnes. 245–58. New York: Simon and Schuster, 2001.

Kendall, Lori. "Recontextualizing 'Cyberspace': Methodological Considerations for On-Line Research." In *Doing Internet Research: Critical Issues and Methods for Examining the Net.* Ed. Steve Jones. 57–74. Thousand Oaks, Calif.: Sage Publications, 1999.

King, Woodie Jr., and Ron Milner, eds. *Black Drama Anthology.* New York: Penguin, Meridian, 1971.

Lauter, Paul, et al., eds. *The Heath Anthology of American Literature.* Boston: Houghton Mifflin, 1989.

LaVere, Stephen C. Liner notes. *Robert Johnson: The Complete Recordings.* Columbia Records, 1990.

Lawrence, D. H. *Studies in Classic American Literature.* 1923. Reprint, New York: Viking Press, 1961.

Lawrence, Rocky. Home page. 16 May 2002 <http://www.rockylawrence.com>.

Leonin, Mia. "The Devil Is in the Details." Review of *Robert Johnson: Trick the Devil,* by Bill Harris. *Miami New Times Online.* 1 March 2001. 11 April 2001 <http://www.miaminewtimes.com/issues/2001-03-01/theater/html>.

Levecq, Christine. "Delta Blues and the City: Walter Mosley's *RL's Dream* as the Ultimate Blues Novel." Conference presentation. The Blues Tradition: Memory, Criticism, and Pedagogy. University Park, Pa., 30 June 2000.

Levi-Strauss, Claude. *The Savage Mind.* Trans. John Weightman and Doreen Weightman. Chicago: University of Chicago Press, 1966.

Lewis, R. W. B. *The American Adam: Innocence, Tragedy, and Tradition in the Nineteenth Century.* Chicago: University of Chicago Press, 1955.

Lhamon, W. T., Jr. *Raising Cain: Blackface Performance from Jim Crow to Hip Hop.* Cambridge, Mass.: Harvard University Press, 2000.

Lieberfeld, Daniel. "Million-Dollar Juke Joint: Commodifying Blues Culture." *African American Review* 29:2 (1995): 217–21.

Lipsitz, George. *Dangerous Crossroads: Popular Music, Postmodernism, and the Poetics of Place.* London: Verso, 1994.

———. *The Possessive Investment in Whiteness: How White People Profit from Identity Politics.* Philadelphia: Temple University Press, 1998.

Lockard, Joseph. "Progressive Politics, Electronic Individualism, and the Myth of Virtual Community." In *Internet Culture.* Ed. David Porter. 219–31. New York: Routledge, 1997.

Lomax, Alan. *The Land Where the Blues Began.* New York: Delta, 1995.

Lott, Eric. *Love and Theft: Blackface Minstrelsy and the American Working Class.* New York: Oxford University Press, 1993.

Marcus, Greil. *Dead Elvis: A Chronicle of a Cultural Obsession.* New York: Doubleday, 1991.

———. *Mystery Train: Images of America in Rock 'n' Roll Music.* New York: Dutton, 1975.

McCaffrey, Larry. "Lusty Dreamers in the Suburban Jungle." Review of *Greasy Lake and Other Stories,* by T. Coraghessan Boyle. *New York Times Book Review,* 9 June 1985, 15–16.

McClary, Susan. *Conventional Wisdom: The Content of Musical Form.* Berkeley: University of California Press, 2000.

McGonigal, Mike. "Interview with Alan Greenberg." *New York Press* 13:28 (2001). 18 May 2001 <http://www.nypress.com/print.cfm?content_id=2255&author_id=185>.

Meyer, Peter. "Peter Meyer's Mystery." Interview. *Borders.com.* 1999. 16 May 2001 <http://go.borders.com/features/ab99003.xcv>.

———, dir. *Can't You Hear the Wind Howl? The Life and Music of Robert Johnson.* Video tape recording. WinStar, 1997.

Milkman, Ocky. "*Living Blues* #150: Tom Freeland on Robt. Johnson." Online posting. 10 May 2000. Blues Music List. 17 May 2002 <http://listserv.brown.edu/archives/blues-l.html>.

Morris, Adelaide. *How to Live/What to Do: H.D.'s Cultural Poetics.* Urbana: University of Illinois Press, 2003.

Morrison, Toni. *Playing in the Dark: Whiteness and the Literary Imagination.* Cambridge, Mass.: Harvard University Press, 1992.

———. *Song of Solomon.* 1977. Reprint, New York: Penguin, 1987.

Mosiman, Bille Sue. Review of *Bone Music,* by Alan Rodgers. 13 July 2001 <http://www.sff.net/people/alanr/books.htm>.

Mosley, Walter. *RL's Dream.* New York: Washington Square Press, 1995.

———. *Workin' on the Chain Gang: Shaking Off the Dead Hand of History.* New York: Ballantine, 2000.

Mugge, Robert, dir. *Hellhounds on My Trail: The Afterlife of Robert Johnson.* Video tape recording. WinStar, 1999.

Nelson, David, and Lauri Lawson. "It's Best to Let Cake Stay Cake." Interview with Lonnie Pitchford. *Living Blues* 91 (November/December 1990): 44–47.

"New Information Found on the Death of Robert Johnson." *Blues Access* 28 (Winter 1997): 108.

Newby, Gregg L. "A Mississippi Odyssey: The Coens' 'O Brother, Where Art Thou?'" *The Movie Vine Home Page.* 16 January 2001. 26 January 2001 <http://movies.thevines.com/leaf/AA0.../&article[cursor]=1&article[id]=AD000000150>.

"News and Notes." *Can't You Hear the Wind Howl?* Official Website. March 2001. 8 May 2001 <http://freehosting1.at.webjump.com/7a1adf1fd/ro/robertjohnson film/Notes/html>.

"Nicotine Fit: A Smokeless Robert Johnson Stamp Gives Its Critics the Blues." *People Weekly,* 10 October 1994, 117.

Noguere, Suzanne. *Whirling round the Sun.* New York: Midmarch Arts Press, 1996.

Oakley, Giles. *The Devil's Music: A History of the Blues.* 2d ed. 1976. Reprint, New York: Da Capo Press, 1997.

Obrecht, Jas. "Robert Johnson." In *Blues Guitar: The Men Who Made the Music.* Ed. Jas Obrecht. 2–15. San Francisco: Miller Freeman, 1993.

Padol, Lisa. Review of *Bone Music,* by Alan Rodgers. *New York Review of Science Fiction* 12:1 (September 1999): 20–21.

Paget, Derek. "Tales of Cultural Tourism." In *Why Docudrama? Fact-Fiction on Film and TV.* Ed. Alan Rosenthal. 47–63. Carbondale: Southern Illinois University Press, 1999.

Palmer, Robert. *Deep Blues.* New York: Penguin, 1981.

Patterson, Gary B. *Hellhounds on Their Trail: Tales from the Rock n Roll Graveyard.* Nashville: Dowling Press, 1998.

Pearson, Barry Lee. "Standing at the Crossroads between Vinyl and Compact Discs: Reissue Blues Recordings in the 1990s." *Journal of American Folklore* 105 (Spring 1992): 215–26.

Pearson, Barry Lee, and Bill McCulloch. *Robert Johnson: Lost and Found.* Urbana: University of Illinois Press, 2003.

Petree, Judy. "Strange Attractor in Chaos Theory." *Chaos without the Math.* 27 July 2002 <http://www.wfu.edu/~petrejh4/Attractor.htm>.

Petronio, Stephen. "Strange Attractors." *Stephen Petronio Company Homepage.* 30 July 2002 <http://www.shaganarts.com/html/petro-strange.html>.

Poster, Mark. "Postmodern Virtualities." In *Media and Cultural Studies: Key Works.* Ed. Meenakshi Gigi Durham and Douglas M. Kellner. 611–25. Malden, Mass.: Blackwell, 2001.

"Postscript." *Juke Blues* 12 (Spring 1988): 27.

Radano, Ronald. "Hot Fantasies: American Modernism and the Idea of Black Rhythm." In *Music and the Racial Imagination.* Ed. Ronald Radano and Philip Bohlman. 459–80. Chicago: University of Chicago Press, 2000.

Ray, Robert B. *A Certain Tendency of the Hollywood Cinema, 1930–1980.* Princeton, N.J.: Princeton University Press, 1985.

Red Rooster. "Rooster Pickin's." *Blues Access* 46 (Summer 2001): 8–10.

Reid, Donald M. "The Symbolism of Postage Stamps: A Source for the Historian." *Journal of Contemporary History* 19:2 (April 1984): 223–49.

Rheingold, Howard. *The Virtual Community: Finding Connection in a Computerised World.* London: Secker and Warburg, 1994.

Richardson, Janine. "Magic and Memory in Sherman Alexie's *Reservation Blues.*" *Studies in American Indian Literatures* 9:4 (Winter 1997): 39–51.

Roach, Joseph. *Cities of the Dead: Circum-Atlantic Performance.* New York: Columbia University Press, 1996.

"Robert Johnson's Death Certificate." *Master Bluesman Robert Johnson. About.com.* 5 August 2002 <http://blues.about.com/musicperform/blues/cs/robertjohnson/index.htm>.

Robins, Kevin. "Cyberspace and the World We Live In." In *The Cybercultures Reader.* Ed. David Bell and Barbara M. Kennedy. 77–95. London: Routledge, 2000.

Rodgers, Alan. *Bone Music.* Stamford, Conn.: Longmeadow Press, 1995.

———. "Re: Robert Johnson in literature." Email to the author. 17 July 2001.

———. "Re: Robert Johnson in literature." Email to the author. 18 July 2001.

Rosenstone, Robert A. *Visions of the Past: The Challenge of Film to Our Idea of History.* Cambridge, Mass.: Harvard University Press, 1995.

Rossinow, Doug. *The Politics of Authenticity: Liberalism, Christianity, and the New Left in America.* New York: Columbia University Press, 1998.

Rubin, Dave. "Robert Johnson: The First Guitar Hero." *Living Blues* 94 (November/December 1990): 38–39.

———. "Somebody Done Hoodooed the Hoodoo Man." *Living Blues* 143 (January/February 1999): 7–8.

Rucker, Leland. "Will the Real Robert Johnson Please Stand Up." *Blues Access* 5:3 (Spring 1991): 3.

Ruelle, David. "Strange Attractors." *Mathematical Intelligencer* 2 (1980): 126–37.

Sante, Luc. "The Genius of Blues." *New York Review of Books,* 11 August 1994, 46–52.

Sardar, Ziauddin. "ALT.CIVILIZATIONS.FAQ: Cyberspace as the Darker Side of the West." In *The Cybercultures Reader.* Ed. David Bell and Barbara M. Kennedy. 733–52. London: Routledge, 2000.

Scherman, Tony. "Chipping Away at the Myths That Encrust a Blues Legend." *New York Times,* 20 September 1998, II: 36, 38.

Senft, Theresa. "Baud Girls and Cargo Cults: A Story about Celebrity, Community, and Profane Illumination on the Web." In *The World Wide Web and Contemporary Cultural Theory.* Ed. Andrew Herman and Thomas Swiss. 183–206. New York: Routledge, 2000.

Shank, Gary, and Donald Cunningham. "Mediated Phosphor Dots: Toward a Post-Cartesian Model of Computer-Mediated Communication via the Semiotic Superhighway." In *Philosophical Perspectives on Computer-Mediated Communication.* Ed. Charles Ess. 27–41. Albany: State University of New York Press, 1996.

Shepard, Jim. "The Damned Outnumber the Rest." *New York Times Books.* 8 November 1998. 3 May 2001 <http://www.nytimes.com/books/98/11/08/reviews/981108.08shepart.html>.

Shields, Rob. "Hypertext Links: The Ethic of the Index and Its Space-Time Effects." In *The World Wide Web and Contemporary Cultural Theory.* Ed. Andrew Herman and Thomas Swiss. 145–60. New York: Routledge, 2000.

Shines, Johnny. "Remembering Robert Johnson." *American Folk Music Occasional* 2 (1970): 30–33.

Silver, David. "Looking Backwards, Looking Forwards: Cyberculture Studies 1990–2000." In *Web.Studies: Rewiring Media Studies for the Digital Age.* Ed. David Gauntlett. 19–30. London: Arnold Publishers, 2000.

Slaven, Neil. "From Channel 4 till Late (or, Where Do We Go from LeVere?) [*sic*]." *Blues and Rhythm, the Gospel Truth* 70 (June 1992): 22.

Slethaug, Gordon E. *Beautiful Chaos: Chaos Theory and Metachaotics in Recent American Fiction.* Albany: State University of New York Press, 2000.

Slevin, James. *The Internet and Society.* Cambridge: Polity Press, 2000.

Smith, Steven G. "Blues and Our Mind-Body Problem." *Popular Music* 11:1 (1992): 41–52.

Sosnoski, James J. "Configuring as a Mode of Rhetorical Analysis." In *Doing Internet Research: Critical Issues and Methods for Examining the Net.* Ed. Steve Jones. 127–43. Thousand Oaks, Calif.: Sage Publications, 1999.

Spencer, Jon Michael. *Blues and Evil.* Knoxville: University of Tennessee Press, 1993.

Stack, Carol B. "Different Voices, Different Visions: Gender, Culture, and Moral Reasoning." In *Women of Color in U.S. Society.* Ed. Maxine Baca Zinn and Bonnie Thornton Dill. 291–301. Philadelphia: Temple University Press, 1994.

———. *All Our Kin: Strategies for Survival in a Black Community.* New York: Harper and Row, 1974.

Staiger, Janet. "Docudrama." *Encyclopedia of Television*. 8 May 2001 <http://www.mbcnet.org/ETV/htmlD/docudrama/docudrama.htm>.

Stasio, Marilyn. "Crime." *New York Times Book Review*, 8 August 1998, 32.

Steinbeck, John. "Paradox and Dream." In *The Contrapuntal Civilization: Essays toward a New Understanding of the American Experience*. Ed. Michael Kammen. 55–65. New York: Crowell, 1971.

Stuart, Andrea. Review of *RL's Dream*, by Walter Mosley. *New Statesman and Society* 8:374 (13 October 1995): 33.

Sublett, Jesse. "Native Son." Review of *Reservation Blues*, by Sherman Alexie. *Austin Chronicle*. 3 July 2001. 9 July 2001 <http://www.auschron.com/issues/vol14/issue44/arts.books.html>.

Sutherland, Sam. "Review of *Can't You Hear the Wind Howl?*" Amazon.com: Editorial Reviews. 8 May 2001 <http://www.amazon.com/exec/obidos/tg/stores/detail/-/video../102-0695971-752250>.

———. "Review of *Love in Vain: A Vision of Robert Johnson*." Amazon.com: Editorial Reviews. 9 September 2003 <http://www.amazon.com/exec/obidos/tg/detail/-/030680557X/qid=1063122766/sr=1–2/ref=sr_1_2/002–9463123–2628846?v=glance&s=books>.

Taylor, Charles. *The Ethics of Authenticity*. Cambridge, Mass.: Harvard University Press, 1991.

Templeton, Ray. "A Special Review." *Blues and Rhythm* 22 (September 1986): 32–33.

Tetzlaff, David. "Yo-Ho-Ho and a Server of Warez." In *The World Wide Web and Contemporary Cultural Theory*. Ed. Andrew Herman and Thomas Swiss. 99–126. New York: Routledge, 2000.

Tharp, Russell. Review of *Crossroads*. Bad Movie Night Web Site. 15 July 2001 <http://www.hit-n-run.com/cgi/read_review.cgi?review=10183_russputen>.

Trynka, Paul. *Portrait of the Blues*. Val Wilmer, photographer. New York: Da Capo Press, 1996.

Turkle, Sherry. *Life on the Screen: Identity in the Age of the Internet*. New York: Simon and Schuster, 1995.

Tysh, George. "Goin' Down Midnight: Bill Harris' Dramatic Vision of Bluesman Robert Johnson's Demise." *Metro Times Detroit*. 19 June 2001. 2 July 2001 <http://www.metrotimes.com/editorial/story.asp?id=1939>.

Ulin, David L. "Where Memory and Reality Intersect." Review of *RL's Dream*, by Walter Mosley. *Los Angeles Times Book Review*, 6 August 1995, 3, 8.

United States Postal Service. "The Criteria Our Postal Service Uses to Select America's Postage Stamps." *Stamps.net*. 6 January 2001 <http//www.stamps.net/newswr24.htm>.

Vickers, Graham. "Picture the Scene." *Creative Review* 15:3 (1 March 1995): 36–37.

Walcutt, Charles C. *American Literary Naturalism: A Divided Stream*. 1956. Reprint, Westport, Conn.: Greenwood, 1973.

Wald, Elijah. *Escaping the Delta: Robert Johnson and the Invention of the Blues.* New York: HarperCollins, 2004.

Wardlow, Gayle Dean. *Chasin' That Devil Music: Searching for the Blues.* San Francisco: Miller Freeman, 1998.

———. Conference presentation. Hellhound on My Trail: Robert Johnson and the Blues Conference. Cleveland, Ohio. 26 September 1998.

———. "Searching for the Robert Johnson Death Certificate." *Blues Revue Quarterly* 6 (1992): 26–27.

Wasserman, Jerry. "'Better Than Anything Else That You Ever Had': Robert Johnson in Recent American Fiction." Conference presentation. Hellhound on My Trail: Robert Johnson and the Blues Conference. Cleveland, Ohio. 26 September 1998.

Waterman, Christopher A. "Race Music: Bo Chatmon, 'Corrine Corrina,' and the Excluded Middle." In *Music and the Racial Imagination.* Ed. R. Radano and P. Bohlman. 167–205. Chicago: University of Chicago Press, 2000.

Waterman, Dick. "To Robert Johnson." *Living Blues* 91 (November/December 1990): 43.

Watson, Nessim. "Why We Argue about Virtual Community: A Case Study of the Phish.Net Fan Community." In *Virtual Culture: Identity and Communication in Cybersociety.* Ed. Steven G. Jones. 102–32. London: Sage, 1997.

Welding, Pete. "Hellhound on His Trail: Robert Johnson." In *Down Beat's Music '66.* 73–74, 76, 103. Chicago: Maher, 1966.

Wells, Jeffrey. "O Brother, Where Art Thou?" Film review. *Showbiz Confidential* 10 June 1999. 25 January 2001 <http://mrshowbiz.go.com/news/Todays_Stories/990610/showcon061099_2.html>.

West, Cornel. "Black Leadership and the Pitfalls of Racial Reasoning." In *Race-ing Justice, En-gendering Power: Essays on Anita Hill, Clarence Thomas, and the Construction of Social Reality.* Ed. Toni Morrison. 390–401. New York: Pantheon Books, 1992.

———. "The New Cultural Politics of Difference." In *Out There: Marginalization and Contemporary Cultures.* Ed. Russell Ferguson, Martha Gever, Trinh T. Minh-ha, and Cornel West. 19–36. New York: The New Museum of Contemporary Art and Massachusetts Institute of Technology, 1990.

White, Hayden. "Historiography and Historiophoty." *American Historical Review* 93:5 (December 1988): 1193–99.

Willson, Michele. "Community in the Abstract: A Political and Ethical Dilemma?" In *The Cybercultures Reader.* Ed. David Bell and Barbara M. Kennedy. 644–57. London: Routledge, 2000.

Winthrop, John. "A Model of Christian Charity." Winthrop Society Home Page. 1630. 24 July 2002 <http://www.winthropsociety.org/charity.htm>.

Woodhead, Leslie. "The Guardian Lecture: Dramatized Documentary." In *Why Docudrama? Fact-Fiction on Film and TV.* Ed. Alan Rosenthal. 101–10. Carbondale: Southern Illinois University Press, 1999.

Woods, Clyde. *Development Arrested: The Blues and Plantation Power in the Mississippi Delta.* London: Verso, 1998.

———. "Opening Remarks." Conference presentation. The Blues Tradition: Memory, Criticism, and Pedagogy. University Park, Pa., 29 June 2000.

Woods, Paula W. "Play Mystery for Me." Review of *RL's Dream,* by Walter Mosley. *San Francisco Review of Books* 20:4 (September/October 1995): 12–13.

Wright, Richard. *Black Boy: A Record of Childhood and Youth.* Cleveland: The World Publishing Company, 1950.

Zane, J. Peder. "Ideas and Trends: Sanitizing History on a Postage Stamp." *New York Times,* 27 October 1996, 4:3.

Index

Patricia R. Schroeder is a professor of English at Ursinus College, where she teaches blues traditions in American literature, African American literature, and American drama. She is the author of *The Presence of the Past in Modern American Drama* (1989) and *The Feminist Possibilities of Dramatic Realism* (1996).

Music in American Life

Only a Miner: Studies in Recorded Coal-Mining Songs *Archie Green*
Great Day Coming: Folk Music and the American Left *R. Serge Denisoff*
John Philip Sousa: A Descriptive Catalog of His Works *Paul E. Bierley*
The Hell-Bound Train: A Cowboy Songbook *Glenn Ohrlin*
Oh, Didn't He Ramble: The Life Story of Lee Collins, as Told to Mary Collins *Edited by Frank J. Gillis and John W. Miner*
American Labor Songs of the Nineteenth Century *Philip S. Foner*
Stars of Country Music: Uncle Dave Macon to Johnny Rodriguez *Edited by Bill C. Malone and Judith McCulloh*
Git Along, Little Dogies: Songs and Songmakers of the American West *John I. White*
A Texas-Mexican *Cancionero:* Folksongs of the Lower Border *Américo Paredes*
San Antonio Rose: The Life and Music of Bob Wills *Charles R. Townsend*
Early Downhome Blues: A Musical and Cultural Analysis *Jeff Todd Titon*
An Ives Celebration: Papers and Panels of the Charles Ives Centennial Festival-Conference *Edited by H. Wiley Hitchcock and Vivian Perlis*
Sinful Tunes and Spirituals: Black Folk Music to the Civil War *Dena J. Epstein*
Joe Scott, the Woodsman-Songmaker *Edward D. Ives*
Jimmie Rodgers: The Life and Times of America's Blue Yodeler *Nolan Porterfield*
Early American Music Engraving and Printing: A History of Music Publishing in America from 1787 to 1825, with Commentary on Earlier and Later Practices *Richard J. Wolfe*
Sing a Sad Song: The Life of Hank Williams *Roger M. Williams*
Long Steel Rail: The Railroad in American Folksong *Norm Cohen*
Resources of American Music History: A Directory of Source Materials from Colonial Times to World War II *D. W. Krummel, Jean Geil, Doris J. Dyen, and Deane L. Root*
Tenement Songs: The Popular Music of the Jewish Immigrants *Mark Slobin*
Ozark Folksongs *Vance Randolph; edited and abridged by Norm Cohen*
Oscar Sonneck and American Music *Edited by William Lichtenwanger*
Bluegrass Breakdown: The Making of the Old Southern Sound *Robert Cantwell*

Bluegrass: A History *Neil V. Rosenberg*
Music at the White House: A History of the American Spirit *Elise K. Kirk*
Red River Blues: The Blues Tradition in the Southeast *Bruce Bastin*
Good Friends and Bad Enemies: Robert Winslow Gordon and the Study of American Folksong *Debora Kodish*
Fiddlin' Georgia Crazy: Fiddlin' John Carson, His Real World, and the World of His Songs *Gene Wiggins*
America's Music: From the Pilgrims to the Present (rev. 3d ed.) *Gilbert Chase*
Secular Music in Colonial Annapolis: The Tuesday Club, 1745–56 *John Barry Talley*
Bibliographical Handbook of American Music *D. W. Krummel*
Goin' to Kansas City *Nathan W. Pearson, Jr.*
"Susanna," "Jeanie," and "The Old Folks at Home": The Songs of Stephen C. Foster from His Time to Ours (2d ed.) *William W. Austin*
Songprints: The Musical Experience of Five Shoshone Women *Judith Vander*
"Happy in the Service of the Lord": Afro-American Gospel Quartets in Memphis *Kip Lornell*
Paul Hindemith in the United States *Luther Noss*
"My Song Is My Weapon": People's Songs, American Communism, and the Politics of Culture, 1930–50 *Robbie Lieberman*
Chosen Voices: The Story of the American Cantorate *Mark Slobin*
Theodore Thomas: America's Conductor and Builder of Orchestras, 1835–1905 *Ezra Schabas*
"The Whorehouse Bells Were Ringing" and Other Songs Cowboys Sing *Guy Logsdon*
Crazeology: The Autobiography of a Chicago Jazzman *Bud Freeman, as Told to Robert Wolf*
Discoursing Sweet Music: Brass Bands and Community Life in Turn-of-the-Century Pennsylvania *Kenneth Kreitner*
Mormonism and Music: A History *Michael Hicks*
Voices of the Jazz Age: Profiles of Eight Vintage Jazzmen *Chip Deffaa*
Pickin' on Peachtree: A History of Country Music in Atlanta, Georgia *Wayne W. Daniel*
Bitter Music: Collected Journals, Essays, Introductions, and Librettos *Harry Partch; edited by Thomas McGeary*
Ethnic Music on Records: A Discography of Ethnic Recordings Produced in the United States, 1893 to 1942 *Richard K. Spottswood*
Downhome Blues Lyrics: An Anthology from the Post-World War II Era *Jeff Todd Titon*
Ellington: The Early Years *Mark Tucker*
Chicago Soul *Robert Pruter*
That Half-Barbaric Twang: The Banjo in American Popular Culture *Karen Linn*

Hot Man: The Life of Art Hodes *Art Hodes and Chadwick Hansen*
The Erotic Muse: American Bawdy Songs (2d ed.) *Ed Cray*
Barrio Rhythm: Mexican American Music in Los Angeles *Steven Loza*
The Creation of Jazz: Music, Race, and Culture in Urban America *Burton W. Peretti*
Charles Martin Loeffler: A Life Apart in Music *Ellen Knight*
Club Date Musicians: Playing the New York Party Circuit *Bruce A. MacLeod*
Opera on the Road: Traveling Opera Troupes in the United States, 1825–60 *Katherine K. Preston*
The Stonemans: An Appalachian Family and the Music That Shaped Their Lives *Ivan M. Tribe*
Transforming Tradition: Folk Music Revivals Examined *Edited by Neil V. Rosenberg*
The Crooked Stovepipe: Athapaskan Fiddle Music and Square Dancing in Northeast Alaska and Northwest Canada *Craig Mishler*
Traveling the High Way Home: Ralph Stanley and the World of Traditional Bluegrass Music *John Wright*
Carl Ruggles: Composer, Painter, and Storyteller *Marilyn Ziffrin*
Never without a Song: The Years and Songs of Jennie Devlin, 1865–1952 *Katharine D. Newman*
The Hank Snow Story *Hank Snow, with Jack Ownbey and Bob Burris*
Milton Brown and the Founding of Western Swing *Cary Ginell, with special assistance from Roy Lee Brown*
Santiago de Murcia's "Códice Saldívar No. 4": A Treasury of Secular Guitar Music from Baroque Mexico *Craig H. Russell*
The Sound of the Dove: Singing in Appalachian Primitive Baptist Churches *Beverly Bush Patterson*
Heartland Excursions: Ethnomusicological Reflections on Schools of Music *Bruno Nettl*
Doowop: The Chicago Scene *Robert Pruter*
Blue Rhythms: Six Lives in Rhythm and Blues *Chip Deffaa*
Shoshone Ghost Dance Religion: Poetry Songs and Great Basin Context *Judith Vander*
Go Cat Go! Rockabilly Music and Its Makers *Craig Morrison*
'Twas Only an Irishman's Dream: The Image of Ireland and the Irish in American Popular Song Lyrics, 1800–1920 *William H. A. Williams*
Democracy at the Opera: Music, Theater, and Culture in New York City, 1815–60 *Karen Ahlquist*
Fred Waring and the Pennsylvanians *Virginia Waring*
Woody, Cisco, and Me: Seamen Three in the Merchant Marine *Jim Longhi*
Behind the Burnt Cork Mask: Early Blackface Minstrelsy and Antebellum American Popular Culture *William J. Mahar*
Going to Cincinnati: A History of the Blues in the Queen City *Steven C. Tracy*

Pistol Packin' Mama: Aunt Molly Jackson and the Politics of Folksong *Shelly Romalis*
Sixties Rock: Garage, Psychedelic, and Other Satisfactions *Michael Hicks*
The Late Great Johnny Ace and the Transition from R&B to Rock 'n' Roll *James M. Salem*
Tito Puente and the Making of Latin Music *Steven Loza*
Juilliard: A History *Andrea Olmstead*
Understanding Charles Seeger, Pioneer in American Musicology *Edited by Bell Yung and Helen Rees*
Mountains of Music: West Virginia Traditional Music from *Goldenseal* *Edited by John Lilly*
Alice Tully: An Intimate Portrait *Albert Fuller*
A Blues Life *Henry Townsend, as told to Bill Greensmith*
Long Steel Rail: The Railroad in American Folksong (2d ed.) *Norm Cohen*
The Golden Age of Gospel *Text by Horace Clarence Boyer; photography by Lloyd Yearwood*
Aaron Copland: The Life and Work of an Uncommon Man *Howard Pollack*
Louis Moreau Gottschalk *S. Frederick Starr*
Race, Rock, and Elvis *Michael T. Bertrand*
Theremin: Ether Music and Espionage *Albert Glinsky*
Poetry and Violence: The Ballad Tradition of Mexico's Costa Chica *John H. McDowell*
The Bill Monroe Reader *Edited by Tom Ewing*
Music in Lubavitcher Life *Ellen Koskoff*
Zarzuela: Spanish Operetta, American Stage *Janet L. Sturman*
Bluegrass Odyssey: A Documentary in Pictures and Words, 1966–86 *Carl Fleischhauer and Neil V. Rosenberg*
That Old-Time Rock & Roll: A Chronicle of an Era, 1954–63 *Richard Aquila*
Labor's Troubadour *Joe Glazer*
American Opera *Elise K. Kirk*
Don't Get above Your Raisin': Country Music and the Southern Working Class *Bill C. Malone*
John Alden Carpenter: A Chicago Composer *Howard Pollack*
Heartbeat of the People: Music and Dance of the Northern Pow-wow *Tara Browner*
My Lord, What a Morning: An Autobiography *Marian Anderson*
Marian Anderson: A Singer's Journey *Allan Keiler*
Charles Ives Remembered: An Oral History *Vivian Perlis*
Henry Cowell, Bohemian *Michael Hicks*
Rap Music and Street Consciousness *Cheryl L. Keyes*
Louis Prima *Garry Boulard*
Marian McPartland's Jazz World: All in Good Time *Marian McPartland*
Robert Johnson: Lost and Found *Barry Lee Pearson and Bill McCulloch*

Bound for America: Three British Composers *Nicholas Temperley*

Lost Sounds: Blacks and the Birth of the Recording Industry, 1890–1919 *Tim Brooks*

Burn, Baby! BURN! The Autobiography of Magnificent Montague *Magnificent Montague with Bob Baker*

Way Up North in Dixie: A Black Family's Claim to the Confederate Anthem *Howard L. Sacks and Judith Rose Sacks*

The Bluegrass Reader *Edited by Thomas Goldsmith*

Colin McPhee: Composer in Two Worlds *Carol J. Oja*

Robert Johnson, Mythmaking, and Contemporary American Culture *Patricia R. Schroeder*

The University of Illinois Press
is a founding member of the
Association of American University Presses.

Composed in 9.3/13 ITC Stone Informal
with Twentieth Century Medium display
by Barbara Evans
at the University of Illinois Press
Designed by Dennis Roberts
Manufactured by Thomson-Shore, Inc.

University of Illinois Press
1325 South Oak Street
Champaign, IL 61820-6903
www.press.uillinois.edu